Social Science and Policy-Making

Social Science *and* Policy-Making

A Search for Relevance
in the Twentieth Century

Edited by
David L. Featherman
and Maris A. Vinovskis

Ann Arbor
THE UNIVERSITY OF MICHIGAN PRESS

Copyright © by the University of Michigan 2001
All rights reserved
Published in the United States of America by
The University of Michigan Press
Manufactured in the United States of America
⊗ Printed on acid-free paper

2004   2003   2002   2001   4   3   2   1

A CIP catalog record for this book is available from the British Library.

Library of Congress Cataloging-in-Publication Data

Social science and policy-making : a search for relevance in the
    twentieth century / edited by David L. Featherman and Maris A.
    Vinovskis.
      p.   cm.
    Includes bibliographical references and index.
    ISBN 0-472-09769-5 (acid-free paper) — ISBN 0-472-06769-9 (pbk. :
acid-free paper)
    1. Policy sciences.   2. United States—Social policy.   I. Featherman,
David L.   II. Vinovskis, Maris.   III. Title.
    H97   .S629   2001
    361.2'5'0973—dc21   00-012182

Contents

Preface   vii

1. In Search of Relevance to Social Reform and
   Policy-Making   1
   David L. Featherman and Maris A. Vinovskis

2. Knowledge for the Public Good: The Emergence of
   Social Sciences and Social Reform in Late-Nineteenth-
   and Early-Twentieth-Century America, 1880–1940   16
   Martin Bulmer

3. Growth and Use of Social and Behavioral Science in
   the Federal Government since World War II   40
   David L. Featherman and Maris A. Vinovskis

4. Designing Head Start: Roles Played by
   Developmental Psychologists   83
   Sheldon H. White and Deborah A. Phillips

5. Policy, Aging, and the Graying of Society   119
   W. Andrew Achenbaum

6. Welfare Reform Policy from Nixon to Clinton:
   What Role for Social Science?   137
   Sheldon Danziger

7. Welfare Reform at the State Level: The Role of Social
   Experiments and Demonstrations   165
   Judith M. Gueron

8. The Making and Analysis of Public Policy:
   A Perspective on the Role of Social Science   187
   Laurence E. Lynn Jr.

Contributors   219

Index   221

Preface

The inspiration and occasion for this work arose from a year-long celebration of the fiftieth anniversary of the Institute for Social Research (ISR). Founded in February 1949 by the Regents of the University of Michigan, ISR became the administrative umbrella for a unique intellectual synthesis between social scientists taking probability samples of American households to study social change with survey data and those exploring the microfoundations of social interaction and intergroup relations through social psychological experiments in small-group labs. The former class of social scientists established the Survey Research Center (SRC) at the University of Michigan in 1946 when Rensis Likert, Angus Campbell, and colleagues relocated their pioneering work on survey sampling and interviewing from a wartime assignment at the U.S. Department of Agriculture. Scientists in the latter category composed the Research Center for Group Dynamics, formed at the Massachusetts Institute of Technology by Kurt Lewin and subsequently headed by Dorwin "Doc" Cartwright, which moved to the University of Michigan to join the SRC unit in 1948. (For a fifty-year history of ISR and of the collateral development of the social sciences at the University of Michigan, see Anne Frantilla, *Social science in the public interest: A fiftieth-year history of the Institute for Social Research,* Bentley Historical Library Bulletin, no. 45 [Ann Arbor: University of Michigan, 1998].)

Union of these two units as components within the newly created Institute for Social Research in 1949 represented more than an integration of different research methodologies in the search for principles underlying changes in behavior and in social institutions. The modus operandi of ISR was from its beginnings multi- and interdisciplinary. The founding generation consisted of social psychologists, sampling statisticians, sociologists, economists, and political scientists working as research teams. It was pragmatic in the sense of using the "abiding problems of civilization" as a contemporary, living laboratory for deriving empirically supported, foundational theories and explanations for phenomena. It was unapologetically positivistic, insofar as it took on the challenge of measuring complex social phenomena with the observational tools of mathematics, probability theory, and statistics and with the aid of experimental designs and manipulations of control and treatment groups. And its scientific evolution was shaped, and continues to be, by its founding charter of semi-independence from the university, that is, to be self-supporting through sponsored research budgets rather than relying on university funds. These elements of ISR's abiding modus operandi inspired the theme of its anniversary celebration in the academic year 1998–99, "ISR, Fifty Years of Social Science in the Public Interest."

This theme also inspired the March 1998 "National Symposium on Social Science and Policy Making: A Centenary Appraisal," held in the Horace Rackham Graduate School as a signature event in the ISR celebration. The fortuitous coincidence of ISR's fiftieth anniversary with the end point of the twentieth century prompted this retrospective review of the coevolution, so to say, of positivist social science in America and of successive efforts to reform society, preserve and strengthen democracy, and make and then analyze policy. ISR's maturation as an institution reflects a part of that history; for example, in the post–World War II period, ISR played a sometimes central role in creating the data and interpretations that entered public discourse and policy debates. But the conference, and this book which emerged from its intellectual content, was never intended to revolve around whatever modest role ISR had in this coevolution. Instead, its goal, and the goal of this book, was to look forward—to anticipate opportunities in the twenty-first century—by looking backward at the coevolution with an analytical eye.

"A search for relevance" is a major theme of this retrospective reconstruction, from the point of view of social science and the course of social reform and policy-making. This theme is elaborated in the initial chapter, which serves both as an introduction and as a concluding synthesis of the historical narratives and case studies that comprise the book. The search for relevance expresses various interrelated paths of development for social science. On one path, social science in America developed as a positivist science of society, encouraged by its early patrons in private philanthropy. Social science's apparent and real effects in meliorating social problems defined one aspect of its relevance, much as medical science gained its relevance in battling illness. On another path, relevance of social science was defined by the ability of an avowedly apolitical social science to speak truth to power. And on still another path, trodden by academic social science, relevance was gained by the abstraction of social science both from the pragmatics of politics and from the urgings of its patrons and funders, perhaps even from the living laboratory problems of the everyday world. All these paths of development appear in the following pages, and their various crossing points mark critical periods in the coevolution of social science and policy-making during the twentieth century.

We pause at the start of this journey along these paths to acknowledge with gratitude those who have contributed to this book. First, we dedicate this effort to the founding generation of ISR, whose individual stories as scientists and scholar/teachers are richly evocative of the golden years of social science:

Angus Campbell, Charles F. Cannell, Dorwin P. Cartwright, Elizabeth M. Douvan, Leon Festinger, John R. P. French Jr., Gerald Gurin, Robert L. Kahn, George Katona, Daniel Katz, Leslie Kish, John B. Lansing, Rensis Likert, Ronald Lippit, Warren Miller, James N. Morgan, Donald C. Pelz, Stanley E. Seashore, Arnold S. Tannebaum, Stephen B. Withey, and Alvin F. Zander.

Second, we are grateful to our authors, who are identified in detail in the list of contributors, and also to the teams of commentators who formed panels and enriched discussions of these materials during the 1998 national symposium: Margret M. Baltes, David K. Cohen, Joseph C. Conaty, Mary E. Corcoran, Ronald Haskins, James H. Johnson Jr., F. Thomas Juster, Ellen Condliffe Lagemann, Valerie Lee, Cora Bagley Marrett, Terrence J. McDonald, Lawrence M. Mead, Samuel J. Meisels, Matilda White Riley, Douglas D. Ross, Janet A. Weiss, Robert J. Willis, and Harriet Zuckerman.

Finally, we thank our staff of assistants and editors without whom the practical side of the project could scarcely have succeeded, and who evoked in us an abiding sense of companionship and pride of purpose. Among these are Anne Frantilla and Francis X. Blouin Jr., of the Bentley Historical Library of the University of Michigan, Tina Smith, Linda Peterson, and Gwen C. Maes. We could not have produced a fluidly readable book without Tanya Hart, the most diligent copy editor one could hope to find.

We shall always be indebted to the University of Michigan Press for its faith in our abilities to convert a set of conference talks into a coherent narrative, and it remains our hope that such faith will be confirmed by the judgment of our readers.

We would wish that such readers, first and foremost, will be the next generation of social scientists and policy analysts who will take up the ever daunting search for relevance and who must chart their own course in ever shifting political and intellectual tides. As they embark upon their own exciting journey, we hope in considerable modesty that this book might read like a pilgrim's progress from an earlier and (probably in retrospect) simpler era, but one whose lessons bear some rereading along their way.

David L. Featherman *and* Maris A. Vinovskis

Institute for Social Research
Ann Arbor, Michigan

CHAPTER 1

In Search of Relevance to Social Reform and Policy-Making

David L. Featherman and Maris A. Vinovskis

In the United States, the role of the federal government in policy-making was modest until national and international cataclysms, particularly the Great Depression and World War II, seemed to justify presidential intervention, federal administrative and judicial decision making, and legislative response in Washington. Prior to the mid-1930s, federal policy-making was less prevalent or potent than city- and state-level politics and local social reform efforts. The modern federal administrative state, the so-called welfare state, emerged in the United States only in the mid-1930s and evolved apace to its apogee in the Johnson and Nixon presidencies of the 1960s and early 1970s. The role of the social sciences as a knowledge base for that administrative state rose in tandem with this evolution; however, the role of social science has become of late more diffused and ambiguous as policy-making and administration have become more decentralized and fractured and as trust in government has waned.

The introductory chapter of this volume concentrates on the history of social science in policy-making as well as the institutional and political contexts in which the contributions of social science research and social scientists to social reform and policy-making have evolved over the twentieth century. The narrative is complex, because the relationship between social science and both social reform and policy-making is fraught with abiding dilemmas that have not been resolved and perhaps may never be. Perhaps the principal dilemma is best captured by the 1920s aspiration of early positivist social scientists—political scientists, economists, statisticians, and later, sociologists—to develop an objective science that can be a legitimate, apolitical instrument in the hands of reformers or policymakers (Prewitt 1995). However, social scientists have continued to seek their relevance to societal reform and public policy during the entire twentieth century.

The aspiration for legitimacy through scientific objectivity sounds oddly out of place at the dawning of the twenty-first century, especially in the environs of Washington. The contemporary landscape of organizations trafficking in social science for policy purposes is strewn with proprietary and not-for-profit think tanks and policy job shops with avowed partisan tendencies if not formal political patrons—for example, the Heritage Foundation and the Progressive Policy Institute. They ring Washington, and they represent—in the worst of cases—defense departments, as it were, in which social science data and analysis are mobilized as political weapons in the service of often preordained policy positions. Some older and comparatively less partisan research and policy organizations, such as the Brookings Institution and the Urban Institute, continue to exist in Washington, but increasingly they compete with less compelling force against these newer advocacy groups for the attention of policymakers.

The contemporary landscape also contains dozens of university-based programs and schools of public policy that have arisen in the past twenty years—with faculties heavily staffed by political scientists, economists, and other social scientists. These academic institutions have ancestral roots in worldly, late-nineteenth-century places like Hull House, which operated in a period just prior to the modern graduate school. Hull House developed in an era when analysts were reformers—standing often at odds with political bosses in city government or with industrial capitalists—and well before the professionalization of the social sciences drove the reformers from would-be legitimate ranks of the emergent disciplines of academe (Bulmer, chap. 2, this vol.; Lagemann 1989). It is perhaps ironic that academics in disciplines such as economics, political science, and sociology—in their quest for professional integrity and scientific objectivity—may have unintentionally undermined these disciplines' long-term relevance to policy and thereby conceded the main battlefield to the private, often partisan, think tanks.

It is particularly ironic to contemplate the evolution of the contemporary relationships of social science to reform and to policy-making from the vantage point of the two decades between the early 1920s and the end of World War II. In that era, the growth of political science, economics, and sociology led the way for social scientists to claim relevance to public affairs, reform, and policy-making by embracing positivism and refining the art and science of social measurement. The Social Survey Movement, sponsored by what became the Russell Sage Foundation in New York City, is but one example. Were it not for a convergence of interest in the leadership of such East Coast private philanthropy—mainly the Laura Spelman Foundation, but ultimately the Rockefeller family—with the burgeoning social science disciplines in that era, America would lack much of today's infrastructure of social science—as exemplified by the University of Chicago and its vaunted Chicago School of social sciences, the Social Science Research Council (SSRC), the National Bureau of Economic Research (NBER), or what became the Brookings Institution (Prewitt 1995). The convergent interests of philanthropy and the disciplines of social science were defined, on the one hand, by creating a science of society—in other words, developing reliable tools for the collection of social, political, and economic data and for the analysis of social change. On the other hand, philanthropy and social science found common cause in educating methodologically sophisticated social scientists—modeled on the investigative methodology of the natural sciences—to measure, analyze, and produce honest numbers (Featherman 1994).

The apogee of this fecund epoch of convergent interests may have been President Hoover's appointment of the blue-ribbon Presidential Research Committee, chaired by economist Wesley Mitchell of the NBER. The committee was funded not by the federal government but by Rockefeller and was staffed at the private SSRC in New York City. Its 1933 report, *Recent Social Trends in the United States,* edited by University of Chicago sociologist William Ogburn, took the view that if the facts and trends in American households, towns, and institutions could be discerned clearly and measured precisely, then surely rational decision makers would use the information in the public interest. However, history does not bear out Ogburn's prediction. Throughout this period and beyond, the annual reports of the SSRC reveal deep intellectual and political reservations among social science leadership regarding both their collaboration with policymakers and the distorting effects of political agenda setting on the course of basic intellectual inquiry. By contrast, the emerging federal policy world dismissed the Ogburn report for its lack of politically inspired analysis and interpretative prescription: the facts could not and would not speak for themselves. In short, in this defining moment for sociology and its sister disciplines—as tools in the service of the public interest—the scholarly proclivities, if not also the needs and interests of academic social science, were revealed to be different from the needs and interests of the emerging administrative state. The growing cadre of administrative decision makers needed knowledge for action in a political arena, knowledge that could be tested against the requirements of political decision making. Policy relevance and scientific objectivity were strange bedfellows from the start.

And yet, during the Johnson presidency of the 1960s, the marriage of policy-making to social science was fully consummated in a so-called golden age of relevance to public administration and policy (Featherman and Vinovskis, chap. 3, this vol.). Though it ultimately proved to be a marriage made in a procrustean bed, the golden age might have lasted longer had the war in Southeast Asia not been so politically divisive, destroying the working partnership with academics and eventually undermining the trust in government that so vitalized the inception of the Great Society era. Robert McNamara, first among others, brought to the Kennedy presidency and governmental administration scientifically grounded, decision-oriented policy analysis, planning, and program evaluation as functions of the public executive and as instruments of political leadership. Political scientists, economists, sociologists, and even historians, based in universities, served as consultants to government. This trend continued apace under President Johnson. But scores of analysts, especially economists, were hired into federal agencies, the Executive Office, congressional staff posts, and service agencies as so-called research brokers (Sundquist 1978). Research brokers translated research into more usable commodities in order to rationalize policy-making and evaluation and assess opportunity costs. It was a golden age for large-scale social experimentation. Consider, for example, the New Jersey Negative Income Tax Experiment and Head Start (White and Phillips, chap. 4, and Gueron, chap. 7, this vol.). Hundreds of social scientists testified in Congress and in federal litigation on Great Society legislation, including school desegregation, voting rights, and crime and civil disorder. (Recall that this was a period not only of the War on Poverty but also of urban race riots and growing civil disorder associated with an increasingly unpopular war in Southeast Asia.) It also was an era when modern schools of public policy were founded, educating cohorts of research brokers and analysts for the swelling administrative state and basing their training in the academic social sciences, namely, economics, political science, and survey-based sociological research. The mission of these cohorts: to speak truth to power, give honest numbers, and provide fairly brokered analysis for the democratic state and its executive and administrative leadership.

But as the founder of one elite school of public policy, Aaron Wildavsky, at Berkeley, put it, "unlike social science, policy analysis must be prescriptive; arguments about correct policy, which deal with the future, cannot help but be willful and therefore political" (cited in Lynn, chap. 8, this vol.). When considered in the context of the 1960s and 1970s, the 1920s-era appeal of positivist social science to policy relevance through its scientific objectivity seems naive: it did not anticipate the difficult pragmatic realities in public administration or the interest group politics that grew apace in the Johnson era and beyond, even though the reaction to the Ogburn report, *Recent Social Trends,* presaged this challenge three decades earlier. And in its moment of ascendancy during the golden age, social science promised too much assistance and delivered too little. Early assessments of the impact of Great Society programs like Head Start, guided into place and emphasis by social science, showed little lasting impact. Efforts to fully characterize the measured effects of other programs often imploded, as methodological debates among scientists left legislators, program administrators, and the courts confused. Two examples are the negative income tax on work effort and, as researched by James Coleman (Coleman and Hoffer 1987), the effect of school expenditures and classroom teaching on narrowing differentials in student achievements and raising overall achievement levels. As the economist Henry Aaron noted: "What is an ordinary member of the tribe to do when the witch doctors disagree?" And political scientist Hugh

Heclo responded: "Experts [make] more sophisticated claims and counter-claims to the point that the nonspecialist becomes inclined to concede everything and believe nothing he hears" (Williams 1998, 248). In short, like Icarus, social scientists of the golden age flew too close to the sun with wings that failed the test of the ascent. Social science lost much of its credibility (if not also its legitimacy) as an objective, useful tool to the administrative state. But unlike Icarus, who fell from soaring heights to his death, university-based social scientists survived to do theory and more modest (in its claims) academic work with limited federal funding.

The 1970s retreat to academic work and the diminution of the demand for honestly brokered social science by the administrative state in the 1980s also were promoted by shifting national politics. Social scientists proved to be out of step with the politics of government. Not only were empirical findings unbelievable or inaccessible to members of the tribe (society at large) but the general alignment with so-called leftist social criticism—and later with postmodern deconstructionism—found little resonance in Washington's politics. Even within the National Science Foundation—created in 1950 to foster basic research within academe as a wellspring for national research and development (R&D)—social science was not initially included but also not explicitly excluded, although the NSF charter hearings of the 1950s echo grave congressional misgivings about our gravitas (Larsen 1992). Indeed, for decades, until the early 1990s, social science was hidden from public view within the biological science directorate. In the Reagan presidency of the 1980s, national politics became more conservative and continued so during the 1990s. Even as recently as 1996, Rep. Robert Walker (R-Pennsylvania), chair of the House Science Committee, questioned the necessity of the decade-old NSF directorate for the social, economic, and behavioral sciences on grounds of its irrelevance to the national scientific interest and of the inherently "applied" (read, political versus scientific) nature of these fields. Social studies, as the social sciences were called in those debates, belong in the humanities and not the sciences. The cultural and historical "turn" (McDonald 1996) of the social sciences in the 1980s, and a growing skepticism if not cynicism about positivist methodologies within its own ranks, made it difficult for social science to counter this critical claim.

A final set of major forces, beginning in the Johnson presidency and accelerating under Nixon and Reagan, further turned academic, honestly brokered social science away from policy relevance (Featherman and Vinovskis, chap. 3, this vol.). The upshot of these forces is the deep politicization of the role of knowledge brokerage for the executive office of the administrative state. A related development, if not also consequence, is a further erosion of the public trust in government and skepticism toward the honesty of numbers reported by the state (e.g., budget forecasts by the Congressional Budget Office versus those of the White House). The Nixon White House assembled great administrative and policy discretion and concentrated it within an elite circle of the president's Executive Office. In turn, each major administrative agency of the Executive Office was linked to this inner circle by a political watchdog. Reports at the U.S. Census, for example, could not be released until such an official had reviewed them. The Office of Management and Budget scrutinized questionnaires that would be used in research supported by federal contracts. President Reagan, under an announced plan to reduce the size of the administrative state, cut the budgets of federal agencies to such an extent that federal funding for nonmilitary R&D—and especially for the social sciences—dropped precipitously, though it recovered somewhat by the late 1980s. For agencies like the Census Bureau and the Social Security Administration, the research programs had to cut major research inquiries and statistical series. For example, in 1988 the General Accounting Office concluded that "the [Reagan] administration had 'gravely eroded' information development capacity in the executive branch and in so doing had failed to execute the 'responsibility of [the federal] government to the people of this country'" (Williams 1998, 248).

Many of the generation of honest research brokers who staffed the federal administrative bureaucracy after World War II and through the 1960s (and of these many were social scientists of professional accomplishment in their fields) either retired or were eliminated by the 1980s. Owing in part to the elimination of rigorous civil service examinations and the requirements for specialized training, some of the new middle-level administrators in federal research and planning posts were not adequately trained in the social sciences. However, the overall number of federal employees did not decline. The replacements were caught up in what we presently describe as "spin doctoring," or what John Burke calls "responsive competence." In contrast to honest research brokerage by a career social scientist, for example, guided by a code of professional ethics and an institutional memory, responsive competence chooses a datum to suit a political need of the moment as a sign of political loyalty. By spreading a network of loyalists across federal agencies, Presidents Nixon and Reagan undermined any safeguards for the production of honest, well-scrutinized numbers otherwise obtained when multiple independent agents, under honest research brokerage, advocate and argue competing points of view from which the president or other executive administrators can make decisions (see Roger Porter as cited in Williams 1998, on "multiple advocacy"). This pattern of selectively using social science studies to bolster policy positions continues into the present. For example, the Department of Education advocates funding of smaller class sizes without regard to mixed scientific conclusions about their efficacy; and as noted by Sheldon Danziger (chap. 6, this vol.), federal welfare programs were "reformed" in Congress and by the White House with highly selective use of research findings.

Although trust in government, and in the work of its bureaucracies, fell during the Vietnam era, public cynicism became palpable in the aftermath of Watergate and the resignation of President Nixon. One can only speculate that this loss of faith in government and its knowledge-brokering agents undergirded wide public support for further reducing the federal administrative bureaucracy and eliminating vestiges of the New Deal welfare state—the rallying cry of conservatives and the Republican Party in the 1990s. Recent partisan debates have focused on the honesty of numbers; when such integrity is announced by a highly politicized federal bureaucracy or countered by equally partisan think tanks and other oppositional spin doctors, credibility and public trust are further undermined. A related trend is decline in the trust of the fourth estate, the news media. One can speculate that a similar disenchantment and skepticism will grow with the Internet as a source of policy-relevant knowledge and analysis. In the burgeoning cyberspace of rapidly available and widely distributed policy-related information and analysis from sources across a wide and often unknowable range of credibility, the placement and pace of academic research and its dissemination may further diminish the role of the social sciences as primary source material for policy decision making.

During the two to three decades prior to the Clinton presidency, most academic social scientists—other than economists and political scientists—have played very peripheral roles in federal policy-making and its inner circles. To the extent that the intellectual production of university-based economists and political scientists, for example, has grown more mathematical and theoretically abstract, the gulf has increased between both the readership of that work and the reward system that expands it, on the one hand, and the absorption and appreciation of this scholarship in Washington, on the other. The exceptions are important, however, and tend to arise from within professional schools of public policy and management or from schools of international affairs in which economists and political scientists (and, to a lesser extent, lawyers) dominate the faculties and student cohorts. At the same time, the demand for such personnel within the federal administrative state may be falling below the growing supply (Williams 1998). In recent decades the training of these workers for the federal administrative state no longer draws exclusively upon the theory and analytical methodology of economics, political science, survey research, operations research, or organizational analysis. Instead, training has been redesigned to reflect the activities of knowledge brokers in their natural habitats, the social roles of analysis in the bureaucracy. Citing the research and interpretations of Martha Feldman on these roles in the Department of Energy in the early 1980s, Laurence Lynn remarks: "Feldman argued that the role of policy analysts in a bureaucracy is not to inform decision making—even the analysts themselves do not see this as their function—but, rather, through negotiating and crossing institutional boundaries, to contribute to the definition of organizational interests and to the interpretation of events and actions" (Lynn, chap. 8, this vol.).

In short, the inner circle of policy-making and analysis of the contemporary administrative state is composed, in part, of specially trained professionals—lawyers and (fewer) policy analysts—with skills that are sharply honed for the political culture of the federal government. What worries some critical observers about that political culture—ever more partisan and demanding of responsive competence rather than honest research brokerage—is that it will either quickly defeat honest research brokers, sending them back to do academic research, or convert or "co-opt" them into partisan spin doctors (Williams 1998). In any case, this development of a professional policy analyst cadre and the partisan nature of its contemporary employers—whether in government or in the think tanks surrounding Washington—introduce additional barriers to the full relevance of academic social science research to the shaping of public policy.

We would be remiss to conclude this overview of the evolution of the federal administrative state, policy-making, and the relevance of social science research to both without commenting on federal support of university-based academic social science and on federal science policy. Like the administrative state itself, federal support for civilian research and development (R&D) grew following World War II, becoming essential to the expanding methodological and theoretical frontiers of the social sciences. For the first part of the century, however, private, East Coast philanthropy built the infrastructure of social science, including institutions of higher education such as the University of Chicago and Rockefeller University in New York, and provided the funding for doctoral training in quantitative statistical and experimental methodologies (Bulmer and Bulmer 1981; Prewitt 1995). The intellectual elite who served as presidents of foundations in the period 1920 through 1945—at the Laura Spelman and the Russell Sage Foundations and in the Social Science Research Council, for example—circulated among the professorate, leadership of philanthropic institutions, and government service. This circulating elite facilitated an extraordinarily high degree of common cause between the foundations, academic social science, and government (mostly state and local but increasingly federal) in creating a science of society able to guide the foundations and government toward better democratic and social reforms and ameliorative public policies.

Though the impact and scope of the philanthropic foundations in reform and public policy were reduced and gradually overtaken by the expanding federal administrative state in the 1960s, philanthropic foundations continued to play an important role in social science research. For example, the Ford Foundation alone made 40 percent of all foundation grants in the United States in 1953 and provided $43 million for university-based social science research over the subsequent seven-year period. Federal investment in university-based research and development expanded after World War II, due in large measure to the perception that American superiority in science and technology was instrumental to winning that war. The architect of federal civilian R&D policy was Vannever Bush, whose report *Science: The Endless Frontier* prescribed a highly decentralized infrastructure of civilian R&D (Zachary 1997). This pre-scription consisted of a network of major research universities and a set of mis-sion-oriented federal agencies, each with an appropriate portfolio of funding opportunities to which researchers could apply in service of agency goals and in pursuit of academic scholarship. It also consisted, of course, of the National Science Foundation (NSF), founded after some delay in 1950, with the mission of promoting basic scientific inquiry. By the 1960s, and on the basis of this infrastructure of science funding, the federal government became the major sponsor of social and behavioral research, with one-half of its funding coming from Washington and another one-third from industry. By contrast, the foun-dations provided about 6 percent. However, as the foundation role declined in shaping public policy and in funding social science, and as the highly decen-tralized mission agencies assumed this responsibility, the social sciences also lost the benefits of committed patronage and common cause resulting from the circulating elite leadership of the pre–World War II era. Except for the decade of the 1990s, during which a Directorate for the Behavioral, Social, and Eco-nomic Sciences was established with the NSF, it is difficult to find an abiding federal patron of social science, per se.

Thus, toward the end of the twentieth century, the social science disci-plines by and large stood at the periphery of the federally supported science establishment and appeared politically vulnerable. These conditions, perhaps consequences in part of a highly decentralized federal science system and of uncoordinated policies affecting the development of all the sciences and tech-nology, seemed to limit the centrality and relevance of social science to the national interest and to public policy.

At the very end of the century, however, contrary signs appeared on the horizon, perhaps signaling a changing political climate in the twenty-first cen-tury. For example, against the background of the longest growth period in the American economy and an apparent federal budgetary surplus, bipartisan sup-port for increasing federal funding for basic research entered the run-up to the presidential election in November 2000. Increases well above the (historically low) inflation rate for the National Science Foundation and especially for the National Institutes of Health—principal funding sources for the social and behavioral sciences—were forecast both in Congress and in the Executive Branch. In the Senate subcommittee hearings on the FY2000 appropriations bill affecting the NSF, an exchange occurred between Daniel Inouye (D-Hawaii) and Christopher "Kit" Bond (R-Missouri) over report language that appeared to refer unfavorably to the social and behavioral sciences as part of the core of the NSF. Responding to Senator Inouye's challenge and query, Senator Bond, chairing the hearings, clarified that "NSF's core mission indeed includes basic research in the behavioral and social sciences, and, let me make it clear, it is my expectation that NSF will continue its strong investment in these areas. . . . Reduced support would jeopardize the development of the multidisciplinary perspectives that are necessary to solve many of the problems facing the Nation" (Consortium of Social Science Associations 1999). One can only wait to see if such a view is sustained throughout subsequent changes in political tides, or by the record of social science achievements as problem-solving, problem-defining tools in the twenty-first century.

A Centenary Appraisal through Historical Narrative and Topical Case Studies

Despite major changes in the use of social and behavioral science in social reform and policy-making in the twentieth century, surprisingly few historical accounts or analytical commentaries chronicle these more recent developments. This volume seeks to fill this void by providing both a detailed overview and topical case studies of the complex relationship between social science and policy-making up through the closing years of the 1900s.

In chapter 2, Martin Bulmer examines the simultaneous emergence of social science disciplines and social reform movements in the late nineteenth and early twentieth centuries. Bulmer traces factors that stimulated the rapid growth of social research in America and analyzes research's changing relationship to efforts to reform institutions and living conditions in that era. He gives particular attention to the role of private philanthropies in fostering early evolution of a "science of society," documenting the growing presence of social science disciplines within colleges and universities during the early twentieth century.

The coeditors of this volume, David Featherman and Maris Vinovskis, focus chapter 3 on developments in the post–World War II period affecting the relevance of social science to policy, the role of social scientists in policy, and the role of social scientists in policy-making and evaluation. They chart the growth and changes in the federal administrative state, shifts in the roles of philanthropic foundations and Washington-oriented think tanks, development of the American research university and of schools of public policy, and intellectual shifts in the social and behavioral sciences themselves. They also analyze the increasing use of academic advisers since the Kennedy administration and investigate the growing disillusionment among policymakers in the 1970s and 1980s with the apparently limited contributions of the social sciences.

The historical narrative provided by chapters 2 and 3 covers most of the twentieth century except for the 1990s. Subsequent chapters and authors focus on specific policy arenas, such as early childhood education or welfare reform. They provide case studies of how social science was used (or not used) and correspondingly shaped through an engagement with federal policy-making and evaluation. Through these case studies, the historical account is extended through the close of the twentieth century.

Sheldon White and Deborah Phillips (chap. 4) investigate the contributions of developmental psychologists in the creation and implementation of Project Head Start. They analyze the role of prominent psychologists, such as Urie Bronfenbrenner and Edward Zigler, in implementing a research-based foundation for this program of early childhood education. They discuss the setbacks faced by the program when the Westinghouse evaluation raised serious questions about the long-term effectiveness of Head Start. White and Phillips document the continuing involvement of behavioral scientists, mostly developmentalists, in setting Head Start policy goals in the 1970s and 1980s and conclude by reviewing their role in the program today.

In contrast to the policy arena of early childhood education, such topics as societal aging—the "graying of society"—and "successful aging" are less well formed as prominent public policy issues. However, in chapter 5 Andrew Achenbaum recalls that the first chapter of the Ogburn report, *Recent Social Trends,* authored by Thompson and Whelpton, concluded that "aging of the population [is] likely to produce significant consequences in our schools, in our business, in our politics and in our social structure" (cited by Achenbaum). New Deal legislation of the 1930s did produce Social Security, based on substantial input from the social sciences. But Achenbaum concludes that, overall, initiatives for elders lagged behind those designed for younger citizens, such as children, mothers, and younger workers. Since the 1930s, a whole new field of academic social science research, gerontology, grew into national and international prominence. Its contributions to policy-making may have been greater abroad—especially in Japan and part of Europe—than domestically. Achenbaum speculates about the reasons underlying the apparent difficulty since the time of the Depression in conceptualizing "productive aging" as a positive agenda in public policy. Apart from the fiscal and political viability of Social Security, the challenging institutional impacts of widespread societal aging among industrial nations have not received attention as federal or state policy priorities, or, perhaps until very recently, as warranting priority investment into social and behavioral research.

Chapters 6 and 7 analyze the complicated interplay of social science and policies related to the welfare of the persistently poor, the working poor, and low-income and single-parent families with dependent children. Since the War on Poverty, extending through President Nixon's Family Assistance Plan, President Carter's Program for Better Jobs and Income, the workfare demonstration projects of the Omnibus Budget Reconciliation Act of 1981, the Family Support Act of 1988, and finally to the Personal Responsibility and Work Opportunity Reconciliation Act of 1996 concluded in the Clinton presidency, welfare policy and programs have been set and reformed with reference to social science research. As noted by Sheldon Danziger (chap. 6), however, research often—especially in recent reforms—has lagged behind policy decisions to redefine baseline welfare standards, program eligibility, or even the goals and responsibilities of individuals versus the welfare state in securing work and an economic foothold in changing market circumstances. He notes: "so much social science, so little policy impact." The Danziger chapter also assesses the likely failure of the 1996 welfare reform, based on the corpus of research to date. Danziger warns that likely changes in the residual welfare population, as implementation of reform policies sends the most employable into the work force, may create new, perhaps unforeseen challenges for policy and research alike.

In chapter 7 Judith Gueron reviews the important role played in policy decision making, in the two decades after the Negative Income Tax Experiment of the 1970s, by demonstration projects and field experiments of program initiatives. Using as her focus the experiences of the Manpower Demonstration Research Corporation (MDRC), created in 1974 by the Ford Foundation and six federal agencies, Gueron recounts the novel research approaches she and her colleagues adopted, given that their primary goal was to affect policy via information dissemination (i.e., putting "rock-solid evidence" into hands of policymakers and practitioners) and "not to fill libraries." In studying the responses of states to federal legislation, MDRC often engaged state welfare commissioners and key agency staff in decisions about design and direction of its research and evaluation projects. In contrast to Danziger's assessment ("so much social science, so little policy impact") that refers mostly to federal policy-making, Gueron concludes that the state-level studies she reviews had unusually large effects on policy. The studies were designed mainly as field experiments and demonstration projects (often) with randomized assignments to hypothetical policy interventions. The apparent success of these studies in the 1980s and 1990s prompts Gueron to offer various lessons to the scientific and the policy communities on how to run these interventions as experiments. However, rather like Danziger, Gueron concludes that the most recent welfare reform in the Clinton presidency "was a radical leap into the unknown." It remains to be seen, she says, how the states—with their new program flexibility and policy responsibilities under the 1996 welfare reform—will use the likes of MDRC and the potential power of experiments and demonstration research to inform and evaluate the (most recent) reformation of welfare as we have known it.

In the final chapter of this volume, Lawrence Lynn views the emergence and evolution of policy analysis as a professional field through the analytical lens of social science. A social scientist looking backward as well as forward, reviewing the century's end and the contexts and conditions shaping the use of social science in policy-making, Lynn notes that knowledge is but one input to the making and the analysis of policy. As to policy-making itself, Lynn defines it as the "use of administrative discretion" and concludes that this discretion is increasingly diffusely located (in government and in nongovernmental interest groups, for example) and requires a more complicated understanding of the premises on which it is exercised. Correspondingly, the roles of policy analysts and researchers in brokering knowledge for the exercise of administrative discretion also have changed over the past thirty years. A challenge for the social sciences, perhaps more acute in the twenty-first century with its partisan think tanks as well as academic schools of public policy, is how its revealed knowledge and research will be used in the contemporary policy arena.

For the twenty-first century, Lynn calls for long-standing and distinguishing values of rigor, rationality, and transparency—honest brokering—in the practice of policy analysis. In the evolving, more decentralized contexts of policy discourse (inside and outside of government, in local and national settings), however, policy analysts also must be "pragmatic and crafty." Meeting these challenges arising with the new century may require drawing from one of the original ideas of the policy analysis movement, according to Lynn. This is "a [backward mapping] vision of social outcomes as foundations for identifying the social practices, resource allocations, institutions, and policies that might appear to be appropriate to achievement, and engagement in the kinds of political communication that might increase chances of their adoption."

This is an appropriate tone of optimism and uncertainty—skeptical realism—on which to end this book. The social sciences have been in search of their relevance to social reform and public policy for an entire century. The twentieth century embraced the full emergence both of these intellectual fields as theoretically rich and methodologically rigorous academic disciplines and of the federal administrative state as the focal point of policy-making for the nation. At the dawning of a new century, therefore, a retrospective assessment of our relevance as social scientists to the policies and policy-making of that administrative state is a worthy undertaking.

Perhaps such an assessment is all the more worthwhile to the extent that it avoids the excesses of either self-congratulation or cynical doubt. The historical record reveals moments and instances of relevance or usefulness to the broad public interest, to discretionary decision making by policymakers and administrators, and to the shaping of policies affecting children, family welfare, and elders, together with other arenas. Our impact as scholars, scientists, and honest research brokers has been episodic, not always positive, sometime

Knowledge for the Public Good: The Emergence of Social Sciences and Social Reform in Late-Nineteenth- and Early-Twentieth-Century America, 1880–1940

Martin Bulmer

From what historical background did social science emerge? What signal developments mark the previous half century of empirical study of society? What factors account for the considerable and early commitment in the United States to produce social science knowledge? What relationship exists between social science and social reform movements? This essay traces interrelated threads in the developing field of pre–World War II social science research in the United States.

Significant national and world events and historical developments impacted the development of social science. A number of distinct developments within social research are noteworthy, including early scientific social surveys, vocational testing administered during World War I, the Social Survey movement, and President Hoover's Commission on Recent Social Trends. Though not addressed chronologically in this essay, some of these distinctive developments are outlined in figure 1. These historical and social research developments can be organized around a series of prevalent themes: the character of American society, politics versus science, faith in the expert, the role of elites, the role of philanthropic foundations, and the place of universities in research. My treatment of the development of social science research is thematic rather than chronological, highlighting prevalent themes in the development of social science in the United States from 1880 to 1940 against the backdrop of the character of American society.

The Character of American Society

Though American exceptionalism is often overplayed, it has some relevance to the development of social science, since social investigation developed differently in the United States than in other parts of the world. For example, the American urge to investigate social conditions is rooted in American society, whereas European social investigation was motivated by the state. What prompted Americans to pursue social inquiry? Social conditions created by urbanization, industrialization, and mass immigration in the northern American cities impinged in the first instance upon the indigenous citizenry of those cities, stimulating reflection on the social consequences of progress. By the late nineteenth century these consequences were plainly evident, fueling the Progressive movement in society and politics,

> a rather widespread and remarkably good-natured effort of the greater part of society to achieve some not very clearly specified self-reformation. Its general theme was the effort to restore a type of economic individualism and political democracy that was widely believed to have existed earlier in America and to have been destroyed by the great corporation and the corrupt political machine; and with that restoration to bring back a kind of morality and civic purity that was also believed to have been lost. (Hofstadter 1962, 5)

Later, the sway of events, particularly the American entry into World War I, the Great Crash of 1929, and the Great Depression that followed, created circumstances in which particular forms of social science research were again in demand.

Roots of Social Science

Systematic social investigation in America, characteristically a phenomenon of the twentieth century, traces its diverse roots and precursors to trends in late-nineteenth-century America. One important contributor to the development of social science was muckraking journalism, which focused upon social conditions in major American cities. Another factor in the development of social science was the burgeoning Settlement House movement, which sought by social intervention to ameliorate the social circumstances of the urban poor. A third precursor lay in the gradual development of better information about labor markets, together with the development of an embryonic system of labor statistics, as part of what Lacey terms the "liberal positivist" project (1993).

Preliminary social inquiry and the urban poor.   The Settlement House studies of urban problems together with the growth of research on juvenile crime illustrate the beginning interest in specific social problems as subjects of scientific inquiry. Public health concerns motivated the first surveys of urban social con-

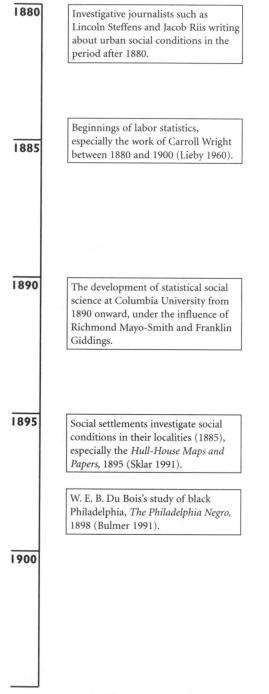

1880	Investigative journalists such as Lincoln Steffens and Jacob Riis writing about urban social conditions in the period after 1880.
1885	Beginnings of labor statistics, especially the work of Carroll Wright between 1880 and 1900 (Lieby 1960).
1890	The development of statistical social science at Columbia University from 1890 onward, under the influence of Richmond Mayo-Smith and Franklin Giddings.
1895	Social settlements investigate social conditions in their localities (1885), especially the *Hull-House Maps and Papers,* 1895 (Sklar 1991).
	W. E. B. Du Bois's study of black Philadelphia, *The Philadelphia Negro,* 1898 (Bulmer 1991).
1900	

Fig. 1. Some major developments in the investigation of society, polity, and the economy in the United States prior to 1940. The following developments are selective, identified particularly in relationship to the development of the social survey and of the disciplines of sociology and political science. The list is not exhaustive but is intended to sketch some of the signposts in the history of social investigation.

1905

The Pittsburgh Survey, 1906–9 (Greenwald and Anderson 1996) and the establishment of the Department of Surveys and Exhibits by the Russell Sage Foundation, 1912–30, the driving force of the Social Survey movement (Eaton and Harrison 1930).

1910

Psychological testing develops as a branch of applied psychology, 1910 onward, especially at Carnegie-Mellon, and is then drawn into the War Department and greatly expanded during World War I.

1915

The development of empirical sociology at the University of Chicago, 1915–35, building upon the work of Thomas under the influence of Robert E. Park, Ernest Burgess, and later William F. Ogburn (Bulmer 1984).

The empirical inquiries of W. I. Thomas at the University of Chicago, culminating in *The Polish Peasant in Europe and America* (1918–20).

1920

L. L. Thurstone develops methods of attitude measurement at the University of Chicago, early 1920s.

The development of the science of politics at the University of Chicago after 1920 under the influence of Charles E. Merriam and his students Harold F. Gosnell and Harold Lasswell.

The establishment of the National Bureau of Economic Research in 1921 under the influence of Columbia economist Wesley Mitchell.

Beardsley Ruml in 1923 becomes the Director of the Laura Spelman Rockefeller Memorial and reorients its program to basic research in the social sciences.

The Social Science Research Council established 1923.

1925

Developments in market research and political polling from 1925 onward (Converse 1987).

President Hoover establishes the President's Committee on Recent Social Trends, 1929–33, directed by Mitchell (chair: economics), Merriam (politics), and Ogburn and Odum (sociology).

1930

ditions in the United States. Labor statistics were collected in some cities by boards whose investigative methods more resembled legislative committees taking oral and written evidence than those of methodical systematic researchers. Firsthand social investigation required close acquaintance with the social worlds under examination. The establishment of settlement houses in poor inner city areas provided the acquaintance necessary to research actively. The University Settlement in New York was established in 1886 and Hull House in Chicago in 1889. Other settlements followed in Boston, New York, and Chicago; by 1910 there were more than 400 settlements. Jane Addams, a friend of John Dewey and George Herbert Mead, headed Hull House, often described as a graduate school of social policy at a time when the subject was little studied in the university. Settlement residents included Florence Kelley, pioneer social investigator and later head of the National Consumer League; Julia Lathrop, first head of the U.S. Children's Bureau; and Edith Abbott, pioneer of social service education. The residents of these settlement houses were young, thoughtful, and socially committed.

The book *Hull-House Maps and Papers,* primarily authored by Florence Kelley, was published in 1895 and included detailed color maps showing the distribution of social characteristics in the areas studied. Influenced by Charles Booth's studies of poverty in London, appearing first in 1889, *Maps and Papers* addressed child labor, sweatshop labor, three neighborhood ethnic groups, and labor organizations for working women, among other issues (Sklar 1991, 1995). Kelley and her colleagues were oriented to social action and what Addams called "constructive work" rather than sociological investigation as an end to itself, although Kelley worked for the U.S. Bureau of Labor while collecting the data that form the study. Hull House residents were concerned about issues such as sweatshop labor and child labor prevalent in Chicago at that time and against which they were actively campaigning. The treatment of juveniles in the court system and bad housing conditions were other issues that they pursued as reform objectives. Robert Hunter's 1904 study *Poverty* had a slightly broader focus, but most studies carried out under the auspices of settlement houses were directly connected to reform in the city in which the houses were located.

Preliminary social inquiry and juvenile crime.   The case of juvenile crime is even more instructive than that of settlement houses in illustrating the development of social research in the United States. In a real sense, late-nineteenth-century society created the category of juvenile crime and identified it as a separate social problem. This categorization resulted from juvenile crime being the focus of reform efforts. Hence, social investigation was harnessed as a means of illuminating societal problems. Social change and the development of investigation have gone hand in hand.

Two crucial developments in the evolution of juvenile justice occurred at this period in history (to oversimplify considerably a complex story): recognition of separate status for "child" as opposed to "adult" offenders, and, through expansion of the legal doctrine *parens patriae,* creation of a special institution, the juvenile court, to assess juvenile offenses and prescribe appropriate treatment (Schlossman 1977). Earlier in the nineteenth century, penal reformers had placed their hopes in the reform school, where residential treatment was supposed to produce social improvement and personal reform. Too often the reform school entirely failed to achieve this objective, held its inmates in insalubrious conditions, and provided a juvenile form of imprisonment for young people who frequently were treated as adults from the perspective of the criminal justice system (Mennel 1973, 32–77).

Philanthropic groups and state agencies began to seek alternatives to the delinquent reform school; the first step in this direction was the establishment of the juvenile court as a separate judicial body to deal with young offenders. The first juvenile court was established in Illinois in 1899, and many other states followed within a short space of time. Within fifteen years, twenty-two states had established such courts. Probation officers were appointed to serve the courts, and the treatment of young offenders changed substantially. "The child was brought before the court," wrote Jane Addams, "with no-one to prosecute him and none to defend him—the judge and all concerned were merely trying to find out what could be done on his behalf. The element of conflict was absolutely eliminated and with it all notions of punishment as such with its curiously belated connotations" (quoted in Mennel 1973, 133). *Parens patriae,* the legal doctrine justifying the state in taking on the responsibilities of a child's parents, was restated and expanded. At the same time, reformers sought to change the basis on which child offenders were treated.

Reformers were frequently disappointed with the results of juvenile courts. Though provided with social work staff and child guidance clinics, the courts often failed to solve problems that home or school also found intractable. An almost naive optimism in the possibilities of social engineering upon a human nature conceived of as a tabula rasa inevitably led to disappointment. But the juvenile courts and those who passed through them served as subjects for research, and in the area of delinquency, this social research was perhaps more analytic than in the study of poverty.

The criminal anthropology and eugenics of the nineteenth century notwithstanding, the earliest research into juvenile delinquency in the present century was psychiatric, conducted by Adolf Meyer in Baltimore and E. E. Southard in Boston. William Healey was hired in 1909 by the Juvenile Protective Association in Chicago to administer the Juvenile Psychopathic Institute, a pioneering body in the establishment of child guidance clinics in the United States. I am not qualified to stray far into the history of psychology but must note this example of the advent of serious applied psychology and psychiatry exercised with delinquent boys. Such an approach was also exemplified at Harvard by the Gluecks in the slightly later study *One Thousand Delinquents* (1934), which challenged the efficacy of the rehabilitative approach.

W. I. Thomas pioneered, then Ernest Burgess seriously developed the study of juvenile delinquency, with the aid of his associates Clifford Shaw and Henry McKay. Frederic M. Thrasher studied the gang, Walter Reckless, vice, John Landesco, organized crime, and Franklin Frazier, black family life. The program that Burgess, Shaw, and McKay pursued was one of the earliest systematic studies of a public policy issue conducted within a scientific framework. The research carried out was both quantitative and qualitative (one myth about Chicago sociology emphasized its mainly qualitative nature), but the quantitative aspect of the study was primarily ecological analysis of the geographical distribution of crime, including the correlation between crime and locality (e.g., Shaw et al. 1929). Delinquency was viewed as the product, not of individual pathology, but of the social setting in which the delinquent passed his or her time, the product of social interaction and the social environment. Delinquency represented the breakdown of the machinery of spontaneous social control, as well as the social and normative constraints through which society is held together.

Thus, in the example of juvenile delinquency, professionals were intimately involved in the development of reform—the judge served as the key figure in the working of the juvenile court. In time, social researchers also assisted with applied work close to the concerns of practitioners, while remaining rooted in a disciplinary perspective, both in psychiatry and sociology in different cases. Thus, social problems became matters for social scientific empirical inquiry (Cravens 1978).

Preliminary social inquiry in immigration and race.   Many examples illustrate the influence of wider social trends upon the development of empirical inquiry. However, the study of immigration and race was a distinctive area of research in the early twentieth century. Indeed, sociology as a discipline established its autonomy, in part, by focusing on this topic. Thomas and Znaniecki's magisterial study *The Polish Peasant in Europe and America* (1918–20), though far from being a social survey, used materials—letters, life histories, court records, the observations of the authors—and responded to the mass migration that left Chicago the second largest Polish city in the world after Warsaw. Twenty years earlier, W. E. B. Du Bois published a pioneering social survey of the black district of Philadelphia, *The Philadelphia Negro* (1898), employing scientific social survey methods closely modeled on the British example provided by Charles Booth's poverty survey of London. Because Du Bois was black, he was confined to teaching at black colleges, and in 1909 he moved from social science to activism, partially due to his frustration at the indifference with which his work was met among mainstream academics (Bulmer 1991; Lewis 1993, 179–210).

In 1922 Robert Park's graduate student Charles S. Johnson carried out a survey of race relations in Chicago for the Chicago Commission on Race Relations. Johnson had worked with Park earlier while investigating the origins of the Great Migration from the American South to northern cities, a phenomenon that gathered pace during World War I (Grossman 1989). The Commission was founded in the wake of the Chicago race riot of 1919, in which thirty-eight people (twenty-three black and fifteen white) died. The Commission's research was a mélange of primitive quantitative interviews, a collection of qualitative life histories, and documentary materials. The research was important because it sought to document extensively not only the events of the riot but also the social conditions from which the riot had sprung. Of all social issues in the American city, white social reformers were perhaps most awkward and uncertain when faced with race questions. Despite the awkwardness, reformers recognized a need for and began to facilitate social inquiry, in this case through the influence of Robert Park upon the Chicago Urban League.

Preliminary social inquiry in marketing and advertising.   The rise of market research and polling in the 1920s and early 1930s was a final and important antecedent of social research (Converse 1987, 87–111). This movement culminated in the 1936 presidential election, which first thrust modern survey research onto the public stage. While Converse chronicles only the development of survey methods, my point here is wider, namely, in the interwar period, American society became less local and more regional and national both in structure and orientation (cf. Karl 1984). Manufactured goods and products (newspapers, magazines, and radio) were evolving, and the techniques of social research were distinctively useful in studying these mass markets. Local studies no longer enabled the researcher to grasp the full range and complexity of the phenomena of mass markets. At the same time, these more extensive methods tended to focus on the atomized individual, aggregating up to the whole from a series of points, rather like a Seurat painting. Thus we see that social research in its fledgling stages was a response to changes in American society.

The Tension between Science and Politics in Social Inquiry

A fascinating antinomy runs through the fifty-year period preceding the establishment of social science, contrasting progress through politics and progress through science. The articulation of one with the other could be conceptualized in a number of ways. "Politics finds its sources," Hugh Heclo has written, "not only in power but in uncertainty—men wondering collectively what to do . . . policy-making is a form of collective puzzlement on society's behalf; it entails both deciding and knowing" (1974, 305).

The Progressive movement allied politics and science, but political objectives often subordinated scientific inquiry in a particular way. Indeed, characteristic of some progressively inspired inquiries was the relationship between inquiry and sociopolitical change that underpinned the inquiry. The Settlement House studies discussed earlier rested on a simple and relatively unexamined assumption that there existed a direct connection between uncovering adverse social conditions and intervention designed to remedy them. Hull House residents were social activists, many of whom later moved on to public positions. Social research was an instrument of alerting civic opinion and initiating legislative action. Consider Jane Addams, herself a public figure. She and many of her colleagues functioned as political animals who used social research as a lever of change.

A slightly different model of the relationship between social research and action developed through the Social Survey movement, at its peak from 1906 to 1926. Because public opinion played a comparatively more important role in the American polity than in Western European democracies, the relationship between social research and local public opinion lay at the center of the Social Survey movement. Significant figures were persuaded that public opinion was of key importance—Robert Park described social research as playing a role in "the illumination of opinion." In the writings of Herbert Croly and Walter Lippmann, the subject became a staple topic in political science discussions even before the advent of the straw ballot, out of which developed the public opinion poll as a technique of survey research. To some extent, researchers believed that once the findings of research were promulgated, the symbiotic relationship between social inquiry and civic opinion would cause remedial action to follow.

The Pittsburgh Survey of 1906–9 was the first major study of the Social Survey movement. It originated in Pittsburgh and is noteworthy, among other reasons, because it marks the first time that local people sought outside expertise in surveying their own locale. Those conducting the survey were closely linked to social work. Paul U. Kellogg, director of the survey, viewed social workers as social engineers, who analyze the nature of social problems and are active in consensus building with local leaders to resolve the problems identified. Kellogg himself was more journalist than social worker, but understanding his links to these two occupations is significant in characterizing the type of inquiry he undertook.

Thus the Pittsburgh Survey provided a comprehensive picture of social conditions in the "steel city," including the use of photographs as a description.

However, prescriptive action was also meant to follow. To ensure that the "illumination of public opinion" occurred, local involvement in the study design was a key feature. Following completion of the study, demonstrations and exhibitions were arranged in Pittsburgh, at which results of the research were presented to the citizenry (Greenwald and Anderson 1996). Though not methodologically pathbreaking, the notion of providing civic feedback was a distinguishing feature of these surveys.

Foundation support was a key factor in the Social Survey movement because of the intimate link to Russell Sage philanthropy. Russell Sage funded the Pittsburgh survey and then in 1912 created Pittsburgh's Department of Surveys and Exhibits, designed to promote Sage-supported social surveys in cities and towns. Shelby M. Harrison directed the department, and between 1912 and 1927 over two and a half thousand such surveys were conducted with department support. The link with social work was perhaps the most salient characteristic of the surveys, and in many respects the surveys more closely resembled investigative journalism than modern social scientific research. In these particular social surveys, investigation and action were closely linked.

A comparison of W. E. B. Du Bois and Charles E. Merriam sheds fascinating light on the relationship between knowledge based on social inquiry and activist involvement. Both men had high-level professional training in the last decade of the nineteenth century, Du Bois in history at Harvard and Berlin, Merriam in political science at Columbia. Du Bois began his research career by moving into sociological research and carrying out both the previously mentioned Philadelphia study and a series of studies at Atlanta University (where he taught for a decade). These studies were scientific, not reformist, in intent and sought to analyze the social situation of black Americans without intervening or recommending action for the alteration of their situation. At the same time, Du Bois as an intellectual wrote *The Souls of Black Folk,* becoming embroiled in arguments with Booker T. Washington about the correct political strategy for black Americans to follow. Du Bois appears to have kept his scholarly and political sides somewhat separate. After a decade of serious research efforts that were almost totally hampered by lack of funding, in 1909 Du Bois accepted an invitation to move to New York to work for the NAACP and edit their magazine *The Crisis.* This move effectively severed his connections with academic research and solidified his prime commitment to politics within a pressure group.

Merriam, who has some claim to the title "father of American quantitative political science in the first half of the twentieth century," moved in the opposite direction. Appointed to teach political science at the University of Chicago in 1900, he was principally preoccupied with involvement in city politics for the first twenty years of his academic career. His father was a staunch Republican, and Merriam grew up with a strong interest in practical politics, which he proceeded to put into practice in Chicago. In 1909 he was elected a city alderman and in 1911 stood unsuccessfully for mayor. He remained involved in city politics for another eight years and in 1919, urged on by Harold Ickes and Jane Addams, stood again. This time he was roundly defeated by the isolationist William Hale Thompson, and as a result left practical politics for good, just as, later, Paul Lazarsfeld abandoned his social democratic political activism when he settled in the United States.

During this period, Merriam's academic publications centered mainly on political theory, but from 1920 onward his interests shifted. Barry Karl suggests that Merriam's political tendencies were shifting from the public stage into the profession (1974, 106). Be that as it may, he adumbrated a program for political science that moved the discipline in a markedly behaviorist direction, and his students, Harold Lasswell and Harold Gosnell, pushed political science even further in the direction that Merriam advocated. In 1920 he was already calling for newer, more modern methods in data collection and a readiness to employ methods of other social sciences. He called for broader use of instruments of social observation in statistics, and of the analytical results and techniques of psychology. And although his own background lay in progressive politics, he sought a sharper distinction between social involvement and academic study. Those conducting social research needed to avoid the status of reformer, particularly in relation to the study of city government, Merriam believed. Unifying this new agenda involved a commitment to organizing the social sciences so that political science could work together with other disciplines—an emphasis that preceded the establishment of social science on team research and interdisciplinary cooperation models by a quarter of a century.

Merriam, together with others, was a national institution builder, concerned with the politics of social science and the building of national capacity in the social sciences. The Social Science Research Council (SSRC), incorporated in New York in 1923, was his chosen instrument, not financed by federal or state government, but acting as a channel for philanthropic resources to contribute to capacity building. SSRC was organized as a representative of seven disciplines: political science, sociology, economics, anthropology, history, psychology, and statistics. SSRC was significant because it articulated growing tendencies in the academic social sciences of the period: to claim to be scientific and to undertake ambitious forms of social inquiry requiring external funding, to create university-based research organizations to carry out these programs, and, to a certain extent, to favor interdisciplinary cooperation, while at the same time building the disciplines separately. Plenty of scope for argument is available concerning the interpretation of the above-mentioned trends. The most recent history (Fisher 1993) frames them in a Gramscian perspective, arguing that SSRC represented class interests and a foundation plan to alter the character of the social sciences. Others maintain that the funders reflected changes already under way in the social sciences, and that the creation of SSRC was a step in the professionalization of the social sciences in America.

At this period, the federal government supported social research only sparingly. Indeed, the school of thought that strongly emphasizes the role of the state in the development of social investigation extrapolates from a few instances, exaggerating the importance of the state. Michael Lacey (1993, 4) argues that an inquiring, would-be problem-solving style of governance was evident from the 1830s onward, and that a receptivity to social investigation reached its zenith near the turn of the century, before becoming solidly established after 1940. To be sure, after 1900 the federal government was more prepared to consider the evidence of contemporary social conditions. However, this readiness did not intimate that the federal government would undertake such studies itself—or extend the responsibilities of government to deal with the problems identified through social research. With the exception of World War I, the government was averse to involvement in studies and solutions. Indeed, the result of "bringing the state back in" has often been to exaggerate its importance. Certainly changes occurred in state responsibility for social policies in the early twentieth century, particularly in Europe, and some of these changes were introduced as a result of political debates influenced by evidence produced by social investigators. But in the United States, the federal government in particular would not assume responsibility for matters that Congress did not consider its concern. Indeed, Congress found itself in the throes of the interwar period, as reflected in the title of the book by Barry Karl, *The Uneasy State* (1984).

Of somewhat more significance were events at the state and local levels, though many occurrences might be interpreted as reaction as much as action. Much of what happened was provoked by the character of local politics and the lack of receptivity to middle-class reformers in major urban centers. The Settlement House social investigators, for example, found themselves frequently at odds with the incumbents of City Hall. In cities like Chicago and New York City, where boss politics reached its zenith, not only middle-class reformers but also various professional groups and academics found themselves on the outside, facing a less than receptive audience among local politicians. The political spoils system was too distinctively American to relinquish in favor of the urge to inquire and document social conditions.

An example of the spoils system at work was evident in Illinois during the 1920s, where Chicago was the scene of particularly glaring excesses in relation to lawlessness, organized crime, and links between the latter and city politicians. John Landesco showed the extent to which 1920s Chicago permitted local judges and other officeholders to act as pallbearers at the funerals of prominent gangland figures. Because of these and other abuses, legal process and reform were vital issues for many members of the legal profession, local civic elites, academics, and moralists. As a result, movements for legal and criminal reform developed, seeking to harness social investigation to address these difficulties. In the case of Illinois, the local and state machines were to an extent separate from one another. Hence, it was possible under the auspices of the state of Illinois to mount investigations into the crime situation in Cook County. These surveys both conducted social inquiries and sought to achieve reform.

The Illinois Crime Survey, which was published as a book in 1929 by the Illinois Crime Commission, was an exhaustive review of all aspects of crime in the state and in the criminal justice system. Some of the contents were of lasting importance to social science, such as Ernest Burgess's analysis of parole and Landesco's monograph on organized crime. The survey was conducted under the auspices of the Illinois Association of Criminal Justice and endeavored to carry out a statewide survey of the administration of criminal justice and of the causes and conditions of crime,

> to initiate and secure the passage of legislation and to take such other remedial action tending to diminish crime and to improve the administration of justice as is deemed necessary or as is suggested by the findings and recommendation of such survey; and to promote and secure intelligent and efficient administration of civil and criminal justice within the state of Illinois. (Illinois Association for Criminal Justice 1929, 11)

In this introduction, jurist John Wigmore identified efficiency as the key aim of the whole exercise, but lamented in strong tones how awful and far from that ideal was the present system and how great the need was for citizens to eschew selfishness and rediscover the spirit of "All for one and one for all." The Illinois Crime Survey, forged out of difficult conditions in the locality, provided a model for the utilization of social science and criminal justice research results in public policy-making. The model was indeed a circumscribed one, but was nonetheless significant in the America of the 1920s—social science could be an ally of reform.

Faith in the Expert and Expertise

We now come to an enduring feature of the American scene, an important element in the relationship under examination in the half century prior to 1940. In this setting, the expert is seen as a worthwhile contributor to the analysis of social problems and an integral part of solution proposals. The social investigator may make claims to expertise himself, or may bring experts in as part of the team, as in the Pittsburgh Survey, to ensure that the investigation is carried out as effectively as possible. But the appeal to expertise provides legitimacy to the investigation and commands some acceptance in the wider society.

In a sense, the belief in expertise may be interpreted as the professionalization of social science. As social inquirers are properly trained and rendered competent, the expertise to which they have access may be used for public policy purposes. The problem with equating belief in expertise with professionalization is that in the early part of the period the techniques of social investigation were poorly codified and by no means confined to university settings where formal training could take place. What, indeed, was considered social investigation during the latter half of the nineteenth century? The history of the American Social Science Association (ASSA) showed clearly that there was no unilinear progress in the field, for the ASSA ended its life in genteel decline (Haskell 1977). What is notable about many of the activities listed in figure 1— for example, the impact of social settlements and the Social Survey movement—is the lack of continuity and the extent to which the consolidation of expertise was not a unilinear process. This incongruous progress solidified the importance of universities, particularly their disciplinary corporations and research centers as bearers of a common approach to social inquiry of lasting import. The twentieth century is marked by the rise of the academic as public policy expert.

Three examples briefly illustrate the impact that an orientation to expertise began to have on social science and society. In psychology, applied psychologists interested in the measurement of ability, aptitude, and performance developed objective tests of these traits, which were given a very powerful fillip by their use in government, particularly the War Department, for the duration of World War I. Testing of ability, aptitude, and performance was one of the first major moves to use applied social research in government in the United States. This move stimulated fields such as occupational psychology and legitimated testing as an activity.

> The war changed the image of testers and of the tested. Intelligence tests were no longer things given by college professors and resident examiners . . . to crazy people and imbeciles in psychopathic institutes and homes for the feeble-minded, but legitimate means of making decisions about the aptitudes and achievements of normal people—an essential means of making objective judgements about individuals in a mass society. (Reed 1987, 76)

Desire for expertise was likewise evidenced through a particular vogue for the survey in the 1920s, when academic experts were mobilized to study urban problems. The Illinois Crime Survey was of this type; it emulated earlier surveys conducted in 1921 by Roscoe Pound and Felix Frankfurter, the Harvard jurists. The 1926 Missouri Crime Survey was directed by Raymond Moley from Columbia, who was later prominent as a member of FDR's brain trust and in 1930s attempts to create planning mechanisms within the federal government. These surveys in some sense echoed the aims of the Pittsburgh Survey but were focused on a single issue, were typically directed by a specialist academic engaged upon a fact-gathering exercise (with others) in the locality, and endeavored to address issues of local policy. In addition to the crime surveys, other local surveys concentrated on public education, recreation, employment, and industrial relations, seeking to harness the skills of the social investigator in delineating and understanding the nature of current social issues. The same faith in the power of expert knowledge was evident throughout these surveys.

Faith in expertise found its apotheosis in the person of Herbert Hoover, an engineer by background, who made a reputation in Progressive circles during World War I by advocating the application of science to government, particularly via scientific management. As Secretary of Commerce after the war, he sought to harness science to industrial development and moved the core staff of the War Industries Board into his department. Shortly after assuming the presidency in 1929, he established the President's Committee on Recent Social Trends, whose scope was no less than to survey the whole of American society so that for the first time in history a whole range of social conditions could be viewed from a rational, scientifically organized perspective. The conception of Recent Social Trends was very different from the goal of the Pittsburgh Survey of righting wrongs and reforming adverse social conditions. Indeed, Recent Social Trends aspired to provide a detached, scientific view of the whole of American society.

Recent Social Trends was chaired by economist Wesley Mitchell and political scientist Charles Merriam. Shelby Harrison, the key figure in the Social Survey movement, was an additional member. Research was driven by director William F. Ogburn of Chicago, assisted by Howard Odum from Chapel Hill, both sociologists. The resulting report was essentially an extremely detailed, factual description of social conditions in the United States of the time, although much debate occurred within the directorate as to what constituted objectivity, and what the relationship was between social science and governmental action. Recent Social Trends' ambitions for expert analysis were never met in governmental reality, symbolized by the fact that by the date of its publication in January 1933, President Hoover had fallen from power. In terms of discontinuities, Recent Social Trends bore no trace whatever of the Social Survey movement, despite Shelby Harrison's involvement.

The Role of Elite Interest in the Development of Social Science

President Hoover's interest in social knowledge as a means to more efficient management of society illustrates the general phenomenon of considerable elite interest in the potential of social investigation and social science contributing to the policy-making process. Elite interest found its most direct expression in the role of philanthropic foundations, discussed in the next section, and is a feature of the period under examination. For much of the fifty years preceding World War II, however, the condition of social investigation was weak, and the occupation of social researcher was a relatively precarious one. The university research base was established only slowly, remaining until 1940 relatively tiny apart from one or two modest centers. Government was not predisposed to commit taxpayers' money to relatively newfangled notions (at either the state or federal levels). Wartime apart, some developments such as psychological testing found their best market in the business world.

A considerable number of studies discussed so far had their origins in either individual initiatives or collective steps taken at the instigation of an elite individual or an elite group in the locality to examine the social state of a city or town or a particular social problem. Influential individuals like Mrs. Ethel Dummer in Chicago, who financed much of W. I. Thomas's research; Susan Wharton, a Quaker member of the committee of the Philadelphia College Settlement, who instigated W. E. B. Du Bois's study; and bodies such as the City Club of Chicago and the Pittsburgh Civic Association were important initiators of several inquiries discussed in this chapter.

Such elite influence may be viewed in different ways. The Gramscian critique of philanthropy, in particular, argues that such initiatives were very much self-interested; members of the ruling class and power elite seeking to safeguard the position of their class encouraged the examination of potentially destabilizing influences and adjusted the social fabric so that the interests of their class would be preserved. While not discounting such explanations entirely, we must note other, more important sources of the impulse to inquire into contemporary social conditions. The following remarks apply both to elite funders of research and individual researchers drawn from elite social strata.

The religious backgrounds of many individuals involved in social research is significant. Perhaps America possessed a successful economy and resulting large resources, but many of a religious cast of mind were uncomfortable with this wealth and the high costs of immigration, industrialization, and urbanization. This unease sometimes led to institutional developments, for example, the late-nineteenth-century establishment of the American Social Science Association. A more specific development in the 1920s and 1930s was the Institute of Social and Religious Research in New York, which emerged from the Interchurch World movement, was concerned with the health of small towns and the countryside, and funded Robert Lynd's notable study of the typical American town, *Middletown*.

Faith in rational analysis of problems was also important to socially concerned Protestants and congruent with the development of a scientific approach to social issues. An ethos of "service" and a belief in the public interest were particularly strong within collective civic associations, which were often criticized by later scholars on grounds of enlightened self-interest. However, these groups ought not be discounted, for they served as a genuine stimulus to discovering social conditions in the cities where they lived. Links between such local political and social elites and senior academics were considerable, and an increasing proportion of the latter were themselves social scientists. With elite interest in social investigation, the perceived value of disinterested inquiry was given due weight, perhaps a reflection of the national belief that scientific solutions to problems existed and should be given a chance.

Some of these reflections are rather speculative, but the Gramscian presentation of elite involvement in the growth of social science involves a considerable element of distortion. Doubtless, some social research was conducted for the gain of some political and social elites. However, a sizable portion of elite-backed social research was valuable for its own sake, or at least for the sake of disinterested inquiry, as much as to bolster the economic interests of the people involved.

The Contribution of the Philanthropic Foundations

In the fifty years before 1940, philanthropic foundations such as Carnegie, Rockefeller, and Russell Sage played an important part in the story of the rise of social investigation. The influence of these foundations was most keenly felt during the last thirty years of the period. University endowment and research in science and medicine in the United States first attracted major funding from these new funding enterprises, but under the influence of some trustees and of the foundation's full-time officers, who by the 1920s had come to exercise as much or more influence than the board members, social science research began to receive financial support. The most notable example of this shift in funding focus was Beardsley Ruml's transformation of the Laura Spelman Rockefeller Memorial into a major funding force in the social sciences (Bulmer and Bulmer 1981). In the years between 1923 and 1929, this fund distributed some $40 million for social research to American and overseas universities.

Foundation-based funding was of signal importance because of the almost total absence of federal or state funding for social science research at public universities, at the federal level because of principle, and at the state level because funding went to support college teachers, not to fund research. The foundations were, in fact, selective by type as well as by choice of recipient. For a long period, the Rockefeller Foundation would only support research at private universities, and therefore the major investments were made in the Ivy League, or at Chicago, Chapel Hill, and other institutions that were not state-supported. The initial foundation of the research system established between 1900 and 1940 was created by these large institutional donors.

Before Ruml's arrival, the Rockefeller Memorial had supported good works in the New York City area, reflecting the interests of John D. Rockefeller Sr.'s wife (after whom it was named). Ruml's policy completely changed the focus to the basic infrastructure of social science research. Still in his twenties, Ruml was a University of Chicago Ph.D. in psychology and a brief assistant to James Angell when he was head of the Carnegie Corporation. In 1923 Ruml framed a policy that argued that basic social science research would provide the soundest basis for making use of social science in the policy process. Such research, he stated, should be empirically oriented, interdisciplinary in its outlook, and directed to identifiable social problems. Although he received counsel from Charles Merriam, Ruml was always particularly careful with proposals for research on municipal reform and kept these at arm's length from the program lest the Memorial be drawn into political wrangling. Ruml was later briefly dean of social sciences at Chicago (1931–34), and Robert Maynard Hutchins claimed hyperbolically that he was "the founder of social sciences in the U.S." This was to claim too much, but Ruml was undoubtedly an extremely important figure in the creation of a funding system and research infrastructure for large-scale empirical research.

Policy at the Carnegie Corporation displayed certain significant differences, both in projects supported and institutional style, but in fact there was a considerable overlap of interests with the Memorial, as well as a lesser tendency to become bureaucratized, compared to events that occurred when the Memorial became the Social Science Division of the Rockefeller Foundation in 1929. Carnegie, for example, funded the study of the American race problem by the Swedish social economist Gunnar Myrdal, published as *An American Dilemma* in 1944 (Lagemann 1989, 123–46).

Philanthropic foundations whose founders were deceased differed from those whose founders were still living. The Russell Sage Foundation became involved in social welfare research and reform through the interests of the donor's widow, who encouraged support for projects like the Social Survey movement. Robert Brookings, a St. Louis businessman who gave up commerce for intellectual pursuits at the age of fifty, was considerably more inclined to question the status quo than the staff of the Institute of Economics that he endowed, because the Institute sought to achieve national efficiency, not to promote alternatives to the present system.

In addition to the controversy over the Gramscian thesis discussed earlier, there has been much debate about the extent to which the foundations changed the character of the social sciences, pushing them in a more empirical direction, particularly during the 1920s. Though philanthropic funding was a necessary condition in institutionalizing empirical social research, for a small number of institutions the argument that the foundations shaped the social sciences decisively is not proven. Foundation officials were in close touch with social scientists, and it is at least as reasonable to argue that these officials were reflecting what they interpreted as predominant tendencies of those in the forefront of their disciplines at the time. It is more plausible to suggest that there was an elective affinity between the aspirations of leading social scientists and the aims of foundation officials, such that they often agreed as to the direction they wished to take. Some, such as European visitor Harold Laski, dissented, and the more critical issue here is perhaps the issue of accountability. As private institutions with no external responsibility, how did foundations affect the balance in social sciences between expertise and democracy (Lagemann 1989, 253–63)? Did foundation officials have a built-in predisposition to support the former over the latter?

The Role of Universities in the Development of Social Research

The final theme is closest to home for myself: the role of universities in the development of social research. Nowadays we take the connection for granted, but this was not the case a century or more ago. Investigative journalists writing about urban social conditions, labor statistics, social settlements, Du Bois's study, the Pittsburgh Survey, and the Social Survey movement—all took place outside the orbit of universities. Settlement houses were a kind of prototype graduate school before university departments fully engaged in policy-making. Growth of university social science departments between 1910 and 1940 created a quite modest presence in social research by the end of our period of inquiry, but the great expansion of university social research occurred post–World War II; its genesis is discussed in the following chapter.

So much could be said about the history of the social sciences in American universities that this is only a sketch. I will focus upon four issues only: the differentiation of disciplines, the rise of science and the faith in science, the institutionalization of empirical social research, and the split between academic and nonacademic research.

As the social sciences developed in the nineteenth century in American universities, they were taught in colleges as part of an undergraduate education (to the extent that they were taught at all). One of the most significant developments of the later nineteenth century was the decline of overseas study (particularly German, by American candidates) for the higher degree, coupled with the establishment of graduate schools, starting at Johns Hopkins in 1876, then at Clark and the University of Chicago, followed by Columbia, and shortly afterward by Harvard and Yale. This growth of graduate education went hand in hand with the growth of the independence and separation of individual disciplines (Shils 1979). For a period, economics had imperialistic aspirations; political economy, particularly at Wisconsin, had a wide reach, but political science, sociology, psychology, and anthropology all became separate disciplines with their own departments, although they often remained extremely small (Higham 1979). One aspect of the development of empirical investigation at this period is the manner in which particular methods, empirical inquiry, and research that was oriented to public policy issues developed within individual disciplines (Platt 1996).

A second theme of great importance played alongside this disciplinary differentiation as the social sciences expanded. From the first and second decades of the twentieth century, the social sciences moved discernibly in a more empirical and scientific direction, placing stronger emphasis upon the collection of original data, measurement, and rigorous testing of ideas, but shying away from armchair theorizing. This was not a uniform development. It affected different disciplines at different rates and did not impact a single discipline uniformly. But Wesley Mitchell in economics, James B. Watson in psychology, Charles Merriam (after 1920) in politics, and William F. Ogburn in sociology were all representative of this trend.

> Institutional economists, most sociologists, and some political scientists, more deeply strained by the rapidity of change and the insecurity of American ideals, sought a different kind of science, an empirical science of the changing liberal world that would allow them technological control. The anxiety to control the careening new world on the one hand, and the narrowed focus and comfortable opportunities for professionalism on the other, turned that scientific impulse towards scientism. Social scientists began to construct a naturalistic social science as an end in itself, and under the influence of instrumental positivism, erected positivist scientific method into the chief standard of inquiry. (Ross 1991, 467–68)

One consequence of this scientific stance was a distancing from the commitment to social intervention and reform, so that surveys like those of the Settlement House and the Social Survey movement tended to be regarded as pre-scientific, not properly at home under a university umbrella.

Empirical methods required resources. With support from the major philanthropies, particularly Ruml at the Memorial, a number of research groups and one or two academic research centers were established. These are of interest as prototypes of what followed, though their resemblance to an organization like the Institute for Social Research, University of Michigan, is cousinly rather than direct. The Local Community Research Committee at the University of Chicago was a network of empirically oriented social scientists with Memorial funds to distribute for individual research support. When the Social Science Research Building opened in 1929, only researchers were housed in the building, and their offices were allocated according to affinity of interest, not purely by department. The Institute for Research in Social Science at the University of North Carolina, Chapel Hill, created by Howard Odum, was set up in 1924 with foundation support and was the first institute of its kind in the nation (Johnson and Johnson 1980). Both at Chicago and Chapel Hill, arrangements were dedicated to cooperation among the social sciences, a goal to which the SSRC and the Memorial (in the person of Ruml) aspired, though they found it more difficult to achieve in reality.

Universities did not have a monopoly on social research prior to 1940, however, and there was significant social research activity outside them. The Institute of Social and Religious Research in New York has already been mentioned, as has the burgeoning growth of market research and the beginnings of political polling. The National Bureau of Economic Research was deliberately founded by Wesley Mitchell in the early 1920s as an independent body not attached to a university, with an independent board of directors, funded initially by the Commonwealth Fund. Its task was to collect data for national income analysis. When Robert S. Brookings endowed an institute to study applied economics, originally called the Institute of Economics (becoming the Brookings Institution in 1927), it was eventually located in Washington, D.C., without an academic affiliation (Critchlow 1985).

In the period between 1920 and 1940, features of the university system of social science research emerged, particularly an increased emphasis on empiricism, stronger disciplines, some models of institutionalization, and much more extensive foundation support, the latter enabling the expansive developments of the post–World War II period. It is appropriate to close this section by again emphasizing the minuscule scale of these activities relative to the expansion that followed.

Conclusion

What made America distinctive in the development of social sciences? The United States is a country that, par excellence, institutionalized the empirical study of contemporary society in the twentieth century. Its wealth, particularly from philanthropic sources, provided the resources for codifying social research, and there has been a faith in the value of the results. Though this faith may not have been fully borne out, the achievement is nonetheless to be admired. But where do the roots of this achievement lie?

The relationship between social science research and public policy may be understood in different ways. The impulse to understand the structure and conditions of society was a very strong one. It appealed to elite groups who felt a responsibility toward those in less fortunate circumstances. Sometimes this responsibility was conceived in terms of noblesse oblige, other times in terms of the ethos of civic education and the town meeting, and still other times in terms of activist research to bring about direct political change. The American people held considerable faith in science as leading to certain types of knowledge and the illumination of opinion. And at times people held the faith that science could provide answers to problems.

The more sophisticated participants, such as Charles Merriam and Beardsley Ruml, were also very concerned to keep relations with politicians at some distance and not to oversell the social sciences. No one who had experienced the fights of social researchers with urban politicians in the early years of the century could be optimistic about the relation between practical politics and scientific research. Too many other considerations came into play for the results of research to feed directly into policy. Moreover, until 1940 Congress remained most reluctant to allow the federal government any scope to undertake significant research activities itself. In the latter part of the period, between 1920 and 1940, the university-foundation nexus was much more significant in shaping a scientific community of social researchers and laying the foundations of a system that has, in many respects, persisted up to the present day. Changes in the initial system, particularly as a result of greater involvement on the part of the federal government, will be made clear in the following essay by David Featherman and Maris Vinovskis.

REFERENCES

Bulmer, Martin. 1984. *The Chicago School of Sociology: Institutionalisation, diversity and the rise of sociological research.* Chicago: University of Chicago Press.
———. 1991. W. E. B. Du Bois as a social investigator. In *The social survey in historical perspective, 1880–1940,* ed. Martin Bulmer, Kevin Bales, and Kathryn Sklar, 170–88. Cambridge: Cambridge University Press.
Bulmer, Martin, and Joan Bulmer. 1981. Philanthropy and social science in the 1920s: Beardsley Ruml and the Laura Spelman Rockefeller Memorial, 1922–1929. *Minerva* 19:347–407.
Converse, Jean. 1987. *Survey research in the United States: Roots and emergence, 1890–1960.* Berkeley: University of California Press.

Cravens, Hamilton. 1978. *The triumph of evolution: American scientists and the heredity-environment controversy, 1900–1941.* Philadelphia: University of Pennsylvania Press.

Critchlow, Donald T. 1985. *The Brookings Institution, 1916–1952: Expertise and the public interest in a democratic society.* De Kalb: Northern Illinois University Press.

Eaton, Allen, and Shelby M. Harrison. 1930. *A bibliography of social surveys.* New York: Russell Sage.

Fisher, Donald. 1993. *Fundamental development of the social sciences: Rockefeller philanthropy and the United States Social Science Research Council.* Ann Arbor: University of Michigan Press.

Glueck, Sheldon, and Eleanor T. Glueck. 1934. *One thousand delinquents: Their treatment by court and clinic.* Cambridge: Harvard University Press.

Greenwald, Maureen, and Margo Anderson, eds. 1996. *Pittsburgh surveyed: Social science and social reform in the early twentieth century.* Pittsburgh: University of Pittsburgh Press.

Grossman, James R. 1989. *Land of hope: Chicago, Black southerners and the great migration.* Chicago: University of Chicago Press.

Haskell, Thomas L. 1977. *The emergence of professional social science: The American Social Science Association and the nineteenth-century crisis of authority.* Urbana: University of Illinois Press.

Heclo, Hugh. 1974. *Modern social politics in Britain and Sweden.* New Haven: Yale University Press.

Higham, John. 1979. The matrix of specialization. In *The organization of knowledge in modern America, 1860–1920,* ed. Alexandra Oleson and John Voss, 3–18. Baltimore: Johns Hopkins University Press.

Hofstadter, Richard. 1962. *The age of reform: From Bryan to F.D.R.* London: Cape.

Hunter, Robert. 1904. *Poverty.* New York: Macmillan.

Illinois Association for Criminal Justice. 1929. *The Illinois Crime Survey.* Chicago: Illinois Association for Criminal Justice in association with the Chicago Crime Commission. Reprint, 1968, Montclair, N.J.: Patterson Smith.

Johnson, Guy B., and Guion G. Johnson. 1980. *Research in service to society: The first fifty years of the Institute for Research in Social Science at the University of North Carolina.* Chapel Hill: University of North Carolina Press.

Karl, Barry D. 1974. *Charles E. Merriam and the study of politics.* Chicago: University of Chicago Press.

———. 1984. *The uneasy state.* Chicago: University of Chicago Press.

Lacey, Michael J. 1993. The world of the bureaus: Government and the positivist project in the late nineteenth century. In *The state and social investigation in Britain and the United States,* ed. Michael J. Lacey and Mary O. Furner, 127–70. Cambridge: Cambridge University Press.

Lagemann, Ellen. 1989. *The politics of knowledge: The Carnegie Corporation, philanthropy and public policy.* Middletown, Conn.: Wesleyan University Press.

Lewis, David Levering. 1993. *W. E. B. Du Bois: Biography of a race, 1868–1919.* New York: Henry Holt.

Lieby, James. 1960. *Carroll Wright and labor reform: The origins of labor statistics.* Cambridge: Harvard University Press.

Mennel, Robert M. 1973. *Thorns and thistles: Juvenile delinquents in the United States, 1825–1940.* Hanover, N.H.: University Press of New England.

Platt, Jennifer. 1996. *A history of sociological research methods in America, 1920–1960.* Cambridge: Cambridge University Press.

Reed, James. 1987. Robert M. Yerkes and mental testing movement. In *Psychological testing and American society,* ed. Michael M. Sokal, 75–94. New Brunswick, N.J.: Rutgers University Press.

Ross, Dorothy. 1991. *The origins of American social science.* Cambridge: Cambridge University Press.

Schlossman, Steven. 1977. *Love and the American delinquent: The theory and practice of "progressive" juvenile justice, 1825–1920.* Chicago: University of Chicago Press.

Shaw, Clifford R., Frederick Zorbaugh, Henry D. McKay, and Leonard Cottrell. 1929. *Delinquency areas.* Chicago: University of Chicago Press.

Shils, Edward. 1979. The order of learning in the United States: The ascendancy of the university. In *The organization of knowledge in modern America, 1860–1920,* ed. Alexandra Oleson and John Voss, 19–50. Baltimore: Johns Hopkins University Press.

Sklar, Kathryn K. 1991. Hull House Maps and Papers: Social science as women's work in the 1890s. In *The social survey in historical perspective, 1880–1940,* ed. Martin Bulmer, Kevin Bales, and Kathryn Sklar, 111–47. Cambridge: Cambridge University Press.

———. 1995. *Florence Kelley and the nation's work: The rise of women's political culture, 1830–1900.* New Haven: Yale University Press.

Sokal, Michael M., ed. 1987. *Psychological testing and American society.* New Brunswick, N.J.: Rutgers University Press.

CHAPTER 3

Growth and Use of Social and Behavioral Science in the Federal Government since World War II

David L. Featherman and Maris A. Vinovskis

The post–World War II period has witnessed numerous intellectual and institutional changes. Perhaps one of the most interesting and important has been the increased use of behavioral and social sciences by the federal government. Prior to World War II, insights from the behavioral and social sciences were employed sporadically in Washington. But it was during that conflict and afterward that the role of behavioral and social sciences expanded and may have reached its golden age of influence in the mid-1960s and early 1970s. Thereafter, while these disciplines continued to have considerable influence with both the legislative and executive branches, a skepticism has grown regarding the usefulness of behavioral and social sciences in effective policy-making.

Many scholars have commented on the increased use of the behavioral and social sciences by policymakers after World War II, and some have even analyzed particular aspects of these developments. Yet few have sought to provide an overall analytical narrative of the diverse relationships between the academic experts and federal policymakers while also taking into consideration changes in federal government, universities, think tanks, and the behavioral and social sciences. In this chapter we explore the impact of World War II on the use of the behavioral and social sciences by the federal government, the great expansion of their usage during the Kennedy and Johnson administrations, and the disillusionment with the usefulness of these disciplines after the mid-1960s. We conclude with some observations on the long-term trends in the relationship between the behavioral and social sciences and federal policy-making.

The brevity of this chapter does not permit complete justice to the complexity of those trends over the entire fifty-year period. Instead, this chapter provides a preliminary analytic and chronological framework for discussing many of these changes, and it highlights some of the more important factors that may have affected these developments.

The Impact of World War II

The behavioral and social sciences gradually emerged in late-nineteenth-century America out of a tradition of reforming society.[1] As these disciplines professionalized in the early twentieth century, they quickly jettisoned the amateur practitioners who had been part of the earlier social science scene. The behavioral and social sciences found a congenial, but sometimes politically restricted home in the steadily growing number of colleges and universities throughout the United States (McCloskey 1994; Matthews 1977; Ricci 1984; Ross 1991). The Social Science Research Council was created in the 1920s to help coordinate the increasingly fragmented social science disciplines and to encourage the use of more rigorous methodology (Lyons 1969, 42–46).

Much of the funding for the new applied social science research was dependent upon the handful of recently established private foundations that supported social reform efforts both at institutions for higher education and at the newly created research agencies such as the New York Bureau of Municipal Research, the Institute for Government Research (later merged into the Brookings Institution), or the National Bureau of Economic Research.[2] The bulk of foundation support for academic research just before World War II came from two institutions—the Carnegie Corporation and the Rockefeller Foundation. Both of these foundations had an interest in behavioral and social sciences and played a key role in fostering worthy projects at a critical stage of their development (Geiger 1986).

The federal government slowly expanded its use of the behavioral and social sciences in its activities in the twentieth century. The federal government had collected and analyzed census and educational statistical information in the nineteenth century but usually had not employed a stable cadre of experts to carry out these functions. In 1902 a permanent Bureau of the Census was established that provided for an ongoing presence of demographic and other social science specialists in the federal government.[3] A few other federal departments also expanded the number of social scientists on their staffs in the early twentieth century. For example, following the economic downturn in farming after World War I, the Department of Agriculture created a Bureau of Agricultural Economics to research the economic problems facing distressed farmers (Kirkendall 1966; Gaus and Wolcott 1940).

In the early decades of the twentieth century, the federal government also expanded its use of outside academic experts and forged closer links with the behavioral and social sciences. For example, President Woodrow Wilson, a former professor and a distinguished scholar himself, turned to academic experts during World War I to help mobilize domestic resources for the war as well as to develop plans for postwar Europe.[4] Herbert Hoover, first as the secretary of commerce and then as the president in 1929, discerned a particularly close connection between research and policy and sponsored such ambitious undertakings as the Research Committee on Social Trends (Karl 1969, 1974). And Franklin D. Roosevelt used the so-called brain trust during his first election campaign to develop some of the ideas for his New Deal (Lyons 1969; Kirkendall 1966; Rosen 1977). While neither Roosevelt nor his predecessors fully understood or always appreciated the complex role played by experts in shaping federal policy, they often brought academic advisers to Washington—especially during periods of national crisis.[5] But as these specialists became more deeply involved in the increasingly contested operations of the federal government, their earlier claims to authority based upon their nonpartisan detachment and intellectual expertise seemed less persuasive to the public.[6]

Opponents of the New Deal attacked the intellectuals who participated in creating and administering those programs and sought ways to curb their influence. The National Resources Planning Board (NRPB), for example, had been created in the 1930s to institutionalize the role of planning experts in the federal government. The NRPB emphasized the close relationship between the natural and social sciences. But conservatives managed to terminate this ambitious, but highly contested experiment in national planning by ending funding for that agency in 1943 (Merriam 1944; Smith 1991b, 86–93).

While behavioral and social scientists frequently provided assistance to the federal government in the decades before World War II, their talents were used intermittently and unsystematically. Roosevelt was neither a rigorous nor a consistent thinker and enjoyed playing one adviser off against another. Often he forced academic advisers to put together contradictory ideas, and he had little patience for intellectual abstractions. While he was committed to trying new ideas and approaches, he was not interested in testing their effectiveness in a more experimental fashion. Moreover, the federal government in the 1930s had few permanently established positions for academic advisers, whose influence therefore was ad hoc and temporary in nature (Lyons 1969, 50–77; Smith 1991b, 73–97).

The experiences of the federal government during World War II led to a major expansion of funding for scientific and medical research and eventually contributed to more support for the behavioral and social sciences as well. Faced with a war of unprecedented scope with major operations in far-flung regions, the U.S. armed forces quickly recognized the importance of new technological developments for military purposes. Under the extraordinary leadership of Vannevar Bush in the new Office of Scientific Research and Development (OSRD), the federal government expanded its research support for the sciences. Federal expenditures on research and development rose from about $100 million in 1940 to approximately $1.5 billion in 1945 (Reagan 1969, 320). Working closely with FDR, Congress, and the military, a small group of elite scientists oversaw and directed the nation's wartime scientific research and produced such important inventions as the atomic bomb, synthetic rubber, and improved radar equipment. In the process, a new and enduring link was forged between eminent scientists at a few prestigious research universities and policymakers in the federal government (Greenberg 1967; Penick et al. 1972; Trenn 1983).

Behavioral and social scientists also contributed to the war effort. Unlike the physical scientists, however, they were scattered throughout federal agencies and lacked any central organization.[7] Yet these scholars made significant contributions in areas such as economic planning, survey research, applied psychology, international affairs, and anthropology. Economists played a prominent role in emerging war agencies such as the Office of Price Administration and the War Production Board (Hauser 1945; Homan 1946; Novick 1947; Somers 1950). Survey researchers helped the Office of Price Administration revamp its stamp-rationing system and drew upon the pioneering work of Rensis Likert at the Department of Agriculture in the late 1930s and early 1940s (Cartwright 1947b; Gosnell and David 1949; Kershaw and Alpert 1947).[8] Social and applied psychologists improved their methodological techniques in order to provide guidance for administrators in several wartime agencies (Cartwright 1947a; Lewin 1943; Stouffer et al. 1949). Historians and other scholars played a leading role in gathering and analyzing foreign intelligence for the newly created Office of Strategic Services (Curti 1942; Smith 1983; Smith 1973; Vinovskis 1999b). And anthropologists set up a social science research unit in a Japanese relocation center in 1942; they also provided assistance in developing plans to deal with the expected fierce resistance in Japan for the anticipated invasion of those islands (Benedict 1946; Leighton 1949; Spicer 1946). Unfortunately, these behavioral and social scientists did not receive recognition and praise comparable to that which was given their medical and hard-science counterparts by policymakers and the public.

Growth of Federal Funding after World War II

Faced with the Soviet threat after World War II, Congress and the military continued to provide massive funding for scientific research. Although considerable disagreement arose over how to coordinate and centralize federal expenditures for scientific research, new institutions such as the National Science Foundation (NSF) were created while existing agencies such as the National Institutes of Health (NIH) were expanded (Kleinman 1995).[9] Federal funding sources for basic research remained scattered and uncoordinated, but the total amount of dollars available for research of all kinds grew rapidly. Behind most of the research expansion in the 1950s was concern about national security and winning the cold war (e.g., Divine 1993). Even as late as 1963, 93 percent of all federal research and development funding came from the Department of Defense (DOD), the Atomic Energy Commission (AEC), or the National Aeronautics and Space Administration (NASA)—and most of the funding went to private industry (Smith 1990, 50; see also Morin 1993). The relative contributions of DOD, AEC, and NASA are more modest, however, when the scope narrows to federal support for university research. These three defense-related federal agencies provided 35.7 percent of all federal support for university research in 1964 (NSF and NIH provided another 60.9 percent) (calculated from Geiger 1993, 186).

At the time of great expansion in postwar federal research and development funding, a shift occurred in the direction of these funds. Prior to World War II, much of the limited federal research had been done directly by government staff; but now funds increasingly went to a select number of research universities, special laboratories, industries, or new institutions such as the RAND Corporation (which had been created initially to work on long-range research for the U.S. Air Force) (RAND Corporation 1963; Smith 1966). More of the federal research dollars went to large-scale university projects that emphasized basic research and to industries that focused on product development. Many federal units such as the Department of Defense used a wide variety of institutions and procurement practices to secure the necessary research and development. Academically oriented agencies such as the National Science Foundation and the National Institutes of Health relied more heavily on grants to individual researchers and used a rigorous peer-review system to maintain high quality standards (Kidd 1959; Geiger 1993; Smith 1990).

Public and legislative enthusiasm for scientific and medical research in the immediate postwar years did not extend equally to the behavioral and social sciences (Klausner 1986). During the five years of debates leading to the founding of the National Science Foundation in 1950, several members of Congress made it clear that they were not interested in seeing the new agency fund social science research.[10] Senator H. Alexander Smith (R-New Jersey) explained: "I have conceived of this . . . as a bill for research in pure science, not in applied science. We are trying to subsidize pure science, the discovery of truth. This has nothing to do with the theory of life, it has nothing to do with history, it has nothing to do with the law, it has nothing to do with sociology" (Lundberg 1944, 398–99).[11]

But other legislators supported NSF funding for social science research. Senator Harley Kilgore (D-West Virginia), one of the originators of the agency, strongly endorsed social science research at NSF. Similarly, President Truman, in discussing NSF, acknowledged the need for social science research as a basic component of the new agency. Rather than provoking further debates, however, Congress decided that while no specific language about social science research would be included in the legislation, the agency itself would be given the option of including the social sciences in their research and development portfolios (Larsen 1992; Miller 1982, 205–9; England 1982).

Initial funding for the National Science Foundation was less than expected. Unanticipated defense expenditures due to the Korean War as well as questions about the value of basic research kept congressional NSF appropriations well below administration requests in the early 1950s. With the dramatic launching of Sputnik in 1957, however, funds for NSF rose dramatically from $16 million in FY1956 to $40 million in FY1957 (Larsen 1992, 34).

Meanwhile, under the able and persistent leadership of Harry Alpert and his successor, Henry Riecken, the social sciences slowly gained NSF acceptance and funding. Emphasizing the more "rigorous" and "objective" social sciences as well as those areas that allowed for a partnership between the natural and social sciences, NSF substantially increased its funding of social science research from $190,000 in FY1956 to $890,000 in FY1959. Nevertheless, the percentage of NSF research funds directed toward the social sciences remained minuscule—rising from 1.2 percent in FY1956 to 1.6 percent in FY1959 (Larsen 1992, 47). Moreover, rather than reflecting a new appreciation for the value of the social sciences, funding increases came from a grudging acknowledgment that while the social sciences were not making great strides, they were not doing anything wrong and should benefit from the overall improvement in NSF funding. Riecken candidly acknowledged:

> It cannot be said too plainly or bluntly: the growth of support for social science at NSF was not the direct result of social scientific achievements as such, much as we might wish it otherwise.
>
> It was the result of strong external support for the program on the part of respected advisors, a rising budget that prevented NSF expansion from being a zero-sum game, a degree of skill at administrative politics within the agency, and the fact that, in the first decade or so, grantees committed no serious gaffes or egregious offenses to the conventional morality or established values of those who controlled authorization and budget.
>
> It was as much the omission of offense as it was the commission of noteworthy acts that allowed the program to flourish. (1986, 219)

While support for the social sciences at NSF was modest, behavioral sciences like psychology also benefited from the rapid growth of biomedical research funding at the National Institutes of Health. NIH was a small agency in 1945 but grew substantially by absorbing medical research projects that had been funded by the Office of Scientific Research and Development during World War II. By the time that the NSF was created in 1950, NIH had already managed to gain control of most of the biomedical work and continued to prosper (Strickland 1972; Spingarn 1976). NIH research and development funds grew rapidly from $33.0 million in 1953 to $274.3 million in 1960 (U.S. Bureau of the Census 1975).

If social science research experienced difficulties even within the generally sympathetic NSF program, support for research and statistics often fared even worse elsewhere.[12] For example, while research and development in science and medicine were flourishing, educational policymakers at the U.S. Office of Education paid relatively little attention to improvements in these areas. Instead, the focus of most educators and legislators was on the debates to provide federal aid to education—especially for the construction of new school buildings to house the postwar baby boom (Ravitch 1983; Vinovskis 1995, 39–46).

With the successful launch of Sputnik in October 1957, concern about Soviet superiority in science and technology immediately led to increased overall federal education funding. The Office of Education expanded its research and statistics staff from 26 to 68 people—thereby expanding and strengthening its in-house data gathering and research capabilities. Previously no funds had been allocated for cooperative research, but now $1 million was appropriated for FY1957 (U.S. Office of Education 1958, 183–85). The National Defense Education Act (NDEA) (PL 85–864) was enacted in September 1958. Much of the administration of NDEA was assigned to the Office of Education. This further expanded the overall role and importance of the agency. NDEA was authorized for $4 billion over a four-year period and received an initial appropriation of $115.3 million (U.S. Office of Education 1965, 235). Appropriations for the cooperative research program reached $2.7 million for FY1959 (U.S. Office of Education 1960).

The additional large amounts of money for scientific and medical research as well as the more modest increases for the behavioral and social sciences helped to support the rapid expansion of colleges and universities after World War II. Similarly, the Serviceman's Readjustment Act of June 22, 1944, created the GI Bill, which provided much needed support for higher education immediately after the war. In 1948 it was estimated that the GI Bill paid 56 percent of student fees in private universities and 67 percent in public institutions (Geiger 1993, 41).[13] With the expansion of colleges and universities, the number of academic researchers grew accordingly, increasing the capabilities of the higher education system to provide assistance and advice for the federal government.

While federal dollars dominated the funding of medical and scientific research after World War II, the behavioral and social sciences continued to rely more heavily on support from private foundations. Particularly with the creation of the Ford Foundation, which provided approximately 40 percent of all foundation grants in 1953, private foundations funded much of the work in the behavioral and social sciences (Geiger 1988, 315–41; 1993, 92–116). The Behavioral Sciences Program at the Ford Foundation dispensed almost $43 million in its seven years of existence and focused most of its support on the disciplines of anthropology, psychology, social psychology, and sociology. Over time, however, the relative role of private foundations in funding behavioral and social science research diminished as the federal government greatly expanded its support in the late 1950s.[14]

Changes in the Federal Government after World War II

Changes in the federal government after World War II increased the opportunities for behavioral and social science advisers and provided many of them with more permanent and influential posts in the bureaucracy. With the conclusion of the war, the number of civilian employees in the executive branch of the federal government dropped dramatically from 3.79 million in 1945 to 1.93 million in 1950; by 1960, however, that number had risen to 2.37 million (U.S. Bureau of the Census 1975). The federal civil service system was reformed and expanded to attract and maintain more highly qualified applicants.[15]

More important than the changes in the size of the federal government were the changes in the role of the presidency that provided more opportunities for policy advisers. Starting with Hoover and Roosevelt, presidents slowly expanded the scope of their influence by adding more staff and playing a more active role in formulating, enacting, and implementing federal policies. The number of full-time civilian officials in the White House who had a substantive interest in policy matters rose steadily during these years: eleven aides at the end of Roosevelt's administration; twenty-two at the close of Truman's tenure; and thirty-four under Eisenhower in 1959 (Walcott and Hult 1995, 8). While the White House staff before World War II was relatively small and organized informally, during the 1940s and 1950s their numbers grew and their activities became more institutionalized. A special science adviser position at the White House was created to provide guidance on issues relating to sciences—though nothing comparable for the behavioral or social sciences was ever developed. As a result, the White House generally became more active and better coordinated in working with federal departments as well as with Congress on all policy matters (Arnold 1986; Henderson 1988; Walcott and Hult 1995; Sander 1989).

Influential positions for advisers were also established in several new federal agencies after the war. The Council of Economic Advisors (CEA), created in 1946, provided for unusually close ties between economists and policymakers (Flash 1965; Nourse 1953; Stein 1984). The development of the Central

Intelligence Agency (CIA) in 1947 offered opportunities for behavioral and social scientists both within and outside that institution (Jeffreys-Jones 1989; Winks 1996). Creation of the National Security Council (NSC) during the Truman administration supplemented advice from the State Department in foreign affairs (Destler 1972; Lord 1988). And the expansion of the Bureau of the Budget (BOB) and its successor under Nixon, the Office of Management and the Budget (OMB), created positions for additional policy analysts in the executive branch (Berman 1979; Mosher 1984).

Reacting to the expansion and centralization of professional staff in the executive branch, the 79th Congress passed the Legislative Reorganization Act of 1946 (PL 79–601), which increased the number and quality of congressional staff. In the ten years after the passage of the Reorganization Act, the number of personal committee staff increased in the House from 1,440 to 2,441 and in the Senate from 590 to 1,115. In the same period, committee staff rose in the House from 193 to 375 and in the Senate from 290 to 558 (Fox and Hammond 1977, 171). Overall, congressional staff, both committee and personal, grew by 79 percent from 1947 to 1957. Moreover, the Reorganization Act created permanent staff for congressional House and Senate committees and encouraged the hiring of better-qualified and better-trained professionals (Fox and Hammond 1977; Heaphey and Balutis 1975; Kofmehl 1962).

Members of Congress were also served by the General Accounting Office (GAO), created by the Budgeting and Accounting Act of 1921, which expanded its activities in the late 1940s by undertaking more comprehensive program audits and evaluations (Mosher 1979, 1984). Similarly, the Legislative Reference Service (LRS), created in 1914 as part of the Library of Congress, expanded under the Legislative Reorganization Act of 1946 to provide more in-depth assistance to the legislators and their staffs (Fox and Hammond 1977, 130–32).

Policy opportunities for behavioral and social scientists increased and became institutionalized during the Truman and Eisenhower administrations. Yet neither Truman nor Eisenhower took full advantage of these new sources of information and advice. Truman, for example, at first did not usually consult with his Council of Economic Advisors on matters of national economic policy; and Eisenhower distanced himself from direct contact with behavioral and social scientists by establishing a more formal and hierarchical model for decision making in the White House. Nevertheless, by the late 1950s the reorganized structure of both the executive and legislative branches provided more frequent and stable communication channels between the federal government and behavioral and social scientists than ever before. These new settings and practices helped to pave the way for the increased presence and influence of academics in Washington in the Kennedy and Johnson administrations (Smith 1991b, 98–121; Wood 1993).

Expansion of Behavioral and Social Science Influence in the Kennedy and Johnson Administrations

The uses and support of social sciences by the federal government grew considerably during the Kennedy and Johnson administrations. Growth in the number of federal employees and social programs as well as increases in federal expenditures were accompanied by more involvement of academics in government and the greater use of the social and behavioral sciences in the development and evaluation of government programs. While a few individuals in the 1960s questioned the value of the expanded uses of the social and behavioral sciences in the federal government, most policymakers and academics welcomed these changes.

The decade of the 1960s saw the rapid expansion of social programs. President John Kennedy called for a more active federal role in social policy, but it was left to President Lyndon Johnson to pass the necessary legislation as part of his Great Society initiatives. New legislation and programs such as the Civil Rights Act of 1964, the Elementary and Secondary Education Act of 1965, Head Start, the Model Cities programs, Medicare and Medicaid, the Neighborhood Youth Corps, Job Corps, and the Community Action Program were created to help disadvantaged Americans.[16] Federal social welfare expenditures rose from $25.0 billion in 1960 to $60.3 billion in 1970 (a 142 percent increase) (U.S. Bureau of the Census 1975, Part 1, Series H32).[17] The number of all civilian federal employees expanded from 2.42 million in 1960 to 2.98 million in 1968 (a 23 percent increase) (U.S. Bureau of the Census 1975, Part 2, Series Y273).

Academics in the 1960s often served as campaign policy advisers. Some prominent intellectuals had been involved in Adlai Stevenson's unsuccessful presidential campaigns in 1952 and 1956 (Martin 1977; Sievers 1983). But it was John Kennedy who worked the hardest to recruit scholars as campaign policy advisers—in part to gain support from liberals and intellectuals in his bid for the Democratic presidential nomination in 1960. East Coast professors were especially singled out and recruited for Kennedy's Academic Advisory Committee. Most of the policy papers and speeches drafted by these intellectuals provided only limited practical assistance during the campaign, but publicity about the involvement of these scholars proved popular with the media and certain segments of the Democratic party. Although the Republicans also mobilized academics on behalf of Nixon, their efforts were more limited and less visible. After the 1960 campaign, recruiting academic advisers on behalf of presidential candidates became an established component of American presidential politics (White 1961; Wood 1993).

Academics were also more involved in staffing the transition teams created to assist incoming administrations. John Kenneth Galbraith and Richard Neustadt, for example, helped to organize the more than two dozen pre-inaugural policy task forces for the Kennedy administration as well as to provide suggestions for possible appointments to federal posts. The creation and use of special task forces was continued by President Johnson who relied heavily upon them to generate many of the new ideas for the Great Society programs (though usually the specific suggestions from these task forces were considerably modified before they were finally implemented) (Brauer 1986; Pfiffner 1996; Wood 1993).

University scholars and other intellectuals were frequently appointed to important posts in the Kennedy and Johnson administrations. During extraordinary crises such as World War I and World War II, many academics had temporarily entered government service. While some academics continued to work with the federal government in the 1950s, their presence and influence were relatively modest. President Kennedy, who particularly enjoyed reading books and discussing new ideas, recruited several prominent academics for his circle of advisers and appointed many others to important positions in federal agencies (Burner 1988; Giglio 1991; Schlesinger 1965).

Johnson was somewhat uncomfortable with academics and intellectuals—especially as hostility toward him among scholars increased as a result of the escalation of the Vietnam War. Johnson tried to duplicate Kennedy's close relationship with intellectuals by designating Eric Goldman from Princeton University as his own in-house intellectual adviser, but that appointment proved disappointing to both parties (Goldman 1969). Johnson was much more successful, however, in recruiting academics to join his numerous task forces as well as to hold key staff positions within the federal bureaucracy. Indeed, after his first thirty months in office, Johnson proudly announced that he had appointed more academics to federal positions than had any other president (Califano 1991; MacKenzie 1987; Wood 1993).

While some Great Society initiatives were hastily assembled and perhaps too quickly enacted as large-scale programs, the White House relied heavily upon social and behavioral scientists for ideas and suggestions about the best ways of helping disadvantaged Americans. In the creation of Project Head Start, for example, specialists in early childhood education and development were consulted (Zigler and Muenchow 1992; Zigler and Valentine 1979). Similarly, educational researchers provided important input in the crafting of the Elementary and Secondary Education Act of 1965 (Graham 1984; Silver and Silver 1991), and the Community Action Program drew upon the work of experts such as Richard Cloward and Lloyd Ohlin of the Columbia School of Social Work (Moynihan 1969). While in retrospect many of the suggestions from academic experts seem somewhat naive and simplistic, they encouraged policymakers to experiment with new and better ways of fighting poverty and inequality in American society (Kaplan and Cuciti 1986; Levitan and Taggart 1976).

Not surprisingly, the federal government also was one of the largest employers of social and behavioral scientists. A survey of scientific and technical personnel in 1966 identified at least 8,400 social and behavioral scientists in the federal government (about 12 percent of all scientific personnel in the federal government at that time). Approximately 40 percent of these social and behavioral scientists were classified as economists, 22 percent as psychologists, and 15 percent as general social scientists (including sociologists). Only 1.5 percent were designated as anthropologists and 6.3 percent as historians (Behavioral and Social Sciences Survey Committee 1969, 214).

In a widely publicized speech on the fiftieth anniversary of the Brookings Institution in 1966, President Johnson acknowledged his debt to intellectuals and the social sciences in the development of the Great Society programs:

> There is hardly an aspect of the Great Society's program that has not been molded, or remolded, or in some way influenced by the communities of scholars and thinkers. The flow of ideas continues because the problems continue. Some ideas are good enough to stimulate whole departments of government into fresh appraisals of their programs. Some are ingenious; some are impractical; some are both. But without the tide of new proposals that periodically sweeps into this city, the climate of our government would be very arid indeed. (Brookings Institution 1966, 13)

The continued growth in the number of the social and behavioral scientists in the 1960s facilitated their increased participation in the federal government. The number of doctorates granted in the social and behavioral sciences grew from 1,677 in 1957 to 3,915 in 1967 (Behavioral and Social Sciences Survey Committee 1969).[18] Another rough index of the expanding pool of social and behavioral scientists is the growth in membership of the seven major behavioral and social science associations. The number of association members grew from 26,255 in 1947 to 51,382 in 1957; by 1967 that number doubled to 103,677. About one-half of these association members in 1967 were estimated to be on the faculties of four-year colleges and universities. The rest worked in areas such as the government, industry, hospitals, K–12 and community college school systems, and specialized research centers (Behavioral and Social Sciences Survey Committee 1969, 22–23).[19]

The 1960s also witnessed large increases in funding for the social and behavioral sciences. Total support for the behavioral and social sciences grew from $384 million in 1961–62 to $803 million in 1966–68. In both periods almost half of the support came from the federal government and one-third from industry. Philanthropic foundations, which had played such a crucial role in financing the social and behavioral sciences in the 1950s, now contributed only 6.0 percent of the funds in 1961–62 and 3.0 percent in 1966–67 (Behavioral and Social Sciences Survey Committee 1969, 15). Despite the relative decrease in overall private foundation support for the social and behavioral sciences, these institutions continued to play an important role in fostering programs on important subjects such as foreign area studies (e.g., see Beckman 1967; McCaughey 1984).

Federal support of the social and behavioral sciences in the 1960s was scattered among many different departments and agencies. Almost half of the federal funding in 1967 was concentrated in the Department of Health, Education, and Welfare—with most of it coming from the National Institute of Mental Health ($50.0 million), the Office of Education ($46.5 million), the Social and Rehabilitation Service ($24.1 million), and the National Institutes of Health ($15.7 million). Yet significant contributions to the social and behavioral sciences stemmed from other federal sources such as the Department of Defense ($32.4 million), the Department of Agriculture ($29.8 million), the National Science Foundation ($24.1 million), and the Office of Economic Opportunity ($18.8 million) (Behavioral and Social Sciences Survey Committee 1969, 236).

The Kennedy and Johnson years witnessed considerable social turmoil in America. Many policymakers and academics cited these difficulties as the rationale for expanding federal support to and use of the social sciences. For example, the influential Behavioral and Social Science Survey Committee sponsored by the National Academy of Sciences and the Social Science Research Council in 1969 concluded:

> We are living in social crisis. There have been riots in our cities and in our universities. An unwanted war defies efforts to end it. Population expansion threatens to overwhelm our social institutions. Our advanced technology can destroy natural beauty and pollute the environment if we do not control its development and thus its effects. Even while scientific progress in biology and medicine helps to relieve pain and prolong life, it raises new problems relating to organ transplants, drugs that alter behavior, and the voluntary control of genetic inheritance.
>
> At the root of many of these crises are perplexing problems of human behavior and relationships. The behavioral and social sciences, devoted to studying these problems, can help us survive current crises and avoid them in the future, provided that these sciences continue to make contributions of two kinds: first, in increased depth of understanding of human behavior and the institutions of society; and, second, in better ways to use this understanding in devising social policy and the management of our affairs. (Behavioral and Social Sciences Survey Committee 1969, 1)

Concerns about the well-being of the nation encouraged more attention to the social and behavioral sciences. At the National Science Foundation these fields were given full divisional status in 1960. NSF funding for the Social Science Division increased from $2.2 million in 1960 to $14.7 million in 1968—but the emphasis within the agency continued to be on basic research (Larsen 1992, 59–90).

Some members of Congress as well as many scholars felt that separate funding and advisory agencies should be created for the social and behavioral sciences. Senator Fred Harris (D-Oklahoma) introduced a resolution to create a new National Foundation for the Social Sciences and held four hearings on the matter in 1966 (Harris 1967; U.S. Congress 1966). Harris wanted the new agency to provide additional support for the social sciences as well as to eliminate the problems caused by having the Department of Defense sponsor such controversial investigations as Project Camelot—the use of social science studies of Latin America for military purposes (see Horowitz 1974). Representative Dante Fascell (D-Florida) sponsored legislation to create an Office of Social Science in the Executive Office of the President, and Senator Walter Mondale (D-Minnesota) called for the creation of a Council of Social Advisors modeled after the Council of Economic Advisors. While none of these legislative proposals was enacted, the introduction and serious congressional consideration of them is further evidence of the growing belief in the 1960s that the behavioral and social sciences could play a key role in revitalizing American society (Klausner and Lidz 1986; Larsen 1992; Lyons 1969).

Yet not everyone in the 1960s was fully persuaded of the usefulness of academics in general, and social and behavioral scientists in particular, in predicting future developments and designing new federal programs. Theodore White, for example, in an influential and generally sympathetic series on action-intellectuals in *Life* magazine in 1967, still concluded pessimistically:

> The action-intellectuals have no certain answers for tomorrow. . . . To measure something does not mean to understand it. . . . Their studies and surveys, however imperfect, are only road maps for the future showing the hazy contours of a new landscape. It is vital work—so long as the mapmakers do not confuse themselves as tour directors. How Americans shall move across the panorama they describe and what structures shall be erected. . . . There is work for other men. (Wood 1993, 39)

As shall be seen, such doubts about the efficacy and usefulness of the social and behavioral sciences would intensify in the 1970s and 1980s.

Second Thoughts about the Usefulness of the Social and Behavioral Sciences in the 1970s and 1980s

Some analysts have argued that the second half of the 1960s and the early 1970s might be considered a sort of golden age in terms of the perceived influence of the social and behavioral sciences in the federal government. For example, Richard Nathan has observed:

> Among western nations, the United States stands out for the optimistic, almost euphoric, belief on the part of social scientists and many politicians that social science scholarship can be useful in the governmental process. The commitment to this idea had its heyday from the mid-1960s to the mid-1970s. Social scientists were feeling their oats. Economists were prominent in government; they were instrumental in the development of national economic policy and in Lyndon Johnson's war on poverty. There was a feeling of ebullience about the potential for applied social science in national domestic policy. (1988, 3)

As discussed in the previous section, prominent social and behavioral scientists in the late 1960s and early 1970s overestimated the efficacy of untested academic theories to solve perplexing social and economic problems. Many academics had optimistically and confidently participated in the development and implementation of President Johnson's Great Society programs. But, in the mid-1970s and 1980s when the problems they were so certain of solving proved to be more intractable than they had hoped, serious questions about the usefulness and relevance of the social and behavioral sciences for policy-making arose, both among academics and the general public. Writing in 1988, Richard Nathan said that "the optimism has faded. In recent years political leaders have been less willing to apply social scientific knowledge in a systematic way in government" (3).

Growth of the Federal Government

Federal domestic spending continued to rise during these two decades. Federal social welfare expenditures grew from $77 billion in 1970 to $303 billion in 1980, and then rose to $617 billion in 1990—though some of that large increase was due to the unusually high rate of inflation during the 1970s and early 1980s (U.S. Bureau of the Census 1996, table 572).[20] Yet in constant 1992 dollars, per capita expenditures on social welfare expenditures did rise substantially, from $1,283 in 1970 to $2,280 in 1980; but per capita social welfare expenditures increased at a much slower rate during the 1980s and reached $2,620 in 1990 (U.S. Bureau of the Census 1996, calculated from table 571). The overall federal civilian labor force, however, remained relatively unchanged during the same period. In the 1970s the number of all federal civilian employees remained nearly the same, rising slightly from 3.0 million in 1980 to 3.2 in 1990 (U.S. Bureau of the Census 1996, table 532).

While federal government expenditures increased substantially and the overall number of federal civilian employees rose only slightly, several other important developments occurred in the federal government. The Nixon administration tried to increase its control of the bureaucracy by creating the Office of Management and Budget to replace the Bureau of the Budget, establishing the Domestic Council, and appointing more lower-level political employees to oversee the operation of the departments and agencies (Nathan 1975; Pfiffner 1988). During the Carter administration, the entire federal civil service system was revamped through the Civil Service Reform Act of 1978, which replaced the Civil Service Commission and established a high-level Senior Executive Service (SES).[21] When Reagan assumed office, some of the key intended benefits and opportunities for the top federal executives under that act were not fully implemented, and approximately one-half of the initial SES members left within three years.[22] Utilizing his Office of Policy Development (OPD) as well as the newly created cabinet council system, Reagan perhaps exerted more control over domestic policies than had any previous president (Warshaw 1995).

One of the more important developments in many federal departments was the growth in the number and use of planning and evaluation staff in the 1960s and 1970s. Drawing upon the experiences in the Department of Defense in the early 1960s, President Johnson in 1965 called for the implementation of that same Planning-Programming-Budgeting (PPB) system in all federal domestic agencies. Yet PPB did not have much direct impact on most agencies. A study of sixteen different agencies found that only three (USDA, HEW, and OEO) made substantial progress in incorporating PPB into their activities (Harper, Kramer, and Rouse 1969).[23] Nevertheless, the system did encourage all federal agencies to try to develop their own planning and evaluation capabilities. For example, by the beginning of 1975, the Office of the Assistant Secretary for Planning and Evaluation in HEW had a staff of about 150 behavioral and social science professionals—mainly economists (Williams 1990, 41–63).[24]

During the Reagan administration, however, a concerted effort was made to minimize or eliminate much of the planning and evaluation staff and activities at the agency level (Williams 1990, 64–104). Eleanor Chelimsky, then the Assistant Comptroller General of the Program Evaluation and Methodology Division in the General Accounting Office, documented the decline in staff and funding for evaluations in fifteen agencies during the early 1980s.

Unfortunately, despite all the good reasons invoked for maintaining a strong program evaluation capability in government, we at GAO have found that, in general, federal program evaluation is not in good health. After tracking the executive branch evaluation investment for a decade, we found that the overall situation (with some exceptions) entails less attention to strong data-supported information (especially information about program or policy effectiveness), less concern with public account-ability and public scrutiny, and a general downgrading of the evaluation function. . . .

Between 1980 and 1984, the number of professional staff in all federal agency evaluation units decreased by 22 percent, from about fifteen hun-dred to about twelve hundred. In contrast, the total number of staff in these agencies decreased by only 6 percent during this period. . . . Reduc-tions in evaluation staff continued between 1984 and 1988. The fifteen agencies most active in 1980 experienced a 52 percent decline in evalua-tion staff between that year and 1988: down from 419 to 200. (Chelimsky 1992, 30–31)[25]

Thus, the expansion of planning and evaluation in federal agencies during the previous administrations was sharply reversed during the Reagan years—unfortunately just at a time when major changes were being proposed that might have particularly benefited from more in-depth planning and analysis.

At the same time that the executive branch of the federal government was expanding its planning and analytical capacity, the U.S. Congress also significantly increased the size of its own staff. The number of personal staff serving members of the House and Senate increased dramatically from 7,706 in 1972 to 11,117 in 1980 and then remained fairly steady, increasing to 11,572 employees in 1991. Similarly, staff of the House and Senate standing commit-tees rose rapidly from 1,137 in 1970 to 3,108 in 1980; thereafter it increased at a much slower pace and by 1991 reached 3,475 employees.[26]

While funding to increase the size of the congressional staffs rose consid-erably, most of those on the staffs did not have extensive training or experience with behavioral or social science research. For example, a study of the educa-tional attainments of congressional professional staffs in the early 1970s found that while almost all had a B.A. degree, only about 16 percent had an M.A. and 5 percent had a Ph.D. Another 32 percent had a law degree—leading some commentators to wonder if lawyers were not overrepresented on congressional staffs (calculated from Fox and Hammond 1977, 175).

Support agencies for the Congress also expanded. The General Account-ing Office grew modestly from 4,704 employees in 1970 to 5,196 in 1980, and by 1991 it had decreased slightly to 5,054 employees. The Congressional Research Service (CRS) grew even more rapidly from a staff of 332 in 1970 to 868 in 1980; by 1991 it also experienced a modest decline to 831 employees. Even more important, the Congressional Budget Office (CBO), established in 1974, provided more overall coordination and in-depth analyses for the Con-gress. Similarly, the Office of Technology Assessment (OTA) began operations in 1973–74 and delivered additional analyses for the legislators.[27]

Continued Use of the Social and Behavioral Sciences in the Federal Government

The Nixon campaign assembled their own set of academic advisers in 1968 under the direction of Martin Anderson. Anderson created several task forces and, somewhat ironically, had to draw upon the scholars who had been initially cultivated by the more liberal former New York Republican governor, Nelson Rockefeller. Despite deep, long-term suspicion of Nixon by many academics, his administration was able to recruit scholars such as Arthur Burns, Stephen Hess, Henry Kissinger, Paul McCracken, Daniel Patrick Moynihan, Richard Nathan, and George Schultz. After the transition period, however, the role of most of these academics diminished considerably; by the early 1970s Nixon relied more heavily on lawyers such as John Ehrlichman, who chaired the new Domestic Council, for advice on domestic policies (Brauer 1986; Kissinger 1979; Nathan 1988; Wood 1993).

Building upon the expanded planning and evaluation efforts in the Johnson administration, the Nixon administration at first showed considerable willingness to support and expand research and evaluation initiatives. For example, under the initial urging and guidance of Moynihan, the Nixon administration in 1973 created the National Institute of Education (NIE) to support additional research and evaluation of school reforms (Sproull, Weiner, and Wolf 1978; Vinovskis 1996). During the debates over the negative income tax and welfare reform, the administration implemented some of the large-scale income maintenance demonstrations and evaluations that had been proposed during the Johnson administration (Anderson 1978; Moynihan 1973; Pechman and Timpane 1975; Robins et al. 1980).

During the late 1960s and early 1970s, some members of Congress pressured the Nixon administration to apply the behavioral and social sciences more directly to the pressing national problems confronting the country. The National Science Foundation, for example, responded by creating a new program in 1971—Research Applied to National Needs (RANN). Some of its goals were the following:

> Identify national needs not being addressed by existing research agencies; provide early warning of potential national problems; and initiate assessments and research that address these needs and problems.
>
> Shorten the lead time between basic scientific discoveries and relevant practical applications, and serve as a bridge between the Foundation's basic research programs and the development, demonstration, and operational programs of Federal mission agencies, State and local governments, and industry.

Assure the communication and use of research results. (Larsen 1992, 93–94)

RANN upset many of the more traditional academics as well as dismayed those in NSF who had always favored basic research. Over its seven years in operation, RANN distributed $468 million to various projects and at its high point in 1975 accounted for approximately one-fourth of the entire NSF research budget (Larsen 1992, 91–127).

The political turmoil over Watergate in 1973–74 distracted most senior officials in the Nixon administration from focusing on the use of research and evaluations to improve federal domestic programs. Academics had less overall impact in the new Ford administration. President Gerald Ford personally was sympathetic to the academic community, and his administration worked closely with scholars such as John Dunlop, Nathan Glazer, Henry Kissinger, Edward Levi, F. David Matthews, Roger Porter, and James Schlesinger. But given the short duration of the Ford administration as well as the political and organizational disarray in the White House, academic involvement in the formulation and implementation of policy was limited. Particularly disappointing and surprising were the internal difficulties Vice President Rockefeller experienced after he was designated to formulate the administration's domestic policies—especially as Rockefeller might have been expected to be able to draw upon his extensive network of scholars that had been established over the years (Greene 1995; Hart 1987; Hartmann 1980; Porter 1980; Wood 1993).

Questions about the Value of the Social and Behavioral Science Research

Even as most scholars and policymakers in late 1960s and early 1970s continued to express faith in the efficacy of the social sciences in general and the Great Society programs in particular, several serious intellectual challenges to those activities arose. Edward Banfield disparaged federal urban renewal programs; Christopher Jencks doubted the ability of schools to reduce inequality; and Moynihan had second thoughts about federal antipoverty initiatives (Banfield 1970; Jencks et al. 1972; Moynihan 1969, 1973).

Perhaps even more troubling for the Great Society programs was a series of large-scale social science evaluations that questioned the effectiveness of the programs in helping disadvantaged Americans. The Westinghouse Learning Corporation's controversial evaluation of Project Head Start claimed that the cognitive gains from that popular program faded quickly (Westinghouse Learning Corporation 1969).[28] Special efforts to help preschool children transition into the regular schools in Follow Through projects were pronounced ineffective (Rivlin and Timpane 1975, 23–45; Rhine 1981; Vinovskis 1999b).

Evaluations of the Elementary and Secondary Education Act of 1965 suggested that the newly enacted Title I compensatory education provided little help, if any, for disadvantaged children (Carter 1984; McLaughlin 1975; Vinovskis 1997).

Supporters of these programs usually challenged the validity and accuracy of these negative evaluations and often tried to introduce more favorable local assessments into the debates (e.g., see Smith and Bissell 1970; House et al. 1978). Yet the public and policymakers usually were left with the distinct impression that these early programs had not worked or that the initially exaggerated claims of their supporters were seriously contested.[29] As a result, scholars such as Henry Aaron now acknowledged that "research tends to be a conservative force because it fosters skepticism and caution by shifting attention from moral commitment to analytical problems that rarely have clear-cut or simple solutions" (1978, i).

During the Nixon-Ford administrations, political leaders also gradually became more disillusioned with the behavioral and social sciences in general. This discontentment was partly a hostile reaction to the anti–Vietnam War movement, which had led to the perception among conservative politicians that many scholars had become so radical and ideological that they no longer could be trusted to provide objective research and evaluations. But it also reflected a frustration with the perceived ineffectiveness of many of the Great Society programs, as well as the growing belief that much of the behavioral and social science work funded by the federal government was irrelevant and wasteful (Aaron 1978).

Conservatives in the 1970s attacked the National Science Foundation for supporting the development of social studies curricula that they felt were subversive and ideologically biased. NSF in the 1960s had funded the development of a fifth-grade anthropological curriculum entitled "Man: A Course of Study" (MACOS). After several local groups had attacked the MACOS project, Representative John B. Conlan (R-Arizona) delivered a harsh attack on the project:

> MACOS is designed to mold children's social attitudes and beliefs along lines that are almost always at variance with the beliefs and moral values of their parents and local communities. . . . Recurring themes of the sixty lessons include communal living, elimination of the weak and elderly in society, sexual permissiveness and promiscuity, violence, and primitive behavior. This is for ten-year-olds. (Dow 1991, 200)

Representative Conlan objected to the participation of behavioral and social scientists in reforming the school curriculum and introduced an amendment that stated that all NSF curriculum projects had to be reviewed by Congress before they could be implemented. While his amendment lost narrowly by a vote of 215 to 196, Representative Robert Bauman (R-Maryland) introduced a more sweeping amendment that called for a congressional review of all NSF grants. Bauman's amendment won by a small margin (212 to 199) but then was dropped during the joint House-Senate conference committee on the NSF authorization. Reacting to the new threats to its independence, NSF quickly and quietly ended its support of MACOS and terminated the funding of several other curriculum projects as well (Dow 1991).

Other members of Congress joined the attacks on the behavioral and social sciences. Senator William Proxmire (D-Wisconsin) ridiculed federal research support by issuing his "Golden Fleece" awards for frivolous-sounding behavioral and social science grants (e.g., see Fields 1980). In the second half of the 1970s, John Ashbrook (R-Ohio) frequently offered unsuccessful amendments to cut NSF social science funding.[30] And Representative Edith Green (D-Oregon), a specialist in educational matters, successfully cut the budget for the National Institute of Education for FY1975 by complaining that thousands of education research grants and contracts were never completed and many of those that were finished were never read or used.

> My studies—that my own congressional office has done research on contracts and grants covering a period of more than 3 years, show that the American people are not getting their money's worth. I say to my colleagues in the House that there has been nothing that I have observed in the 20 years that I have been in Congress that I think is such an appalling waste of money as the billions of dollars which this Congress votes for research, for contracts and grants, for studies, for evaluations[,] for reports that are never read. (*Congressional Record* 1974)

As an increasing number of policymakers questioned the value of funding behavioral and social science research and evaluations in the mid-1970s, the scholarly community obtained a growing recognition that the golden age of their influence and assistance was rapidly and perhaps even properly receding. Robert Nisbet wrote in the *New York Times Magazine* in 1975 about the public disenchantment regarding the efforts of scholars and social science research to solve national problems. Several scholars were invited to respond in a special symposium in the *American Scholar* (Social Science 1976). On the one hand, Robert Lekachman, professor of economics at Herbert H. Lehman College (CUNY), believed that Nisbet had greatly exaggerated the decline in the prestige of the behavioral and social sciences:

> I doubt (a) that the more extravagant claims of social scientists were ever widely accepted beyond the learned journals; (b) that in public esteem social scientists have declined more precipitously than other establish-

ment types—corporate managers, politicians, lawyers, doctors, et al.; (c) that the public was ever wrong in applying a pound or two of salt to the wisdom of pundits. (Social Science 1976, 342)

On the other hand, Harry G. Johnson, professor of economics at the University of Chicago, agreed with the basic premises of Nisbet's argument but was much more charitable toward his colleagues in judging their behavior:

> It seems to me indisputable both that there has been a loss of public confidence in the usefulness of social scientists, and that this loss is merited by the behavior of the social scientists themselves. One must, however, be wary of the American tendency to blame people for responding to the social forces that act on them, and particularly for not sternly refusing to accept greatness when public opinion seems to be thrusting it upon them. . . .
>
> In short, the social sciences have lost prestige because they have claimed to be able to deliver more than they can possibly deliver. And worse, the claim has been based on a very superficial understanding of the nature of a social system, and on a consistent refusal to understand the basic constraints on social possibilities imposed by the overall limitations of economic resources and the manifold defects of the human social being as an instrument from which to forge the ideal society. (Social Science 1976, 340–41)

By the second half of the 1970s, there was growing disillusionment among many policymakers, scholars, and the general public with the role of the behavioral and social sciences. Jimmy Carter, however, continued the practice of assembling academic advisers for his presidential campaign. While no major scholars became part of Carter's inner circle of domestic advisers, he did rely more heavily upon the permanent policy and planning experts in the executive offices and departments. Carter often placed himself at the center of the policy process but tended to focus on the technical and scientific details of the proposals, paying less attention to the overall strategy or approach (Hargrove 1988; Kaufman 1993; Lynn and Whitman 1981; Shoup 1980; Wood 1993).

Reagan was quite suspicious of academics in general yet did not hesitate to use them in both his 1976 and 1980 presidential campaigns. Many of these scholars, such as Richard Allen, Alan Greenspan, Martin Anderson, and George Schultz, had served in the Nixon-Ford administrations. President Reagan was especially successful in recruiting some prominent economists, though often he did not try to resolve or follow their conflicting advice. Moreover, given Reagan's strong personal ideological orientation, he was determined to control the bureaucracy and impose severe budget and staff cuts on most federal agencies and programs—including those that had dealt with the collection and analysis of behavioral and social science data. During the Reagan years, the behavioral and social scientists felt particularly threatened as conservative appointees in agencies such as the National Institute of Education tried either to eliminate those programs or ideologically redirect their efforts. Yet at the same time, the Reagan administration was quite supportive of basic scientific research, engineering, and defense-oriented research (Hess 1988; Larsen 1992; Nathan 1988; Palmer 1986; Palmer and Sawhill 1982; Williams 1990; Wood 1993, 139–61).

Throughout the tumultuous decades of the 1970s and 1980s, behavioral and social science analyses continued to be funded and consulted by policy-makers. While the impact of these studies and evaluations usually was more limited and less clear-cut than scholars and analysts initially might have predicted or hoped, overall the work often provided modest, useful additional information and different perspectives for policymakers and their staffs.[31] On some highly controversial issues, however, policymakers sometimes knowingly misused behavioral and social science studies to promote a particular point of view. For example, in the early 1980s the Reagan administration proposed that parents of unemancipated adolescents had to be notified if their daughters received prescription contraceptives from federally funded family planning clinics. Both the U.S. Office of Adolescent Pregnancy Programs (OAPP) and its opponents misled the public and other policymakers by deliberately withholding crucial information about the medical and social science studies they cited during the controversy (Vinovskis 1988, 87–130; 1989).[32]

Challenges to Higher Education

The period of the 1970s and 1980s was a difficult time for colleges and universities. Student turmoil, initially due to the civil rights movement and then furthered by opposition to the Vietnam War in the late 1960s and early 1970s, divided campuses and often created an antimilitary, anti-Washington atmosphere. Many scholars and institutions of higher education moved away from military-related research altogether. At the same time, a push toward a more practical and socially conscious mission at many colleges and universities raised concerns among some critics about the objectivity and disinterestedness of researchers and scholars (Fleming 1996; Geiger 1993; Ladd and Lipset 1975; Lipset and Schaflander 1971; Rorabaugh 1969).

Higher education had prospered during the 1960s, but the next two decades were more challenging economically to institutions of higher learning. As faculty salaries and administrative costs rose, colleges and universities scrambled to increase their revenues. Current fund expenditures for higher education rose from $23.4 billion in 1970 to $64.1 billion in 1980; in 1990 they reached $146.1 billion. But the federal share of the overall costs dropped from 17.9 percent in 1970 to 12.5 percent in 1990. Meantime, the proportion of total current expenditures covered by tuition and fees rose from 21.5 percent in 1970 to 25.6 percent in 1990. Overall, colleges and universities used increases in tuition and alumni contributions to keep up with the rising costs (calculated from U.S. Bureau of Census 1996, table 284).

While, in real dollars, federal spending for sponsored academic research declined slightly in the 1970s, it rose nearly one-fifth during the 1980s. Federal support of basic research increased relative to applied research. While federal funding for psychological research increased in 1987 constant dollars from $282 million in 1980 to $401 million in 1990, funding for the social sciences dropped from $742 million in 1980 to $563 million in 1990. As a result, while the Reagan years proved to be less disastrous for academic research overall than many scholars had predicted, they presented particular hardships for the social sciences, which lost almost one-quarter of their federal funding in real dollars during the 1980s (U.S. Bureau of the Census 1996, table 968).[33]

As colleges and universities faced financial challenges in the 1970s and 1980s, the number of Ph.D.'s granted in the social sciences declined slightly from 3,660 in 1971 to 3,230 in 1980; by 1990 it dropped to 3,010—making for a 17.8 percent drop in that nineteen-year period. Ph.D. degrees in psychology, however, rose significantly from 2,144 in 1971 to 3,395 in 1980; they then increased to 3,811 in 1990—giving a 77.8 percent increase during that same period. The composition of those Ph.D.'s in the 1970s and 1980s became more diversified as larger numbers of women and minorities completed their degrees. Meantime, the job market for new faculty in the behavioral and social sciences became much worse in the 1970s and 1980s (U.S. Bureau of the Census 1996, table 303; Bowen and Rudenstine 1992).

The number of permanent full-time faculty in the behavioral and social sciences had increased rapidly in the 1960s and early 1970s but did not grow as much in the mid-1970s and 1980s, partly because many of those retiring were replaced by part-time adjunct lecturers and instructors. At the major research universities, however, the use of part-time faculty was less common and there-fore had less impact on those most likely to have the time and resources to con-duct policy-related research (Blackburn and Lawrence 1995; Bowen and Rudenstine 1992; Bowen and Sosa 1989).

Growth of Public Policy Programs

One of the major institutional developments during these two decades was the rapid growth in public policy schools or programs. While some of these public policy institutions taught undergraduates, many of them offered master or doctoral degrees. The orientation of these institutions varied by the disciplinary composition of their faculty as well as the location of the programs in the academic structure. Many of the public policy school programs emphasized basic training in economic-oriented public policy analysis, while others had a more political science orientation. Graduates from these schools and programs played an increasingly important role in staffing government positions and introducing academic and behavioral social science knowledge into the broader policy world. While debate about the depth or usefulness of some of that training abounds, public policy schools and programs are an important additional source of training for students interested in working in the government or in nonprofit organizations.[34]

Important changes in the behavioral and social sciences in the 1970s and 1980s affected policy analyses. On the one hand, the more quantitative behavioral and social sciences became more sophisticated and more rigorous conceptually and methodologically in these decades. Many behavioral and social scientists also emphasized the historical and socioeconomic context in their analyses and developed a more realistic understanding of the limitations of any empirical investigations. On the other hand, many behavioral and social science practitioners moved away from positivist quantitative models and analyses toward a more nuanced and theoretical multidisciplinary cultural approach. William Dunn and Rita Kelly summarized the impact of these developments on public policy analysis by the end of these two decades.

> In any case, by the 1990s numerous modifications of the applied social science approach to policy inquiry had occurred. Values were more readily seen as critical and inseparable from policy inquiry. Grounded theory and an understanding of the limits of time, space, and specific contexts were widely recognized as vital to adequate social science research as well as to policy analysis, giving rise to a renewed respect for qualitative as well as quantitative analyses. Perhaps most dramatically, a simple correspondence theory of truth had been replaced with either a consensus or a coherent theory of truth. The sum total impact of these basic changes in orientation was to move policy inquiry away from a dominant emphasis on prediction, forecasting, and control of "manipulable" variables, toward an emphasis on expanding our understanding of contingency and chance. These changes clearly make policy inquiry multiple in orientations and less unified in its assumptions about reality, in the training needed to be part of the policy community, and in the type of research on analytic products accepted as valid and useful. (1992, 13–14)

While public policy analysis became an important academic subfield during the 1970s and 1980s, considerable skepticism about its lack of theoretical sophistication and methodological rigor continued to persist among other scholars. Nevertheless, the topic of public policy ranked fourth in the proportion of articles appearing in major journals, such as the *American Political Science Review,* from 1978 through 1988 (Palumbo 1992, 59–80).[35] Most of these articles focused on analyzing the policy process rather than addressing a specific substantive policy area or question. As a result, Dennis Palumbo suggested

> that policy research of political scientists is seldom relevant to policymakers because it seldom makes recommendations (only 7 percent of the time) and it does not often focus on implementation or evaluation of a specific policy area (only 30 percent of the time). The latter stages are more likely to be of interest to policymakers than formulation. Moreover, the 30 percent of the articles that do focus on implementation or evaluation most often are concerned with formulating generalizations rather than recommending action to improve policy. (1992, 67, 70)

Thus, the growth of public policy schools and programs provided valuable training for students planning to enter government service and encouraged many faculty members to explore this subject matter in their classrooms as well as in their own research. Yet as valuable as the efforts of these public policy scholars might have been from a more theoretical and disciplinary perspective, they do not appear to have generated as much direct and immediate assistance to policymakers who were more narrowly focused on a particular problem area.

At the same time that many faculty became more aware of their political and ideological orientations, many intellectuals disengaged themselves from government service in the 1970s and 1980s. For some scholars, the divisions over the Vietnam War spurred this separation between academe and participation in government. The detachment was reinforced by the reluctance of many behavioral and social scientists to serve in the more conservative, Republican administrations in those years. The growing general distrust and separation between scholars and the federal government in the 1970s and 1980s also reflected the lack of interest by more conservative political leaders to reach out to many prominent behavioral and social science analysts whom they regarded as radical or too liberal to suit their particular policy needs (Anderson 1992; Brint 1994; Damrosch 1995; Fink, Leonard, and Reid 1996; Finkelstein 1984; Levine 1993).

Proliferation of Washington Think Tanks

The other major institutional development affecting policy-making during these decades was the rapid proliferation of Washington-based think tanks. We have already mentioned the development and importance of institutions such as the Brookings Institution, the RAND Corporation, the Russell Sage Foundation, and the Urban Institute—many of which tended to have a profederal government and liberal bias. These were joined in the mid-1970s by organizations such as the Manpower Demonstration Research Corporation, which specialized in large-scale social science evaluations. At the same time, however, some of the older and more conservative institutions like the American Enterprise Institute for Public Policy Research; the Hoover Institution on War, Revolution, and Peace; and the Hudson Institute were revitalized. Several major new conservative think tanks were established including the Cato Institute, the Heritage Foundation, the Institute for Contemporary Studies, and the Manhattan Institute for Policy Research. Liberals countered by creating the Center on Budget and Policy Priorities, the Center for National Policy, the Economic Policy Institute, and the Progressive Policy Institute. It has been estimated that by 1990 there were at least one hundred major policy research groups in Washington—two-thirds of which had been established since 1970 (Smith 1991b).

During these years, political leaders relied more and more upon these think tanks. Conservatives, who were deeply suspicious of the liberal orientation of most behavioral and social scientists in the major research universities, worked especially hard to create and use the resources of these think tanks to provide themselves with staff and new policy ideas. It would be easy to exaggerate, however, the importance of these more conservative organizations as agents of change since the general ideas espoused by them reflected in large part what many in the public already had come to believe. Yet James Smith has pointed to the special role of these think tanks in helping to develop a conservative policy elite:

> The long-term success of the conservative think tanks lay less in their efforts to persuade and exhort the public—market metaphors notwithstanding—than in helping to shape a conservative policy elite that could claim that it was capable of governing. Indeed, in fostering a counter elite, the work of the conservative think tanks paralleled, though in a much foreshortened way, developments that had taken place over more than half a century in the older research institutions. Think tanks of the Right did not make a revolution; rather, they prepared the revolutionary cadres who ascended to power in 1980. These self-conscious revolutionaries used policy research organizations in new ways, challenging the assumptions on which Brookings, RAND, the Urban Institute, and others had operated while casting further doubt upon the long-term political contributions of experts who were trained in the social sciences. (1991b, 203)[36]

Disappointment with the claims and help from behavioral and social scientists in the 1970s and 1980s forced many policymakers to look elsewhere for assistance. Other factors contributing to their disillusionment were the increasingly specialized and difficult language of scholars as well as challenges to the desirability and effectiveness of federal domestic programs. In part, this deviation encouraged a growing reliance upon experts and information from more ideologically oriented think tanks supported by both the left and the right. Again, James Smith observes how this shift has helped to undermine the use of more rigorous behavioral and social science research in policy-making.

> The potent modern metaphors of marketing and intellectual combat, now so much in vogue within the research enterprise (as elsewhere in society), arose out of disappointments with scientific claims of social research. Yet despite their popularity among researchers themselves, they are far more damaging to a proper understanding of the process of policymaking—and the role of experts in it—than are even the most grandiose scientific metaphors. These influential images suggest that the enterprise of experts largely involves creating and peddling innovative policy measures to citizen consumers or battling for ideas in a hostile arena in which the winner takes all. They seek persuasion of the most superficial sort, not understanding or reflection. Furthermore, the current emphasis on marketing techniques and relentless intellectual combat has little to do with either sustained research (and the steady, cumulative nature of the knowledge enterprise) or the deliberative and educational processes that best serve a democratic society and that require a structured dialogue among experts, leaders, and citizens. (1991b, 237)

Thus, the decades of the 1970s and 1980s saw considerable changes. On the one hand, there was growing disillusion with the excessive promises and expectations for the Great Society programs of the 1960s and the ability of behavioral and social scientists to provide meaningful and lasting ways of helping disadvantaged Americans. On the other hand, policy analysts and evaluation experts became permanent and accepted additions to the federal bureaucracy. On college and university campuses, as well as in the proliferating Washington think tanks, policy analysis and program evaluations were widely accepted and practiced—though often without much agreement on how these tasks should be pursued.

Conclusion

Many changes have developed in the relationship between the behavioral and social sciences and federal policy-making during the past half century. From 1940 to the present, the federal government has grown considerably in the overall amount of money it spends, the number of individuals it employs, and the number of domestic programs it supports. Much of this expansion in federal activities and responsibilities occurred during the New Deal and World War II. But the development of the Great Society programs of the 1960s also stimulated federal government expansion, which then continued during the Nixon, Ford, and Carter administrations. While the Reagan administration hoped to cut back or eliminate many of these federal domestic programs, it merely slowed their growth temporarily. Over the past fifty years, the American people have come to expect much more from the federal government even though their personal trust of the leaders has diminished considerably over the past three decades.

Paralleling the growth of the federal government has been the expansion in the number and type of specialized agencies that provide or use behavioral and social science studies and ideas. Since World War II the Executive Office not only expanded the number of professionals on its immediate staff but also created new agencies such as the Council of Economic Advisors, the Central Intelligence Agency, and the National Security Council. Building upon the experiences of biological and social science research in the Department of Agriculture, many other federal departments created their own policy and evaluation units after the mid-1960s. Not to be left behind, Congress expanded its own professional staffs and created new organizations or restructured old agencies such as the Congressional Research Service, the General Accounting Office, and the Congressional Budget Office.

Thus, the role of the federal government in American society has expanded dramatically in the past fifty years. At the same time, the federal government has increased the organizational specialization and capacity to hire its own behavioral and social science experts as well as its ability to solicit and fund outside analysts.

To facilitate the demands for service in this arena, the United States's higher education system increased its capacity to provide behavioral and social science research for policymakers after World War II and its ability to train experts necessary in these fields. Not only did the existing major research universities expand during these decades, but they were joined by many other institutions that had not been particularly research-oriented before the war. Federal research and development funds grew rapidly, though unevenly, during these years. While the bulk of the federal research and development monies still went to private industry, colleges and universities benefited tremendously from the increased funding—especially in the sciences. Although the number and sophistication of the behavioral and social scientists at the colleges and universities grew, the interest or willingness of many of them to work closely with federal policymakers diminished considerably in the 1970s and 1980s. This reduction of interest reflected in part the growing alienation between academia and the federal government over the Vietnam War, the mutual distrust between many academics and the more conservative Republican administrations of the 1970s and 1980s, and the intellectual and public disappointment regarding the ability of academic experts to find solutions for the most pressing social problems.

Nonprofit private organizations such as the Brookings Institution and the Russell Sage Foundation have existed since the early twentieth century and provided advice and assistance for federal policymakers. These institutions played a vital role in doing and supporting behavioral and social science research and sharing that knowledge with policymakers. These organizations continued to contribute to the revitalization and expansion of the behavioral and social sciences after World War II, though their relative overall funding contributions shrank as the federal government expanded its role in the 1950s. They were also joined after World War II by new quasi-government institutions such as the RAND Corporation and the Urban Institute.

These more traditional nonprofit organizations were soon joined in the 1970s by a large number of new or revitalized institutions such as the Heritage Foundation and the Hoover Institution. Many of these new so-called think tanks provided more conservative policy advice and relied less upon doing extensive, in-depth research than on disseminating policy position papers to sympathetic legislators. Perhaps somewhat ironically, while there also has been a sizable expansion of public policy schools and programs during the 1970s and 1980s, the new conservative and liberal think tanks appear to be having a more immediate, though perhaps only short-term, impact on policy-making today.

While most twentieth-century presidents relied upon academic advisers to some extent, Presidents Kennedy and Johnson can be credited with being the first to make systematic use of them during their campaigns and during the transitions from one administration to the next. Following their lead, it has now become routine for presidential aspirants to recruit scholars for their campaigns and to use them extensively on ad hoc task forces in setting up the incoming administrations. While the actual influence of these academic advisers usually has been quite limited during presidential campaigns and administration establishment, a few advisers have survived to become significant participants and contributors in the regular administration.

Perhaps equally important has been the sizable number of behavioral and social scientists employed by the federal government, often in more specialized planning and evaluation units. These professionals have not only produced policy-relevant studies, but have served as potentially useful links between policymakers and the behavioral and social scientists located outside the government. Although the direct and overall impact of the behavioral and social sciences on federal decision making and program implementation usually has been quite modest or even negligible, it certainly has expanded considerably in amount, scope, and sophistication since 1940. At the same time, policymakers and the public have been left with considerable disillusionment about the usefulness and objectivity of the behavioral and social sciences. While the ability to do first-rate behavioral and social science work in policy-oriented areas has improved and the capacity and need of the federal government for such assistance has grown in the past fifty years, it still remains to be seen how that everchanging relationship will evolve as we face the great social and economic challenges of the twenty-first century.

NOTES

1. On the development of the social sciences in the late nineteenth century, see Furner 1975; Haskell 1977.

2. On the role of private foundations during this period, see Lagemann 1989; Sealander 1997.

3. On the role of the federal government in collecting and analyzing educational data, see Vinovskis 1996; Warren 1974. On the development and uses of the federal censuses in the nineteenth century, see Anderson 1988. For an analysis of the development of the Bureau of the Census, see Willcox 1914. On the development of the new non-profit research agencies in the early twentieth century, see Smith 1991a, 1991b.

4. At first President Wilson appointed few university-trained individuals and did not tolerate conflicting opinions among his advisers. During World War I, however, he increasingly turned to academic experts for assistance (Cuff 1973; Gelfand 1963). On the role of academics in the federal government during these years, see Cook 1982.

5. It is estimated that in 1938 there were nearly 7,800 social scientists working for the federal government, most of them as economists scattered throughout the increasing number of federal agencies (Smith 1991b, 79). On the role of the economists in the New Deal, see Barber 1996.

6. James Allen Smith writes in *The Idea Brokers:*

Before the New Deal, their authority had rested on their assertion of detachment from partisan wrangling. The independent institutions they had created and the advisory patterns that had evolved tried to preserve this respectable distance by presenting the experts primarily as fact-finders who were seeking to reconcile ideological or "value" differences. But the 1930s had brought some experts into political advisory positions and many more into positions as planners and administrators of government programs. Accordingly, their expertise began to operate on the political process in a different way. Instead of a disinterested knowledge that fostered a consensus on policy solutions, theirs was now a knowledge that served political actors, justifying policies and rationalizing political convictions. (1991b, 94)

7. For a useful overview, see Lyons 1991, 80–123.

8. After the war, Likert and some of his colleagues set up the Survey Research Cen-

ter at the University of Michigan (later merged into the newly created Institute for Social Research).

9. Funding for NIH rose rapidly during the 1950s. By 1960 NIH appropriations totaled $430 million—most of which went to support research and training at medical schools (Geiger 1993, 183). On the development of NIH during the postwar period, see Deignan and Miller 1952; Strickland 1972.

10. The following discussion of NSF and the social sciences draws heavily upon the useful analysis by Otto Larsen (1992).

11. Similarly, Representative Clarence Brown (R-Ohio) had earlier warned:

If the impression becomes prevalent in Congress that this legislation is to establish some sort of organization in which there would be a lot of short-haired women and long-haired men messing into everybody's personal affairs and lives, inquiring whether they love them and so forth, you are not going to get your legislation. (England 1982, 50)

12. There were some other federal agencies, however, that were more supportive of social science research. The Office of Naval Research, for example, expanded its support of social science research through its Human Resources Division from $100,000 in 1946 to $1.5 million in 1950 (and then even more due to the outbreak of the Korean War) (Darley 1957). In general, each of the three branches of the military had its own system of social science research that featured the use of psychology for understanding personnel issues in the armed forces. For a useful discussion of the role of social science research by the military after World War II, see Lyons 1969, 136–47.

13. For a more in-depth discussion of the impact of the GI Bill on postwar education, see Bennett 1996.

14. On the creation and development of the Ford Foundation, see MacDonald 1956; Sutton 1987, 41–91.

15. On the evolution of the federal civil service system, see Ingraham 1995; Johnson and Libecap 1994.

16. For an introduction to the Great Society programs of the 1960s, see Bernstein 1996; Kaplan and Cuciti 1986; Levitan and Taggart 1976.

17. Much of that increase was in social insurance programs (such as Social Security) that rose from $14.31 billion in 1960 to $35.39 billion in 1968 (U. S. Bureau of the Census 1974, Part 1, Series H33).

18. The major disciplines included in this tabulation were anthropology, economics and agricultural economics, history, political science, psychology and educational psychology, sociology, and geography.

19. The associations used in this calculation and their membership in 1967 (in parentheses) were the American Psychological Association (25,800), the American Economic Association (23,305), the American Historical Association (17,839), the American Political Science Association (14,685), the American Sociological Association (11,000), the American Anthropological Association (6,634), and the Association of American Geographers (4,414). Naturally, some social and behavioral scientists did not belong to any of these organizations, and a few belonged to more than one.

20. The data on federal social welfare expenditures cited earlier for the period 1960

through 1970 are not identical to the information presented here because the latter includes some additional programs.

21. The Civil Service Commission was replaced by the Office of Personnel Management (OPM) and the Merit Systems Protection Board (MSPB) (Ingraham 1995, 73–91).

22. The reasons for the departure of large numbers of SES employees is complex, but certainly one factor was the reduction in the number of them who would be eligible for the sizable bonuses. Some left or were forced out because their political orientation did not match that of the new administration (Ingraham 1995, 84–86; Moe 1985).

23. On the evolving role of policy analysts in the federal bureaucracy, see Meltsner 1976.

24. For a more in-depth analysis of the development of planning and evaluation activities in HEW, see Abert 1979.

25. For a discussion of these problems, see Vinovskis 1999a.

26. For information on the changing numbers and functions of these congressional staff members, see Fox and Hammond 1977; Mann and Ornstein 1993, 68–75; Ornstein et al. 1982; U.S. Bureau of the Census 1996, table no. 445.

27. See Fox and Hammond 1977, 175, for the sources on the numbers and functions of the staff. The Office of Technology Assessment (OTA) has recently been abolished. For a useful discussion of OTA, see Bibber 1996.

28. For discussions of the controversies over Head Start, see Vinovskis 1993; Zigler and Muenchow 1992.

29. For example, in reporting the results of the Westinghouse Learning Corporation's evaluation of Head Start, the *New York Times* ran the headline "Head Start Pupils Found No Better Off Than Others" (April 14, 1969).

30. For an elaboration of Representative Ashbrook's attacks on social science funding at NSF, see Ashbrook 1980, 12–14; Prewitt 1980, 15–16.

31. On the uses of behavioral and social science analyses for policy-making during the 1970s and 1980s, see Arrow and Abt 1979; Bulmer 1987; Lyons 1975; McCall and Weber 1984; Nagel 1975; Nathan 1980; OECD 1980.

32. The public was also misled in regard to the "epidemic" nature of teenage pregnancies in the late 1970s (Luker 1996, 81–108; Vinovskis 1988, 22–46).

33. The cuts in the social sciences were particularly severe during the first term of the Reagan administration and then recovered somewhat afterward. See also Cohen and Noll 1992.

34. On developments in the 1970s and 1980s in the public policy schools and programs, see deLeon 1988; Dunn and Kelly 1992.

35. Palumbo found similar results in four other journals as well—*American Journal of Politics, Polity, Western Political Quarterly,* and *Policy Studies Review.* His findings are similar to those advanced by James Rogers (1989).

36. See also Stefancic and Delgado 1996.

REFERENCES

Aaron, Henry J. 1978. *Politics and the professors: The Great Society in perspective.* Washington, D.C.: Brookings Institution.

Abert, James G., ed. 1979. *Program evaluation at HEW: Research versus reality.* 3 vols. New York: Marcel Dekker.

Anderson, Margo J. 1988. *The American census: A social history.* New Haven: Yale University Press.

Anderson, Martin. 1978. *Welfare: The political economy of welfare reform in the United States.* Stanford: Hoover Institution Press.

————. 1992. *Impostors in the temple: American intellectuals are destroying our universities and cheating our students of their future.* New York: Simon and Schuster.

Arnold, Peri E. 1986. *Making the managerial presidency: Comprehensive reorganization planning, 1905–1980.* Princeton: Princeton University Press.

Arrow, Kenneth J., and Clark C. Abt, eds. 1979. *Applied research for social policy: The United States and the Federal Republic of Germany compared.* Cambridge, Mass.: Abt Books.

Ashbrook, John M. 1980. A critique of NSF. *Society* 17 (September/October): 12–14.

Banfield, Edward C. 1970. *The unheavenly city: The nature and future of our urban crisis.* Boston: Little, Brown.

Barber, William J. 1996. *Designs within disorder: Franklin D. Roosevelt, the economists, and the shaping of American economic policy, 1933–1945.* Cambridge: Cambridge University Press.

Beckman, George M. 1967. The role of the foundations in non-western studies. In *U.S. philanthropic foundations: Their history, structure, management, and record,* ed. Warren Weaver, 395–409. New York: Harper and Row.

Behavioral and Social Sciences Survey Committee. 1969. *The behavioral and social sciences: Outlook and needs.* Englewood Cliffs, N.J.: Prentice-Hall.

Benedict, Ruth. 1946. *The chrysanthemum and the sword.* Boston: Houghton Mifflin.

Bennett, Michael J. 1996. *When dreams came true: The GI Bill and the making of modern America.* Washington, D.C.: Brassey's.

Berman, Larry. 1979. *The Office of Management and Budget and the presidency.* Princeton: Princeton University Press.

Bernstein, Irving. 1996. *Guns or butter: The presidency of Lyndon Johnson.* New York: Oxford University Press.

Bibber, Bruce. 1996. *The politics of expertise in Congress: The rise and fall of the Office of Technology Assessment.* Albany: State University of New York Press.

Blackburn, Robert T., and Janet H. Lawrence. 1995. *Faculty at work: Motivation, expectation, satisfaction.* Baltimore: Johns Hopkins University Press.

Bowen, William G., and Neil L. Rudenstine. 1992. *In pursuit of the Ph.D.* Princeton: Princeton University Press.

Bowen, William G., and Julie Ann Sosa. 1989. *Prospects for faculty in the arts and sciences.* Princeton: Princeton University Press.

Brauer, Carl M. 1986. *Presidential transitions: Eisenhower through Reagan.* New York: Oxford University Press.

Brint, Steven. 1994. *In an age of experts: The changing role of professionals in politics and public life.* Princeton: Princeton University Press.

Brookings Institution. 1966. *Government and the critical intelligence: An address by President Lyndon B. Johnson.* Washington, D.C.: Brookings Institution.

Bulmer, Martin, ed. 1987. *Social science research and government: Comparative essays on Britain and the United States.* Cambridge: Cambridge University Press.

Burner, David. 1988. *John F. Kennedy and a new generation.* Glenview, Ill.: Scott, Foresman and Little, Brown.

Califano, Joseph A. 1991. *The triumph and tragedy of Lyndon Johnson: The White House years.* New York: Simon and Schuster.

Carter, Launor F. 1984. The sustaining effects study of compensatory and elementary education. *Educational Researcher* 13 (August/September): 4–13.

Cartwright, Dorwin. 1947a. Social psychology in the United States during the Second World War. *Human Relations* 1 (November): 333–52.

———. 1947b. Surveys of the war finance program. In *Measurement of consumer interest,* ed. C. West Churchman, Russell L. Ackoff, and Murray Wax, 198–209. Philadelphia: University of Pennsylvania Press.

Chelimsky, Eleanor. 1992. Executive branch program evaluation: An upturn soon? In *Evaluation in the federal government: Changes, trends, and opportunities,* ed. Christopher G. Wye and Richard C. Sonnichsen. San Francisco: Jossey-Bass.

Cohen, Linda R., and Roger G. Noll. 1992. Research and development. In *Setting domestic priorities: What can government do?,* ed. Henry J. Aaron and Charles L. Schultze, 223–65. Washington, D.C.: Brookings Institution.

Congressional Record. 1974. 120, June 27, pt. 16: 21677.

Cook, Paul B. 1982. *Academicians from Roosevelt to Roosevelt.* New York: Garland.

Cuff, Robert. 1973. *The War Industries Board.* Baltimore: Johns Hopkins University Press.

Curti, Merle. 1942. The American scholar in three wars. *Journal of the History of Ideas* 3 (June): 241–64.

Damrosch, David. 1995. *We scholars: Changing the culture of the university.* Cambridge: Harvard University Press.

Darley, John G. 1957. Psychology and the Office of Naval Research: A decade of development. *American Psychologist* 12 (May): 305–23.

Deignan, Stella L., and Esther Miller. 1952. The support of research in medical and allied fields for the period 1946 through 1951. *Science* 115:321–43.

DeLeon, Peter. 1988. *Advice and consent: The development of the policy sciences.* New York: Russell Sage Foundation.

Destler, I. M. 1972. *Presidents, bureaucrats, and foreign policy: The politics of organizational reform.* Princeton: Princeton University Press.

Divine, Robert A. 1993. *The Sputnik challenge: Eisenhower's response to the Soviet satellite.* New York: Oxford University Press.

Dow, Peter B. 1991. *Schoolhouse politics: Lessons from the Sputnik era.* Cambridge: Harvard University Press.

Dunn, William N., and Rita Mae Kelly. 1992. Introduction: Advances in policy studies. In *Advances in policy studies since 1950,* ed. William N. Dunn and Rita Mae Kelly, 13–14. New Brunswick, N.J.: Transaction Publishers.

England, J. Merton. 1982. *A patron for pure science: The National Science Foundation's formative years, 1945–57.* Washington, D.C.: National Science Foundation.

Fields, Cheryl M. 1980. A social scientist recounts some lessons he learned from winning Proxmire's "Golden Fleece." *Chronicle of Higher Education* 27 (15 September).

Fink, Leon, Stephen T. Leonard, and Donald M. Reid. 1996. *Intellectuals and public life: Between radicalism and reform.* Ithaca: Cornell University Press.

Finkelstein, Martin J. 1984. *The American academic profession: A synthesis of social scientific inquiry since World War II.* Columbus: Ohio State University Press.

Flash, Edward S., Jr. 1965. *Economic advice and presidential leadership: The Council of Economic Advisors.* New York: Columbia University Press.

Fleming, Robben W. 1996. *Tempest into rainbows: Managing turbulence.* Ann Arbor: University of Michigan Press.

Fox, Harrison W., Jr., and Susan Webb Hammond. 1977. *Congressional staffs: The invisible force in American lawmaking.* New York: Free Press.

Furner, Mary O. 1975. *Advocacy and objectivity: A crisis in the professionalization of American social science.* Lexington: University Press of Kentucky.

Gaus, John M., and Leon Wolcott. 1940. *Public administration and the United States Department of Agriculture.* Chicago: Public Administration Clearinghouse.

Geiger, Roger L. 1986. *To advance knowledge.* New York: Oxford University Press.

———. 1988. American foundations and academic social science, 1945–1960. *Minerva* 26:315–41.

———. 1993. *Research and relevant knowledge: American research universities since World War II.* New York: Oxford University Press.

Gelfand, Laurence. 1963. *The inquiry: American preparations for peace.* New Haven: Yale University Press.

Giglio, James N. 1991. *The presidency of John F. Kennedy.* Lawrence: University Press of Kansas.

Goldman, Eric F. 1969. *The tragedy of Lyndon Johnson.* New York: Alfred A. Knopf.

Gosnell, Harold F., and Moyca C. David. 1949. Public opinion research in government. *American Political Science Review* 43 (June): 564–72.

Graham, Hugh D. 1984. *The uncertain triumph: Federal education policy in the Kennedy and Johnson years.* Chapel Hill: University of North Carolina Press.

Greenberg, Daniel S. 1967. *The politics of pure science.* New York: New American Library.

Greene, John Robert. 1995. *The presidency of Gerald R. Ford.* Lawrence: University Press of Kansas.

Hargrove, Erwin C. 1988. *Jimmy Carter as president: Leadership and the politics of the public good.* Baton Rouge: Louisiana State University Press.

Harper, Edwin L., Fred A. Kramer, and Andrew M. Rouse. 1969. Implementation and use of PPB in sixteen federal agencies. *Public Administration Review* 29 (November/December): 623–32.

Harris, Fred R. 1967. The case for a National Social Science Foundation. *Science* 157 (August 4): 507–9.

Hart, John. 1987. *The presidential branch.* New York: Pergamon.

Hartmann, Robert L. 1980. *Palace politics: An inside account of the Ford years.* New York: McGraw Hill.

Haskell, Thomas L. 1977. *The emergence of professional social science: The American Social Science Association and the nineteenth-century crisis of authority.* Urbana: University of Illinois Press.

Hauser, Philip M. 1945. Wartime developments in census statistics. *American Sociological Review* 10 (April): 160–69.

Head Start pupils found no better off than others. 1969. *New York Times,* April 14.

Heaphey, James J., and Alan P. Balutis, eds. 1975. *Legislative staffing: A comparative perspective.* New York: Sage.

Henderson, Phillip G. 1988. *Managing the presidency: The Eisenhower legacy—From Kennedy to Reagan.* Boulder, Colo.: Westview.

Hess, Stephen. 1988. *Organizing the presidency.* 2d ed. Washington, D.C.: Brookings Institution.

Homan, Paul T. 1946. Economics in the war period. *American Economic Review* 37 (December): 855–71.

Horowitz, Irving Louis, ed. 1974. *The rise and fall of Project Camelot.* Rev. ed. Cambridge: MIT Press.

House, Ernest R., Gene V. Glass, Leslie D. McLean, and Decker F. Walker. 1978. No simple answer: Critique of the follow through evaluation. *Harvard Educational Review* 48 (May): 128–60.

Ingraham, Patricia Wallace. 1995. *The foundation of merit: Public service in American democracy.* Baltimore: Johns Hopkins University Press.

Jeffreys-Jones, Rhodri. 1989. *The CIA and American democracy.* New Haven: Yale University Press.

Jencks, Christopher, et al. 1972. *Inequality: A reassessment of the effect of family and schooling in America.* New York: Basic Books.

Johnson, Ronald N., and Gary D. Libecap. 1994. *The Federal Civil Service System and the problem of bureaucracy: The economics and politics of institutional change.* Chicago: University of Chicago Press.

Kaplan, Marshall, and Peggy Cuciti, eds. 1986. *The Great Society and its legacy: Twenty years of U.S. social policy.* Durham, N.C.: Duke University Press.

Karl, Barry D. 1969. Presidential planning and social science research: Mr. Hoover's experts. *Perspectives in American History* 3:347–409.

———. 1974. *Charles E. Merriam and the study of politics.* Chicago: University of Chicago Press.

Kaufman, Burton I. 1993. *The presidency of James Earl Carter.* Lawrence: University Press of Kansas.

Kershaw, Joseph A., and Harry Alpert. 1947. The invalidation of food ration currency, December 1944. *Journal of Social Issues* 3 (July): 40–48.

Kidd, Charles V. 1959. *American universities and federal research.* Cambridge: Harvard University Press.

Kirkendall, Richard S. 1966. *Social scientists and farm politics in the age of Roosevelt.* Columbia: University of Missouri Press.

Kissinger, Henry. 1979. *The White House years.* Boston: Little, Brown.

Klausner, Samuel Z. 1986. The bid to nationalize the social sciences. In *The nationalization of the social sciences,* ed. Samuel Z. Klausner and Victor M. Lidz, 3–40. Philadelphia: University of Pennsylvania Press.

Klausner, Samuel Z., and Victor M. Lidz, eds. 1986. *The nationalization of the social sciences.* Philadelphia: University of Pennsylvania Press.

Kleinman, Daniel L. 1995. *Politics on the endless frontier: Postwar research policy in the United States.* Durham, N.C.: Duke University Press.

Kofmehl, Kenneth. 1962. *Professional staffs of Congress.* Purdue, Ind.: Purdue University Studies.

Ladd, Everett Carll, Jr., and Seymour Martin Lipset. 1975. *The divided academy: Professors and politics.* New York: McGraw Hill.

Lagemann, Ellen Condliffe. 1989. *The politics of knowledge: The Carnegie Corporation, philanthropy, and public policy.* Middletown, Conn.: Wesleyan University Press.

Larsen, Otto N. 1992. *Milestones and millstones: Social science at the National Science Foundation, 1945–1991.* New Brunswick, N.J.: Transaction Publishers.

Leighton, Alexander H. 1949. *Human relations in a changing world.* New York: E. P. Dutton.

Levine, Arthur, ed. 1993. *Higher learning in America, 1980–2000.* Baltimore: Johns Hopkins University Press.

Levitan, Sar A., and Robert Taggart. 1976. *The promise of greatness: The social programs of the last decade and their major achievements.* Cambridge: Harvard University Press.

Lewin, Kurt. 1943. Forces behind food habits and methods of change. In *The problem of changing food habits,* 35–65. Washington, D.C.: National Academy Press.

Lipset, Seymour Martin, and Gerald M. Schaflander. 1971. *Passion and politics: Student activism in America.* Boston: Little, Brown.

Lord, Carnes. 1988. *The presidency and the management of national security.* New York: Free Press.

Luker, Kristin. 1996. *Dubious conceptions: The politics of teenage pregnancy.* Cambridge: Harvard University Press.

Lundberg, George A. 1944. The Senate ponders social science. *Scientific Monthly* 44 (May): 398–99.

Lynn, Laurence E., Jr., and David deF. Whitman. 1981. *The president as policymaker: Jimmy Carter and welfare reform.* Philadelphia: Temple University Press.

Lyons, Gene M. 1969. *The uneasy partnership: Social science and the federal government in the twentieth century.* New York: Russell Sage Foundation.

———. 1975. *Social research and public policies.* Hanover, N.H.: University Press of New England.

MacDonald, Dwight. 1956. *The Ford Foundation: The men and the millions.* New York: Reynal.

MacKenzie, G. Calvin, ed. 1987. *The in-and-outers: Presidential appointees and transient government in Washington.* Baltimore: Johns Hopkins University Press.

Mann, Thomas E., and Norman J. Ornstein. 1993. *A second report of the renewing Congress project.* Washington, D.C.: American Enterprise Institute and Brookings Institution.

Martin, John Barlow. 1977. *Adlai Stevenson of Illinois.* New York: Anchor Books.

Matthews, Fred H. 1977. *Quest for an American sociology: Robert E. Park and the Chicago School.* Montreal: McGill-Queen's University Press.

McCall, George J., and George H. Weber, eds. 1984. *Social science and public policy: The roles of academic disciplines in policy analysis.* Port Washington, N.Y.: Associated Faculty Press.

McCaughey, Robert. 1984. *International studies and academic enterprise: A chapter in the enclosure of American learning.* New York: Columbia University Press.

McCloskey, Donald N. 1994. *Knowledge and persuasion in economics.* Cambridge: Cambridge University Press.

McLaughlin, Milbrey Wallin. 1975. *Evaluation and reform: The Elementary and Secondary Education Act of 1965, Title I.* Cambridge, Mass.: Ballinger.

Meltsner, Arnold J. 1976. *Policy analysts in the bureaucracy.* Berkeley: University of California Press.

Merriam, Charles E. 1944. The National Resources Planning Board: A chapter in American planning experience. *American Political Science Review* 38 (December): 1075–88.

Miller, Roberta B. 1982. The social sciences and the politics of science: The 1940s. *American Sociologist* 17 (November): 205–9.

Moe, Terry. 1985. The politicized presidency. In *The new direction in American politics,* ed. John Chubb and Paul Peterson, 260–72. Washington, D.C.: Brookings Institution.

Morin, Alexander J. 1993. *Science policy and politics.* Englewood Cliffs, N.J.: Prentice-Hall.

Mosher, Frederick C. 1979. *The GAO: The quest for accountability in American government.* Boulder, Colo.: Westview.

———. 1984. *A tale of two agencies: A comparative analysis of the General Accounting Office and the Office of Management and Budget.* Baton Rouge: Louisiana State University Press.

Moynihan, Daniel Patrick. 1969. *Maximum feasible misunderstanding: Community action in the War on Poverty.* New York: Free Press.

———. 1973. *The politics of a guaranteed income: The Nixon administration and the Family Assistance Plan.* New York: Vintage Books.

Nagel, Stuart S. 1975. *Policy studies and the social sciences.* Lexington, Mass.: Lexington Books.

Nathan, Richard P. 1975. *The plot that failed: Nixon and the administrative presidency.* New York: Wiley.

———. 1988. *Social science in government: Uses and misuses.* New York: Basic Books.

Nourse, Edwin. 1953. *Economics in the public service.* New York: Harcourt Brace.

Novick, David. 1947. Research opportunities in the War Production Board Records. *American Economic Review* 37 (May): 690–93.

Organisation for Economic Co-operation and Development (OECD). 1980. *The utilization of the social sciences in policy making in the United States.* Paris: OECD.

Ornstein, Norman J., Thomas E. Mann, Michael J. Malbin, and John F. Bibby. 1982. *Vital statistics on Congress, 1982.* Washington, D.C.: American Enterprise Institute.

Palmer, John L., ed. 1986. *Perspectives on the Reagan years.* Washington, D.C.: Urban Institute Press.

Palmer, John L., and Isabel V. Sawhill, eds. 1982. *The Reagan experiment.* Washington, D.C.: Urban Institute Press.

Palumbo, Dennis J. 1992. Bucking the tide: Policy studies in political science, 1978–1988. In *Advances in Policy Studies since 1950,* ed. William N. Dunn and Rita Mae Kelly, 59–80. New Brunswick, N.J.: Transaction Publishers.

Pechman, Joseph A., and P. Michael Timpane, eds. 1975. *Work incentives and income guarantees: The New Jersey Negative Income Tax Experiment.* Washington, D.C.: Brookings Institution.

Penick, James L., Jr., Carroll W. Pursell Jr., Morgan B. Sherwood, and Donald C. Swin. 1972. *The politics of American science: 1939 to the present.* Rev. ed. Cambridge: MIT Press.

Pfiffner, James P. 1988. *The strategic presidency: Hitting the ground running.* Chicago: Dorsey Press.

———. 1996. *The strategic presidency: Hitting the ground running.* 2d rev. ed. Lawrence: University Press of Kansas.

Porter, Roger B. 1980. *Presidential decision making: The Economic Policy Board.* Cambridge: Harvard University Press.

Prewitt, Kenneth. 1980. A defense of NSF. *Society* 17 (September/October): 15–16.

RAND Corporation. 1963. *The RAND Corporation: The first fifteen years.* Santa Monica, Calif.: RAND Corporation.

Ravitch, Diane. 1983. *The troubled crusade: American education, 1945–1980.* New York: Basic Books.

Reagan, Michael D. 1969. *Science and the federal patron.* New York: Oxford University Press.

Rhine, W. Ray, ed. 1981. *Making schools more effective: New directions from follow through.* New York: Academic Press.

Ricci, David M. 1984. *The tragedy of political science: Politics, scholarship, and democracy.* New Haven: Yale University Press.

Riecken, Henry W. 1986. Underdogging: The early career of the social sciences in the NSF. In *Nationalization of the social sciences,* ed. Samuel Z. Klausner and Victor M. Lidz. Philadelphia: University of Pennsylvania Press.

Rivlin, Alice M., and P. Michael Timpane, eds. 1975. *Planned variation in education: Should we give up or try harder?* Washington, D.C.: Brookings Institution.

Robins, Philip K., Robert G. Spiegelman, Samuel Weiner, and Joseph G. Bell, eds. 1980. *A guaranteed annual income: Evidence from a social experience.* New York: Academic Press.

Rogers, James. 1989. Social science disciplines and policy research: Politics, scholarship and democracy. *Policy Studies Review* 9 (autumn): 13–29.

Rorabaugh, W. J. 1969. *Berkeley at war: The 1960s.* New York: Oxford University Press.

Rosen, Elliot A. 1977. *Hoover, Roosevelt and the Brains Trust: From Depression to New Deal.* New York: Columbia University Press.

Ross, Dorothy. 1991. *The origins of American social science.* Cambridge: Cambridge University Press.

Sander, Alfred Dick. 1989. *A staff for the president: The executive office, 1921–52.* New York: Greenwood Press.

Schlesinger, Arthur M., Jr. 1965. *A thousand days: John F. Kennedy in the White House.* New York: Fawcett.

Sealander, Judith. 1997. *Private wealth and public life: Foundation philanthropy and the reshaping of American social policy from the Progressive Era to the New Deal.* Baltimore: Johns Hopkins University Press.

Shoup, Lawrence H. 1980. *The Carter presidency and beyond: Power and politics in the 1980s.* Palo Alto, Calif.: Ramparts Press.

Sievers, Rodney M. 1983. *The last Puritan: Adlai Stevenson in American politics.* Port Washington, N.Y.: Associated Faculty Press.

Silver, Harold, and Pamela Silver. 1991. *An educational war on poverty: American and British policy-making, 1960–1980.* Cambridge: Cambridge University Press.

Smith, Bradley F. 1983. *The shadow warriors: OSS and the origins of CIA.* London: Andre Deutsch.

Smith, Bruce L. R. 1966. *The RAND Corporation: Case study of a nonprofit advisory corporation.* Cambridge: Harvard University Press.

———. 1990. *American science policy since World War II.* Washington, D.C.: Brookings Institution.

Smith, James Allen. 1991a. *Brookings at seventy-five.* Washington, D.C.: Brookings Institution.

———. 1991b. *The idea brokers: Think tanks and the rise of the new policy elite.* New York: Free Press.

Smith, Marshall S., and Joan S. Bissell. 1970. Report analysis: The impact of Head Start: A reply to the report analysis. *Harvard Educational Review* 40:51–104.

Smith, R. Harris. 1973. *OSS: The secret history of America's first Central Intelligence Agency.* New York: Delta.

Social science: The public disenchant. 1976. *American Scholar* (summer): 335–59.

Somers, Herman M. 1950. *Presidential agency.* Cambridge: Harvard University Press.

Spicer, Edward H. 1946. The use of social scientists by the War Relocation Authority. *Applied Anthropology* 5 (spring): 16–36.

Spingarn, Natalie Davis. 1976. *Heartbeat: The politics of health research.* Washington, D.C.: Robert B. Luce.

Sproull, Lee, Stephen Weiner, and David Wolf. 1978. *Organizing an anarchy: Belief, bureaucracy, and politics in the National Institute of Education.* Chicago: University of Chicago Press.

Stefancic, Jean, and Richard Delgado. 1996. *No mercy: How conservative think tanks and foundations changed America's social agenda.* Philadelphia: Temple University Press.

Stein, Herbert. 1984. *Presidential economics: The making of policy from Roosevelt to Reagan and beyond.* New York: Simon and Schuster.

Stouffer, Samuel A., Arthur A. Lumsdaine, Robin M. Williams Jr., M. Brewster Smith, Irving L. Janis, Shirley A. Star, and Leonard S. Cottrell Jr. 1949. *The American Soldier.* 4 vols. Princeton: Princeton University Press.

Strickland, Stephen P. 1972. *Politics, science, and dread disease: A short history of United States medical research policy.* Cambridge: Harvard University Press.

Sutton, Francis X. 1987. The Ford Foundation: The early years. *Daedalus* 116 (winter): 41–91.

Trenn, Thaddeus J. 1983. *America's golden bough: The science advisory intertwist.* Cambridge, Mass.: Oelgeschlager, Gunn and Hain.

U.S. Bureau of the Census. 1975. *Historical statistics of the United States, colonial times to 1970.* Bicentennial Edition, Parts 1 and 2. Washington, D.C.: U.S. Government Printing Office.

———. 1996. *Statistical abstract of the United States: 1996.* 116th ed. Washington, D.C.: U.S. Government Printing Office.

U.S. Congress, Senate, Subcommittee on Government Research. 1966. *Hearings on the*

National Foundation for the Social Sciences. 90th Cong., 1st Sess. Washington, D.C.: U.S. Government Printing Office.

U.S. Office of Education. 1958. *Annual report, 1957.* Washington, D.C.: U.S. Government Printing Office.

———. 1960. *Annual report, 1959.* Washington, D.C.: U.S. Government Printing Office.

———. 1965. *Annual report, 1964.* Washington, D.C.: U.S. Government Printing Office.

Vinovskis, Maris A. 1988. *An "epidemic" of adolescent pregnancy? Some historical and policy considerations.* New York: Oxford University Press.

———. 1989. The use and misuse of social science analysis in federal adolescent pregnancy policy. In *Distinguished lectures in the social sciences.* DeKalb: Northern Illinois University.

———. 1993. Early childhood education: Then and now. *Daedalus* 122 (winter): 151–75.

———. 1995. Changing views of the federal role in educational statistics and research. Office of Educational Research and Improvement (OERI), September. Draft.

———. 1996. The changing role of the federal government in educational research and statistics. *History of Education Quarterly* 36 (summer): 111–28.

———. 1997. The development and effectiveness of compensatory education programs: A brief historical analysis of Title I and Head Start. In *Giving better, giving smarter: Working papers of the National Commission on Philanthropy and Civic Renewal,* ed. John W. Barry and Bruno V. Mano, 169–92. Washington, D.C.: National Commission on Philanthropy and Civic Renewal.

———. 1999a. Missing in practice? Systematic development and rigorous program evaluation at the U.S. Department of Education. Paper prepared for Conference on Evaluation of Educational Policies, American Academy of Arts and Sciences. Cambridge, Mass. May 13–14.

———. 1999b. *History and educational policymaking.* New Haven: Yale University Press.

Walcott, Charles E., and Karen M. Hult. 1995. *Governing the White House from Hoover through LBJ.* Lawrence: University of Kansas Press.

Warren, Donald R. 1974. *To enforce education: A history of the founding years of the United States Office of Education.* Detroit: Wayne State University Press.

Warshaw, Shirley Anne. 1995. White House control of domestic policy making: The Reagan years. *Public Administration Review* 55 (May/June): 24–53.

Westinghouse Learning Corporation. 1969. The impact of Head Start: An evaluation of the effects of Head Start on children's cognitive and affective development. Report presented to the Office of Economic Opportunity, contract B89–4536. Washington, D.C.: Clearinghouse for Federal Scientific and Technical Information.

White, Theodore H. 1961. *The making of the president: 1960.* New York: Atheneum.

Willcox, Walter F. 1914. The development of the American Census Office since 1890. *Political Science Quarterly* 29 (March): 438–59.

Williams, Walter. 1990. *Mismanaging America: The rise of the anti-analytic presidency.* Lawrence: University Press of Kansas.

Winks, Robin W. 1996. *Cloak and gown: Scholars in the secret war, 1939–1961*. 2d ed. New Haven: Yale University Press.

Wood, Robert C. 1993. *Whatever possessed the president? Academic experts and presidential policy, 1960–1988*. Amherst: University of Massachusetts Press.

Zigler, Edward, and Susan Muenchow. 1992. *Head Start: The inside story of America's most successful educational experiment*. New York: Basic Books.

Zigler, Edward, and Jeanette Valentine, eds. 1979. *Project Head Start: A legacy of the War on Poverty*. New York: Free Press.

CHAPTER 4

Designing Head Start: Roles Played by Developmental Psychologists

Sheldon H. White and Deborah A. Phillips

Head Start was launched in 1965 as part of the War on Poverty, providing a highly visible symbol of the federal government's concern about disadvantaged children. Because its emergence coincided with a period when behavioral and social scientists were perceived to have much to say about the best ways of ameliorating poverty in America (see Featherman and Vinovskis, chap. 3, this vol.), they became inextricably linked to this fledgling program. Since then, the program and the scientific community that has grown alongside it have been profoundly shaped by what has arguably been one of the most enduring collaborations between public policy and the behavioral and social sciences to emerge from the Great Society era.

What began as an arm's-length friendship between child developmentalists and Washington bureaucrats, built on a shared recognition of the importance of the endeavor and the need to document its efficacy, grew into a virtual industry of Head Start research. This research has weathered the vicissitudes of shifting views of social science as a guide for policy and of policy as an effective mechanism for changing lives. Head Start has served as both social intervention and laboratory, rich with lessons about the evolving relationship between researchers and policymakers, a relationship fraught with ambivalence on both sides and negotiated in an ever-changing political context. Yet, in this case, it is a relationship that has been mutually sought and sustained for over three decades. The themes of this story echo those of this volume as a whole: the uneasy place of science in an arena that relies on bargaining, obfuscation, and compromise; the challenges posed to the credibility of science by its association with "intractable" and politicized problems; and the growing fragmentation of both political decision making and the research enterprise that informs it.

Head Start lives today, thirty years after its founding, in a somewhat contentious political climate. It has grown. It is being imitated by state-level early childhood programs. The program is popular, and the majority of Americans support it. Not everyone is fully persuaded that the program "works"; nor does everyone agree on the criteria by which "working" is to be judged. In fact, Head Start has been afflicted from the start by competing claims about what it was designed to accomplish. The community action vision that emphasizes community empowerment and civil rights stands alongside the child development vision that emphasizes social competence, school readiness, and quality services to facilitate these outcomes (Greenberg 1990a; Zigler and Muenchow 1992; Zigler 1999). The organizational theorist Donald Schon has argued that the need to contend with dilemmas and trade-offs is an inescapable fact of life for people in organizations. There remains an uneasiness, a tentativeness, about Head Start that must be given serious thought when considering what the program represents in policy terms.

Developmental psychologists, who have been involved with the program from the very beginning, do not ordinarily deal with matters of national policy, prominent individual exceptions notwithstanding. They typically study small samples of children, at times projecting their findings toward the mythical "average child" or "typical adolescent" or "twos," though these statistical universalizations often come to grief when cross-regional, or cross–social class, or cross-school comparisons are made. Yet the research activities of developmental psychologists have led them again and again, from the turn of this century on forward, to explore the ways in which social practices, programs, and policies might reasonably be harmonized with norms or ideals of human development.

What Is Head Start?

Head Start is a heterogeneous program with a unity-in-diversity that is not so easy to spell out in words. It is composed of approximately 2,000 programs across the country and a total budget in FY1999 of $4.7 billion. Enrollment reaches about 800,000 poor children per year—that is, in terms of the standards of FY1996, children living in a four-person family that has an income less than $16,036. A total of almost 17 million children have been served by the program since it began in 1965. The conventional stereotype pictures Head Start's clientele as urban African-American children, but presently 36 percent of Head Start's children are African American, 31 percent Caucasian, 26 percent Hispanic, 4 percent Native American, and 3 percent Asian American. Approximately 13 percent of the children enrolled in Head Start have disabilities. It is estimated that the program serves 38 percent of the children in this country who are eligible for it in terms of the poverty standards.

In 1994, the Head Start reauthorization set aside a small share of funds (growing to 10 percent) for services to families with infants and toddlers. This was not the first time that Head Start has reached down to this younger age group. For example, in 1967, the Parent and Child Centers were launched as demonstration programs to serve children from birth to three and their families. In contrast to earlier initiatives, however, the 1990s form of Early Head Start is viewed as a core element to be evaluated and sustained alongside the preschool program. There are now over 300 Early Head Start programs. Estimates indicate that by the year 2000 Early Head Start will serve 45,000 infants and toddlers at a cost of $420 million.

Although Head Start is commonly viewed as a set of preschools for the poor, it was designed as a comprehensive program offering combinations of early education, health screening and immunizations, direct services to parents, referrals to social services, and the stimulation of community action on behalf of the poor. Head Start does not mandate a specific mix of services nor have a standard curriculum, but it is decidedly not the case that anything goes. Since the 1970s, all programs have been monitored on their compliance with national performance standards dictating certain staffing patterns, nutrition and health services, and requirements for parent involvement. Revised performance standards, explicitly cast as criteria for program accountability, became effective in 1998. They cover all children from birth through age five and provide detailed guidance with respect to the child development, child health, and family and community elements of the program, as well as regarding overall program design, staffing, management, and safety. Beyond this, Head Start centers are free to vary their services depending on the needs of the population of children they serve. This provision for local variation seems essential because Head Start centers serve differing cultural mixes of children in various parts of the country. Over half of Head Start centers are bicultural; a few centers serve children coming from as many as ten different cultural backgrounds.

The Establishment of Head Start

Head Start came into existence with explosive speed in the 1960s. In a few short months well over 1,000 centers opened, offering summer programs to disadvantaged children across the United States. Four cross-cutting historical accounts picture the creation of Head Start from differing perspectives. Zigler and Valentine's (1979) *Project Head Start* is an edited volume examining the history of the program thirteen years after its establishment. Administrators and planners—people such as Joseph Califano, Mrs. Lyndon B. Johnson, Sargent Shriver, Urie Bronfenbrenner, Jule Sugarman, Julius B. Richmond, Edward Davens, and others—discuss what happened and what they thought they were doing when planning and initiating Head Start. Other sections of the volume reflect on the preschool component of Head Start, other services (health, mental health, social services, parent involvement, career development), changes in Head Start across time, and evaluations of the program. A subsequent book by Zigler and Muenchow (1992) traces Head Start's history through the twenty-seven years of Zigler's work with it, from his membership on the Planning Committee through his service as the first director of the Office of Child Development and subsequent consultantships. These volumes offer a history of Head Start as seen from a top-down perspective, with a particular focus on federal planning and management activities.

Publications by Polly Greenberg (1990a,b) enrich and complicate our historical understanding. Greenberg is an early educator who was serving on the staff of Sargent Shriver, the director of the Office of Economic Opportunity under whose auspices Head Start was administered, when the idea of Head Start first came to life. She argues that Head Start was a second-stroke initiative of the War on Poverty developed by Sargent Shriver's staff to support the first-stroke War on Poverty programs—VISTA, Job Corps, the Community Action Program—which they knew were politically difficult.

> Sargent Shriver was worried about who the recipients of the War on Poverty would be: teenage dropouts, many from minority populations, the type Job Corps was to serve, are not popular in our society. To be politically viable, the War on Poverty would have to serve people perceived as "the deserving poor." Many people . . . made suggestions about what to do "next summer." Older people and handicapped people . . . were mentioned, and young children. Everyone present grabbed the idea! Young children! Surely they are the *victims* of poverty, not the perpetrators of it. (Greenberg 1990b, 43)[1]

Greenberg provides an excellent picture of a rapid, informal, tumultuous series of political planning discussions carried out by Sargent Shriver "in his characteristic cyclonic manner," his staff, and assorted friends and experts reached by telephone or in person. The planning process assembled a multidisciplinary group of experts who were loosely guided by some pragmatic ideas Shriver and his staff wanted to emphasize. These included a "health first" orientation, the idea that attending to health was the surest thing government could offer a disadvantaged child. The "health first" priority was initially promoted by the appointment of Dr. Robert E. Cooke, Chief of Pediatrics of the Johns Hopkins Hospital, as Chairman of the Head Start Planning Committee, and reinforced with the appointment of Dr. Julius B. Richmond, Dean of the Upstate Medical Center at Syracuse, to serve as Head Start's first director. The concept of "maximum feasible participation," the idea that families served by the program should be closely involved in its operations, was also prominent from the beginning. The experts who composed the planning committee lent substance to Shriver's loose conceptions of the program along the lines of their backgrounds. As noted by Zigler, "the mental health people wanted mental health, the early childhood educators wanted early education, and the pediatricians wanted physical health and nutrition" (personal communication, March 1999). Maximum feasible participation evolved into a two-pronged approach to parent involvement—part parent governance and part parent education.

When applications for Head Start centers were sought, Greenberg was one of those sent out from Washington to help poor communities prepare proper applications. She became interested in the Child Development Group of Mississippi (CDGM) and eventually left Washington to help the group put together its program. Greenberg's (1990a) book describes the establishment of a group of Head Start centers in the state of Mississippi in the 1960s. Her story offers a useful contrast to high-level accounts of federal committees negotiating coolly and rationally about commodities such as health, early education, cognitive development, community action, parent involvement, and the like. "Hot knowledge" radiates out of Greenberg's vibrant, beautifully written book. She provides a clear picture of ordinary people moved by hope, despair, fear, compassion, defiance, and idealism to assemble and defend Head Start programs in political surroundings full of opposition and menace.[2]

Since domestic policies grow out of local politics and eventually must return to be interpreted and used by actors at the local level, viewing Head Start from the top-down perspective of Zigler and Valentine (1979) and the bottom-up perspective of Greenberg (1990a) is extraordinarily useful. Since policy formation at the federal level takes place in a sea of multiple voices and interests negotiating their way toward a rough harmony of purposes, it is useful to have Greenberg's (1990b) backroom account of the creation of Head Start combined with the accounts of the formal planning and management processes described in Zigler's books (Zigler and Valentine 1979; Zigler and Muenchow 1992).

The long-term alliance between developmental psychology and social policy-making for children (White 1996) was called into play in the formation of Head Start. It is not a purpose of this account to argue that developmental psychology and developmental psychologists have had a large influence on the creation and subsequent development of Head Start, nor to argue that the influences they have had were wholly positive. Developmental psychologists have played a relatively small part in the creation and maintenance of the reality of Head Start. At times they have helped, and at times they have hindered or made mischief for the program. On balance:

1. Developmental psychologists have assisted in the articulation of Head Start policy, building bridges between policies-in-practice and declared policies.
2. They have played this bridging role through (a) *representation,* (b) *demonstration,* (c) *idealization,* and (d) *evaluation.*

3. Developmental psychologists have also assisted in the crystallization of policy positions and proposals propounded in opposition to Head Start.
4. The involvement of developmental psychologists with Head Start over the past thirty years has had a reciprocal effect. Developmental psychology has changed, and is still changing, because of the work of some of its members with Head Start.

Policies and Practices in Head Start

Suppose we define *policy* as an organized, directed course of action agreed to by members of a political group through some legitimate political process. The group purpose may or may not be in accord with the articulated wishes or purposes of any one member of the group, but members of the political group negotiate and "go along with" the course of action for a variety of reasons. Any sustained and ongoing federal program might then be said to represent, ipse dixit, the implementation of a national policy. However, the exact purposes and goals of a policy-in-practice such as Head Start are not easily articulated. Proponents and friends of the program speak for it but, to the present day, their multiple and often diffuse goal statements have militated against a coherent public understanding of the program. In the name of comprehensiveness, various objectives have been attached to Head Start over time—school readiness, empowerment of the underclass, multiculturalism, parent literacy. There is no one reason for Head Start, of course. Researchers, bringing toward Head Start their concepts and methods, bring also their habits of inquiry . . . there is, or ought to be, a hypothesis behind Head Start. But historical accounts, such as those noted above, make it clear that those who created and supported Head Start did so on the basis of a number of beliefs, purposes, and goals.[3] Is it possible to articulate the goals of that course of action upon which all converged?

In 1965 the Planning Committee for Head Start, chaired by Robert Cooke, recommended seven goals for Head Start:

1. Improving the child's health and physical abilities.
2. Helping the emotional and social development of the child by encouraging self-confidence, spontaneity, curiosity, and self-discipline.
3. Improving the child's mental processes and skills, with particular attention to conceptual and verbal skills.
4. Establishing patterns and expectations of success for the child that will create a climate of confidence for future learning efforts.
5. Increasing the child's capacity to relate positively to family members and others, while at the same time strengthening the family's ability to relate positively to the child and his problems.

6. Developing in the child and his family a responsible attitude toward society, and encouraging society to work with the poor in solving their problems.

7. Increasing the sense of dignity and self-worth within the child and his family.[4]

These recommendations were, in one language, a declaration of the purposes to be pursued by the Head Start program. At a more operational level, the Planning Committee called for a comprehensive intervention into the lives of disadvantaged children, and the components necessary for comprehensiveness were specified by Julius B. Richmond, first Director of Head Start, as (1) a health component, (2) a social-service component, (3) an early childhood education component, (4) parent involvement, (5) volunteer effort, (6) community participation in the government of the program, and (7) career ladders and in-service training (Zigler and Valentine 1979, 125–26).

Therefore one could say that Head Start's policy, at a human level, was to further those changes in the development of poor children and in their families specified in Cooke's memo. Head Start's policy, at an operational level, was to offer those comprehensive services to poor children and their families spelled out by Richmond. Policies articulated to this degree were by no means sufficient. Jule M. Sugarman served as executive secretary of the Head Start Planning Committee, as associate director of Head Start in its early years, and as an interim director when Head Start was moved from the Office of Economic Opportunity to the Department of Health and Human Services under President Nixon. In his recollections, he remarks:

> The most difficult tasks the administrators of Head Start faced were the fleshing out of the principles recommended by the Planning Committee. It was very clear that there should be educational, health, nutrition, social-service, and parent-participation activities. It was very clear that the program should be comprehensive. . . . But the Planning Committee had only established the policy. It was up to the administrators to set rules and guidelines. . . . [We] found that "experts" were not very deep in their knowledge. No one could tell us, based on real evidence, what the proper child-staff ratios or length of program should be. Despite their lack of depth, experts were vigorously committed to their point of view and often rejected other views in irrational and unproductive ways. Many of the decisions eventually had to be made by administrators because the professionals could not reach decisions among themselves. (Zigler and Valentine 1979, 118–19)

The Head Start planning process arrived at the "big" decisions, and the essential "little" decisions were made partly by administrators and partly by

Head Start center directors and parents doing what came naturally. By design, discretion was left to the local level. It was not until the mid-1970s that performance standards were issued to provide common guidance to all Head Start programs. Sugarman points out:

> We found that very little of what was written for Head Start participants was read or fully understood by those who received the materials. Finally, we learned that what Washington and the "experts" said didn't necessarily make that much difference. There are instinctive understandings and skills in working with children that are widely distributed in America. Given the resources, people can help children in effective ways, and they will invest a lot of themselves in doing so. They may even turn out to "know" through experience and intuition a lot more than the experts. (Zigler and Valentine 1979, 119)

It is difficult to understand the evolution of Head Start without appreciating the tension that has historically existed between the top-down, expert-guided conceptions of Head Start and the bottom-up, antielitist spirit that is so palpable in this quote. It manifested itself in the Office of Economic Opportunity where the language of empowerment and community mobilization prevailed in stark contrast to the voices of the developmentalists and pediatricians who conceived of Head Start as a child development program. A particularly telling incident is recounted by Zigler in his account of the early years of Head Start. When he was director of the Office of Child Development,

> a number of local Community Action Program leaders came to present me with some "non-negotiable demands." Finally, one man . . . said, "Dr. Zigler, you don't understand. We are interested in systemic change. We are willing to give up a whole generation of our children in order to get it." I said that I was not, and that was not my mission in OCD. His children had a right to be all they could be, I said, and that was what Head Start was about. (Zigler and Muenchow 1992, 110–11)

The tension remains today in the form of debates between those who are seeking to increase the professional qualifications of Head Start staff and those who resist this as a deterrent to the employment of local community parents.

Roles Played by Developmental Psychologists

Representation

Three developmental psychologists, Edward Zigler, Mamie Clark, and Urie Bronfenbrenner, were active participants in the planning process that led to

Head Start. Other psychologists such as Jerome Kagan, Jerome Bruner, Benjamin Bloom, and B. F. Skinner were called upon by Sargent Shriver or his staff from time to time about possibilities for improving the lives of poor children. What functions did the psychologists serve? In part, they represented children in the deliberations leading to Head Start, just as social scientists more generally represented the poor in deliberations about the Great Society programs (Featherman and Vinovskis, this vol.). The planning process was conducted by "distal bureaucrats" (Siegel and White 1982; White 1978) who lived lives distantly removed from those of poor children whom programs such as Head Start hoped to affect. Meanwhile, developmental psychologists, among other behavioral and social scientists, translated the enormously complicated worlds of children living in poverty into the symbols and ideas that mobilized the nation's leaders to want to help them and to believe that they could be helped.

A long-standing function of the social sciences—indeed, a substantial impetus for their creation—has been to describe the poor in such a way as to build public awareness and understanding of their circumstances and needs. People have crowded into cities in modern times, distributing themselves into rich or poor districts or various ethnic ghettos. Great distances have opened up between the lives of the rich and the poor. In mid-nineteenth-century England, journalist Henry Mayhew wrote about the street people of London, and novelist Charles Dickens told stories about the lives of poor children. Many journalists and writers like them used symbols to make the well-to-do conscious of the poor around them (Cunningham 1991; Himmelfarb 1991). Near the turn of this century, symbolic representations took a more systematic and scientific form. Settlement houses such as Toynbee Hall in London and Hull House in Chicago were centers for major studies of the conditions of the poor. The research at Hull House (Residents of Hull-House 1895) was clearly ancestral, on the one side, to a brilliant first generation of social science research at the University of Chicago and, on the other, to the data-gathering of the Children's Bureau that, in Julia Lathrop's hands, was a powerful stimulant to political action for young children.

The active work of developmental psychologists and other social scientists in describing and characterizing the lives and needs of the poor was undoubtedly useful in the deliberations that led to Head Start in the 1960s. Distance and lack of understanding existed then, as always, between the well-to-do and the poor.[5] Academics do not lead lives that easily familiarize them with the lives of the poor. Instead, they do studies comparing people with different backgrounds, experiences, levels of language, degrees of education, or SES membership. The studies' representations of poor children and families were of mixed value. Well-meaning but careless stereotypes abounded. Zigler and Valentine (1979) describe the picture of the poor offered by such studies in these terms:

Unfortunately, social-science professionals reinforced these popular mis-conceptions by creating a stereotype of the American poor family on the basis of very meager research. According to this stereotype, the poor child was deprived not only of the health and nutritional care that the family could not afford, but of proper maternal care and environmental stimula-tion as well. Poor mothers (fathers were assumed to be absent) were char-acterized as immature, harsh disciplinarians, unable to love because of their own dependency. The environment was either understimulating (insufficient toys, insufficient interaction and attention) or overstimulat-ing (noise, fighting), or both. Verbal activity in the poor household was supposed to consist of body language, monosyllables, shouts, and grunts. (8–9)

In the early 1970s, a systematic review of 182 references dealing with the special psychological characteristics of disadvantaged children and their families found the following attributions:

Imaginative capacity (lack); Need for achievement (low); Sense of exter-nal vs. internal control (external); Anxiety about school (high); Voca-tional and educational aspirations (low); Self-esteem and self-concept (low); Attention span (short); Aggression (high); Visual and auditory per-ception (less acute); Range of time perspective (short); Fatalistic attitude (present); Sense of power—effectance (low); Ability to delay gratification (low); Adequacy of verbal reinforcement only (low); Use of language (restricted); Ability to use language as a tool of communication (low); Ability to speak decontextually (low); IQ score (low); Achievement scores (low); Conceptual thought ability (low); Cognitive style (non-analytic). (White et al. 1973, 1:67–69, table 2.3)

The use of psychological research procedures to characterize groups of indi-viduals eventually generates a scientific pointillism, the person pictured as a swarm of particulate dependent variables.

At present, other and more complex characterizations of the circum-stances and problems of disadvantaged children are coming into use as a grounding for idealizations and evaluations of Head Start. Fueled by growing sophistication within the research community about the vast variability that characterizes poor children, the older sweeping characterizations have given way to models that emphasize the balance of risk factors and resilience among children and families living in poverty. Extensive research has now identified an array of child characteristics, family factors, school/peer influences, and social context effects that converge to predict which children will emerge healthy and well-adjusted, and which will develop problems (Masten, Best, and Garmezy 1990; Masten and Coatesworth 1998; Sameroff 1995; Sroufe 1997).

Demonstration

The second role played by developmental psychologists was as participants in experimental and demonstration studies exploring the possibilities of pro-grammatic interventions in the lives of poor children and their families. Some important projects established in advance of Head Start included the experi-mental preschool program of Gray and Klaus (1965) in Nashville, Tennessee; the early childhood enrichment program of Cynthia and Martin Deutsch (1968) in New York; the Perry Preschool Project established by Weikart (Weikart et al. 1971) in Ypsilanti, Michigan; and the preschool intervention program created by Bereiter and Engelmann in Illinois (1967).[6]

These were among the best known of several dozen experiments in early education established around the country. There is, again, something classic about the role of the developmental psychologist in creating and exploring such model programs. After creating his famous Laboratory School at the Uni-versity of Chicago, John Dewey explored and wrote about a number of the model schools of his day with his daughter, Jane. He would ultimately argue that it is the eternal role of the philosopher (read "social scientist") to assist in the translation of the values and goals of older institutions into the design of the institutions of the future (White 1991b). Campbell (1988) has put forth a similar vision of the work of the social scientist in his description of an "exper-imenting society."

The model preschool programs demonstrated concrete possibilities to those who considered early childhood programs for deprived children. One did not have to imagine or speculate about what a Head Start center ought to look like. Washington poverty warriors often visited Susan Gray's Nashville program and the Deutsches' program in New York City in the early years of the War on Poverty. Before Julius Richmond took the directorship of Head Start, he had collaborated with Bettye Caldwell in the establishment of an education-ally oriented day-care center for infants and toddlers (Caldwell and Richmond 1964), and this experience undoubtedly colored his view of what might be pos-sible in Head Start Centers. Foundation-supported studies of model programs mobilized support for Head Start, suggested guidelines for the program, and provided important information in the history of evaluations of Head Start. Again, however, the studies had special biases and emphases because of the developmental psychologists' concentration on cognitive development at that point in history.

Developmental psychology, it should be noted, was in the process of being born again in the 1960s (White 1991a). Part of that rebirth was undoubtedly stimulated by the events and public concerns leading up to the implementation of the War on Poverty. Though developmental psychologists generally see themselves as the descendants of a continuous history of child study going back to the work of G. Stanley Hall in the 1890s (Siegel and White 1982; White

1990), there is reasonable evidence for a rising-and-falling pattern in their history. A first wave of activity was the Child Study questionnaire studies that peaked between 1894 and 1904, a second wave of work was the Child Development movement organized in interdisciplinary centers and institutes in the 1920s and early 1930s, and a third began with the rise of developmental psychology in the early 1960s.[7]

The new developmental psychology that emerged in the 1960s was strongly influenced by the "cognitive revolution" taking place in mainstream American psychology and, more locally and specifically, by the theory and research program of Jean Piaget (White 1991a). With the present hesitancies about Piaget's psychology, it is well to recall the genuine excitement with which his work was greeted in the 1960s. The strength of Piaget's program was in its philosophical and methodological sophistication. His vision of a "genetic epistemology" to be pursued through studies of children's cognitive development was a continuation of a powerful evolutionary vision of the development of mind first put forward by the sadly underestimated American James Mark Baldwin at the turn of this century. Piaget's *clinical method*, which he devised for research on children's thinking, was far more sophisticated and subtle methodologically than either the tests-and-measurement approach that had dominated studies of children in the 1930s and 1940s or the experimental child psychology that had a brief ascendancy in the United States in the 1950s and early 1960s.

In the 1960s, American developmental psychologists directed their attention upon studies of intellectual development, and many took *cognitive development* as virtually synonymous with *child development.* They introduced their philosophical framework into a good number of the model programs. Such programs did not have a large influence on Head Start at the beginning, in part because Head Start's administration wanted flexible, customized programming:

> Jule Sugarman was the leading proponent of the conviction that there are people in every community who know how to provide wholesome, helpful happy childhood experiences for children. "We wanted a flexible program customized in every community." Jule opposed the idea of model program clones being mechanically planted in widely diverse settings. He was backed by everyone on the CAP staff. (Greenberg 1990b, 45)

Surveys of the goals of Head Start preschool directors in the early years of the program have regularly shown that the majority of them did not favor cognitive-developmental goals but rather espoused goals of social and self-development for their children. In fact, Greenberg recently argued that the model programs have been largely irrelevant to the practices of Head Start preschools:

Although during the next 25 years an enormous amount of energy and talent was invested in exemplary and model programs of many "planned variations," the basic educational program Head Start recommends to its grantees is still the sensible, intellectually stimulating, nonacademic, play and projects nursery/kindergarten program conventional in the 1940s, '50s, and early '60s, currently called "developmentally appropriate." (1990b, 44)

Greenberg's skepticism must be taken seriously; she has been for some years the editor of *Young Children*, the leading practitioner journal of early childhood education in the United States. However, contemporary evidence suggests that the ideas and methods of at least some of the models have diffused into working Head Start programs. For example, a sizable share of Head Start programs have adopted the High/Scope curriculum that was derived from the Perry Preschool Project.

The question of the effects of the model and demonstration programs on Head Start deserves some serious examination. If, in fact, they have had relatively little influence on actual Head Start preschool programs, much energy and many human resources invested in the creation and maintenance of such programs were wasted. Furthermore, the model programs are peculiarly strategic for current political deliberations about the value and meaning of Head Start. The best data about the long-term effects of early intervention programs stem from studies of graduates of such programs. Most assume that the findings obtained with such programs provide meaningful yardsticks, at least to a degree, by which to judge the achievements of Head Start programs. While these comparisons have bolstered Head Start's popularity, they have also backfired as conservatives exposed the distinctions between model and national programs (Hood 1992). In a careful analysis of these distinctions, Zigler and Styfco (1994) suggest that generalizations from a short-lived model program that served fifty-eight children in Ypsilanti, Michigan, to an enduring comprehensive program that has served millions of children are dubious at best. However, High/Scope has just provided a first report of long-term benefits for actual Head Start children (Oden, Schweinhart, and Weikart 1999).

Idealization

The third role played by developmental psychologists was a conceptual one, assisting in projecting the larger meaning of the Head Start program—the "theory of intervention" that might be said to guide it and justify it. This is not quite the question of articulating a Head Start policy, discussed earlier, though it lies close to it. Polly Greenberg (1990b) remarks that, even though Head Start may have been created to enhance the political acceptability of the War on Poverty, a portion of the staff nevertheless rejoiced:

> Be that as it may, Head Start (as it later came to be called) was an obvious, common sense Right Thing to Do. A number of us went downtown and celebrated till dawn. (43)

Why was Head Start a "Right Thing to Do?" What was its purpose? What good could such a program effect? The planners and administrators held wide-ranging views about the possibilities. Such a program might benefit children's health. It might empower parents by involving them. It might give jobs to poor parents and, with such jobs, train them in parenthood and possibly encourage them to seek further education. It might serve as a catalyst for community action. It might coordinate services to disadvantaged children and their families. It might help schools accommodate to the needs of disadvantaged children. The planners held both positive views of the program's potential results as well as more political and indirect views.[8]

Remarkably, these early accounts of Head Start's origination reveal the limited extent to which possible direct changes in children's development played a part in the discussions of the backroom planners or the grassroots people of Mississippi who looked forward to the reality of Head Start. The lack of discussion regarding children's development contrasts sharply with the views of the formally appointed members of the Planning Committee. As noted by Zigler, "The community action people in OEO [Office of Economic Opportunity] wanted to man the barricades and change the system; we wanted to opportunize the development of children" (personal communication, March 1999).

Yet shortly after Head Start began, public discussions about the program began to focus more and more upon a purely technical conception of the program as an experiment in modifying the IQ of disadvantaged children in its care. Two books—Hunt's (1961) *Intelligence and Experience* and Bloom's (1964) *Stability and Change in Human Characteristics*—were largely responsible for catalyzing the discussion. The books were repeatedly discussed in the media as scientific justifications for Head Start—to such an extent that many believed then, and some persist in believing now, that Head Start was fundamentally an experiment in IQ modification.

During the 1930s and 1940s, a heated controversy had arisen regarding studies that seemed to indicate that children's IQ scores could be raised by nursery-school experiences. The controversy galvanized and polarized the researchers of that time. Iowa took the environmentalist position, facing off against Minnesota and Berkeley, which took the hereditarian position. The argument was prolonged, noisy, and, at times, bitter.[9] After two decades of controversy, the majority conclusion—though by no means unanimous—was that children's IQ scores arc largely determined by heredity and not significantly changed by experience (cf. Jones 1954). Hunt wrote his book to challenge that conclusion. He reviewed three bodies of research: the nursery schools and other environmental enrichment studies of the past, contemporary research on the effects of early experiences on animal behaviors, and the work of Jean Piaget (then little known in this country) on the early organization of children's intelligence. The weight of all this research, Hunt thought, justified the conclusion that human intelligence can be easily and significantly modified by experience.

In his book, Bloom presents his correlational study of the stability of human characteristics. He analyzed the degree to which children's later IQ scores could be predicted from their earlier IQ scores, using the data of the California longitudinal studies. Bloom concluded that human IQ is extremely "plastic" in the early years, capable of being modified by experience until about five years of age, but "hardening" thereafter to become relatively resistant to environmental influence. The theories of both Hunt and Bloom seemed to indicate that Head Start could substantially elevate the IQ scores of disadvantaged children at a critical period in their development.

Hunt's and Bloom's conclusions were widely quoted and discussed by the media as authoritative scientific statements. Most research psychologists, we would estimate, would characterize the books as legitimate and interesting, but argumentative. Although people raised IQ modification as a scientific justification for Head Start at the very beginning, the major players in the creation of Head Start did not subscribe to the theory that many policymakers and the public were so eager to accept. Indeed, Zigler repeatedly debated Hunt in public platforms, arguing that IQ modification was not and should not be the goal of Head Start (see Zigler and Trickett 1978; Zigler and Freedman 1987).

Vinovskis has credited Sargent Shriver with emphasizing the power of Head Start to increase IQ when testifying before Congress (Vinovskis 1999a, 1999b; Dombkowski, Smith, and Vinovskis 1999). But in this testimony, Shriver gave equal time to the significance of parental involvement, community action, and the role of Head Start in the early detection of health problems and disabilities (1966, 186). In 1967, when testifying before the House Committee on Education and Labor, Shriver stated that Head Start "was not undertaken as an educational program exclusively; never was. The objective of Head Start was, first of all, to prepare the child, but in reaching the child to do something about the family and to do something about the cultural conditions in which the child grows up" (1394).

Dr. William Brazziel may have most accurately captured the sentiments of the early planners of Head Start in his testimony before the Committee on Education and Labor in 1969 on behalf of the National Urban League:

IQ gains are eye-catching and emotion-generating but the true test of preschool experience is the performance of the children in learning to read, write, and do numbers in school; their understanding and appreciation of school routines; and their achievement motivations for school work. This performance is measured by achievement tests, analyses of age-grade records, school persistence and attrition, and teacher opinion. IQ tests are not the correct instrument here. (1969, 2436)

Of the forty-eight individual testimonies before congressional committees between 1966 and 1969, three mentioned IQ modification as a positive goal of Head Start.[10] IQ modification apparently was grafted as an issue onto Head Start, illustrating the peculiar power of psychologists to form the concepts and propositions on which public discussions center. In this instance, psychologists, coming in from the side, so to speak, managed to make the question of IQ modification seem like the issue for Head Start when, in the minds of the players, it was not the central focus. Yet, Head Start administrators did not challenge the IQ-modification model of the program—possibly because, in a somewhat politically embattled situation, one does not pick a quarrel with friends.

These "friendly" analyses ultimately jeopardized Head Start by setting firmly into many people's minds what Zigler has called an "inoculation model" of the program's goals. In its crudest form, the "inoculation model" implies that one year of Head Start ought to produce in a child's development irreversible, long-standing change, which should be detectable years after the child has left Head Start. To this day, Head Start administrators struggle to deal with the demands imposed by this model.

If, in fact, the IQ-modification model was not the true basis for the establishment of Head Start, why did it seize such a prominent place in public conceptions of the program? One can only conjecture. The model was simple, and easy to grasp and remember. In contrast, the true purposes of the various planners who designed Head Start were multiple and heterogeneous. Years ago, Allport and Postman (1947) described a "leveling and sharpening" phenomenon in their classic study of the psychology of rumor. Complex issues are regularly resolved into simplifications and stereotypes as they pass from one person to another. Something like this phenomenon seems to happen repeatedly in media discussions of Head Start issues.

The IQ model re-aroused an old dispute about nursery school effects that was part of the collective memories of developmental psychologists and early educators. It was testable, far more so than the "softer" and more complex objectives set forth by Robert Cooke's Planning Committee. The IQ model fit together with the peculiar fact that early evaluators of Head Start programs, being woefully short of meaningful and credible research instruments to detect program effects, tended to use IQ tests to measure Head Start's achievements. Finally, the IQ model silently addressed an important, rarely spoken conservative objection to Head Start: that such a program was a liberal fantasy because most of the children it served were not sufficiently intelligent to become successful in school or life.

The role of developmental psychologists in helping to set forth philosophies or idealizations of programs such as Head Start goes back to the turn of this century. Margaret McMillan drew on the psychological writings of her time when designing her nursery school (White 1995). The ideas of G. Stanley Hall, John Dewey, and Edward L. Thorndike were important in the development of Conservative and Progressive forms of kindergartens at the turn of this century (White and Buka 1987). In recent years, the High/Scope preschool curriculum of David Weikart, one of the most successful and influential preschool educators of our time, is based on thoughtful and sophisticated translations of Piagetian developmental psychology into key experiences for preschool children (Hohmann, Banet, and Weikart 1979).

Evaluation

The fourth and most prominent role played by developmental psychologists, among a number of social scientists, was in the design, implementation, and interpretation of evaluation studies of Head Start. The War on Poverty occurred during a time of significant change in the federal management of social programs. In the past, professionals who managed services for children, youth, and families traditionally spoke to government about the needs and efficacies of their services. During the time of the War on Poverty, however, program planning and budgeting offices began to appear in the administrations of human service agencies with the expectation that data would be used in a much more systematic fashion to determine the needs of client populations and the efficacy of policies and programs established to serve them. Federal legislation regularly called for scientific program evaluations. So began a series of efforts to study the effects of Head Start. Such efforts provoked debates, discussions, and a learning process that continues today. This discussion focuses on the learning process and explores three periods of time during which evaluators approached Head Start in various ways.

The "Bang for the Buck" Period

At the very beginning of evaluation research on Head Start, it was assumed—without, apparently, much discussion or debate—that systematic scientific evaluations could and should be mounted to judge the value of the program as a whole. In the terminology of the time, a "summative" evaluation was expected to provide data about the overall effectiveness of the program, in contrast to a "formative" evaluation that provided information useful in shaping and guiding the program's activities. The focus of almost all of the evaluation studies directed at Head Start was on the presumptive impact of the program on children's development. Children who had experienced Head Start were compared with control children to determine whether the program had made a difference. In the first few years, from 1965 to 1968, small studies directed at the work of one or a few centers tended to show immediate, small benefits. Head Start children showed small but meaningful gains on IQ tests or other cognitive instruments.

A nationwide "National Impact" study of Head Start conducted by the Westinghouse Learning Corporation (1969) became a major political issue because it cast serious doubt on the efficacy of Head Start and, some say, also cast a shadow on the War on Poverty as a whole. The Westinghouse study, a cross-sectional study of various-aged children who had experienced Head Start, provided information about the dynamics of Head Start effects over time. The study seemed to show that summer Head Start programs had little or no effect on children. Although full-year Head Start programs benefited children's school achievement, such effects tended to fade out by the third grade. Instruments designed for the Westinghouse study to obtain indices of the social and emotional development of the children showed no positive benefits as a result of children's Head Start experience. Since the meaning of these instruments was not well understood, no clear interpretation could be attached to the results. In addition to collecting test data on the children, the Westinghouse study surveyed parental satisfaction with their Head Start programs and found a very high degree of parental approval.[11]

The negative effect of the National Impact study was augmented by the near-simultaneous (but almost certainly coincidental) publication of Jensen's (1969) article claiming that compensatory education programs cannot be expected to work because the scholastic difficulties of many disadvantaged children stem from hereditary and unchangeable IQ deficiencies. The combination of the Westinghouse study, the widely known IQ-modification rationale for Head Start, and the Jensen article produced a coherent story. Head Start was a psychological experiment that had failed.

The many difficulties and technical problems resulting from the timing and design of the Westinghouse study were thoroughly discussed in the aftermath of the study. But large numbers of other studies supported the overall conclusion of Westinghouse—that Head Start children attained short-term benefits that faded by third or fourth grade (cf. White et al. 1973, 2:108–99). Researchers debating the Westinghouse study unfortunately tended to focus on issues of methodology while avoiding questions about the conception and aims of the study. A few of those questions follow.

Should the direction of the evaluation study have been decided by researchers?
During the design of the Westinghouse study, the researchers who designed the
study were largely responsible for selecting the positive outcomes to assess.
From a purely technical point of view, the researchers' role was wise because
limitations of instrumentation and procedure are greatly related to the possibilities of action in a study such as Westinghouse. From a policy perspective,
however, this abdicates the decision about what Head Start should be expected
to achieve to "value-free" scientists. The problem is quite common in evaluation studies (Rein and White 1977). It brings to mind Isaiah Berlin's ironic
remark that "the fundamental business of bureaucracies is the conversion of
moral problems into technical ones."

Were any instruments capable of detecting Head Start's effects?   A small war
broke out repeatedly in the design of the Westinghouse study and other evaluation studies like it. On one side were the developmental psychologists who
argued, either from practical psychometrics or from a faith in Piagetian cogni-
tive-developmentalism, that gains on cognitive instruments provide the best
indication of a program's success. On the other side were experienced
preschool teachers, memorably Barbara Biber of Bank Street College, arguing
that the only meaningful goals of a preschool education program lie in a child's
enlargement of his or her sense of self and in social and emotional development.[12] These teachers viewed questions about behavioral objectives as narrow
and trivial, and as particularly objectionable if such questions encouraged the
early childhood program to focus its activities on behavior engineering. They
viewed short-term gains on achievement tests as "quick tricks."

The small war usually ended in compromise. The studies used achievement tests and/or cognitive skills tests and, in addition, imported or developed
hundreds of "noncognitive" instruments (Walker 1973). Because the
researchers did not have theories or observational instruments sufficient to
address the full reality of the preschool teachers' experience with children, the
findings obtained with the available measures were almost uninterpretable.
This difficulty is hardly surprising in a world in which even psychologists committed to psychotherapy have trouble locating instruments to detect its effects.

Shortly after the release of the Westinghouse study, the Office of Child
Development commissioned the Educational Testing Service to construct a
battery of instruments for the assessment of social competence (Anderson and
Messick 1974), viewed by many as the critical construct on which to judge
Head Start's success (Raver and Zigler 1997; Zigler and Trickett 1978). A stag-
gering amount of effort to produce appropriate measures ensued, but funding
was terminated after almost a decade of work, leaving only the cognitive battery completed. To this day, the field lacks a consensus definition of social com-

petence that can guide evaluation, although promising efforts in this area are under way (Raver and Zigler 1997; Malakoff, Underhill, and Zigler 1998).

Whose principles or policies should determine the goals of evaluation studies? The Head Start Planning Committee included individuals with a number of conceptions about goals for an early childhood program. The implementation of the program deliberately left open options to local Head Start centers, in order to allow them opportunities to operate effectively in their distinct environments with differing clientele. Could a single study thoroughly explore the spectrum of issues, values, and concerns represented by those parties involved with Head Start?

To the present day, debates continue regarding what it means to evaluate Head Start. Those connected to the Westinghouse study and its aftermath learned many lessons, around which thinking has evolved gradually over the past thirty years. It was summarized most recently by the Blueprint Committee (see the following section, "The Blueprint Committee Period"). Among them were the following points: (1) There is no one Head Start program and no solid guarantee that what is true for one is true for another. Efforts to understand its effects share all the challenges of assessing a conglomerate and then deciphering the primary sources of the outcomes. (2) Researchers face the severe limitations of available instruments. Only a limited number are suitable for use in large-scale studies. Researchers do not know how to assess in psychometric terms many legitimate and important goals and meanings of Head Start. (3) An accurate understanding of whether and how Head Start works will involve estimation and a reconstructive process of gathering and synthesizing evidence derived from a range of studies. (4) The multiple audiences for the results of Head Start evaluations—high-level legislators and administrators, Head Start center directors, advocates across the political spectrum, assorted professionals whose work intersects with Head Start, and parents—require different kinds of information and utilize different mechanisms for obtaining information.

The "Sleeper Effect" Period
The Westinghouse findings plunged Head Start into a period of uncertainty. The program survived, staunchly supported by advocates, parents, and friends. There were good reasons to be deeply skeptical about the several elements that had been the presumptive determinants of the program's "failure"—the IQ-modification legend, Jensen's arguments that depended heavily upon that legend, and the somewhat equivocal meaning of the fade-out phenomenon (Should one expect a one-year program to inoculate a four-year-old child forever against the baneful effects of impoverished life circumstances?). But, still, a large national program cannot live on alibis. Where could one find a positive vision of what one could hope to achieve with the Head Start program?

A new wave of studies suddenly turned the picture around. David Weikart had been pursuing the graduates of his Perry Preschool Project as they grew up. In a remarkable series of studies in which he traced the lives of the Perry Preschool children to age twenty-seven, he showed that students could obtain success after fade-out (Weikart et al. 1970; Weikart, Bond, and McNeil 1978; Schweinhart and Weikart 1980; Berruetta-Clement et al. 1984; Schweinhart, Barnes, and Weikart 1993). In the short term, the children were less often enrolled in special classes and retained in grade than those who had not attended the preschool. In the long term, they had more often graduated from high school and college, were more often employed, and had been less often detained or arrested. Female Perry Preschool graduates had had far fewer teenage pregnancies than had girls in the control group. Corroborating some of these findings were the data of the Developmental Consortium, a group of eleven directors of model preschool programs, with Weikart as the twelfth member of the group, joined together to obtain longitudinal data about longer-term outcomes from the graduates of their preschool programs (Lazar and Darlington 1982). Reports from the eleven other model programs confirmed, on the whole, the Perry Preschool's earlier longitudinal findings. Looking beyond fade-out, alumni of the programs were less often in special classes and more often at grade level for their age in elementary school.

Apparently a "sleeper effect" was occurring. Some positive effects of the early interventions, not detected in earlier years, emerged in the later years of elementary school and continued into early adulthood. The longitudinal findings of Weikart together with those of the Developmental Consortium for-ever changed the nature and possibilities of Head Start evaluation studies. Advocates for Head Start, assisted by the media in its leveling-and-sharpening manner, instantly understood the findings as positive proof that Head Start really works. This conclusion was discussed repeatedly in the 1980s. Unfortu-nately, the conclusion went considerably beyond the findings of the longitudi-nal studies. What had been found was that model programs, implemented in or near universities, with resources of funding and personnel that are not gen-erally available in Head Start programs, had produced significant long-term benefits to their children. Even now, similar longitudinal data for actual Head Start children are just beginning to be available (Oden, Schweinhart, and Weikart 1999; Currie and Thomas 1995; Garces 1999). One might argue that Head Start programs must logically be producing similar benefits or that the large differences in the two classes of programs make any such inference impossible. Haskins (1989) offers a careful, conservative review of the possible significance of the long-term intervention studies. A more optimistic review is provided by Barnett (1995, 1998) who nevertheless concludes that Head Start has been less effective than better-funded public school programs.

However they were interpreted from a policy perspective, the studies of long-term effects of the model programs made it forever impossible to return to the evaluation studies of the earlier, bang-for-the-buck period. Such studies, regularly leading to an apparent fade-out, were misleading. Interestingly, the children in the longer-term studies never seemed to recover from their psychometric appearance of fade-out. Their earlier gains on IQ or achievement or cognitive skills tests never reappeared. Somehow, they pushed past the third or fourth grade period to do better according to simple, credible, face-valid indicators of success in school and in later phases of life. It would be impossible for any later evaluation study of Head Start to rely completely on short-term psychometric indicators of a program's consequences. The findings of the long-term studies uncovered the need to look beyond short-term data to examine the child's performance in ordinary life circumstances.

The Blueprint Committee Period
An important reconsideration of how and when Head Start should be evaluated began in the latter years of the Bush administration (U.S. Department of Health and Human Services 1990) and continues to evolve today. A "Blueprint Committee," composed of experienced researchers and administrators, considered briefly the possibility of another summative study of Head Start's effectiveness and decisively rejected it as impossible to design and defend in the climate of understanding prevalent in the 1990s. Instead, the committee proposed the establishment of a program of studies that would systematically explore the effects of various components of Head Start's program, the consequences of its programs for the several cultural groups being served, its activities with special populations such as migrant children or handicapped children, and other factors. Such programmatic studies could be of service to administrators and legislators needing to arrive at judgments about the overall effectiveness of Head Start. The studies could not automate the judgment, subjecting the program to an exact cost-effectiveness analysis, as had once been hoped, but they could provide for richer and more informed processes of political judgment about the program. At the same time, the committee proposed studies that could be of service to Head Start center directors and parents, whose questions about the program and needs for useful research might not always coincide with those of high-level administrators.

The strength of the Blueprint Committee's recommendations was that they took into account the reality of Head Start as a program in a new way—its pluralism, its decentralized nature, the several audiences and interests it served. But the problem with the recommendations is that they demanded a new level of sophistication and reflective planning in the organization of Head Start's research. Someone, somewhere would have to "keep score"—remember what the findings of earlier studies indicated, recognize the lacunae in existing information, and balance the needs and interests of the several stakeholders who were to be recognized as having legitimate claims on Head Start's resources for research and evaluation.

To further articulate portions of the Blueprint Committee's recommendations, the Clinton administration supported a Roundtable on Head Start Research at the National Research Council and the Institute of Medicine, which met periodically between 1994 and 1996 (Phillips and Cabrera 1996). The Roundtable members specifically identified four areas requiring study. How do family-level dynamics and development affect Head Start, and how are they affected by Head Start? How can new methods of studying social and emotional development, as well as mental health problems, among the Head Start population be identified? How can Head Start best face the relatively new challenges posed by welfare reform, the vacillation of low-wage work, and increasing ethnic and linguistic diversity of the families it serves? How can a broader array of Head Start programs use tools of research to harvest and disseminate local programmatic inventions? In this tentative, exploratory period, it is yet to be discovered if this research and evaluation program can be conducted in a meaningful way.

Today: Renewed Contestation

Head Start is once again at the center of controversy, fueled in part by politics and in part by the changing sociodemographic context to which it must adapt. Research is again a conspicuous player in the drama, though it too is facing a changed landscape.

Newly elected President Clinton proposed full funding for Head Start, effectively breaking open the delicate truce made under Republican presidents between those who favored and those who opposed the expansion of Head Start. The resolution consisted of incremental funding increases over the period of a decade, signifying steady survival of a popular program with no major expansion or large new initiatives. The only interruption to this pattern consisted of the Charlottesville Education Summit in September 1989 when President Bush and the governors agreed to make early childhood education a top priority for any increased federal funding—an event that some believe paved the way for the increased interest in early education (Vinovskis 1999b). This interest, in turn, facilitated President Clinton's successful efforts to substantially increase funding for Head Start. Yet, once the budgetary resolution between Democrats and Republicans was upset, Head Start again became vulnerable to serious criticism from those on the political right. The criticism focused on the uneven quality of Head Start, its unusual funding structure that circumvents state regulation and sets it apart from all other early childhood and child care programs, and its weak evaluation literature.

The Clinton administration countered with the formation of an Advisory Committee on Head Start Quality and Expansion that called, among other things, for improvements in the consistency of the quality of Head Start programs and for efforts aimed at coordinating Head Start with other early childhood programs. By-products included the revised Program Performance Standards that emphasize accountability and program management and the need for partnerships with other community services; the initiation of Early Head Start; and establishment of the Advisory Committee on Services for Families with Infants and Toddlers. The cadre of researchers with links to Head Start stepped up to the challenge and played important roles on these advisory groups, reminiscent of Head Start's earliest years. They provided vision, projected the larger meaning of Head Start, called for new data and monitoring, and, perhaps most important, lent credibility to efforts to shepherd Head Start safely into the new century.

To date, the expansionists have the upper hand. Head Start is growing and is moving into new territory with Early Head Start. It is bolstered with new performance standards and an elaborate data-gathering and monitoring effort to lend legitimacy to the standards. It is mounting a major new evaluation initiative focused on program impacts with a final report due in 2003. But Head Start's advocates and administrators continue to view the program as vulnerable. They may be right.

The poor face difficulties today (Danziger, this vol.; Gueron, this vol.) that reach far beyond the problems of poverty in 1965. The effective implementation of welfare reform poses serious challenges to early childhood programs, most of which operate on a part-day basis and sustain themselves on parent involvement. The highly credible U.S. General Accounting Office recently issued a scathing analysis of the adequacy and outcomes of research on Head Start's effectiveness (General Accounting Office 1997) at the request of the Chairman of the House Budget Committee. And, as noted by Featherman and Vinovskis (chap. 3, this vol.), politically motivated think tanks are now well positioned to embed such pieces in research summaries that challenge positive assertions about Head Start, often made by other think tanks (see, for example, Olsen 1999).

The terrain of Head Start has also changed dramatically. Surrounding Head Start is a virtual bedlam of new early childhood programs and policies, ranging from expansions of home visiting programs in states and counties all around the country (Gomby, Culross, and Behrman 1999) to publicly funded prekindergarten programs now operative in the majority of states. The so-called new brain research has effectively upped the ante on interventions for very young children. While the research has provided a solid rationale for Head Start, it has also challenged its special status as a unique program with a distinct and sizable funding stream tied to particular performance standards and with resources earmarked for quality improvements. In some parts of the country, solid partnerships between Head Start and other community services have been forged; in others, strong jealousies and turf battles persist.

These are not the issues that researchers are adept at addressing. Indeed, they call to mind James March's characterization of the "conspicuous disparity" between science and politics: "The prototypic scientist engages in an experiment; the prototypic politician engages in a logroll" (1979, 29). It remains to be seen who will remain standing when this current logroll is over. Whatever its impetus, the new focus on program accountability and data gathering promises to benefit Head Start. It is also time to gather new evaluation evidence on Head Start, guided by new understandings of how to evaluate a work in progress and by an awareness of the diverse audiences whose needs can and should be addressed by a major evaluation initiative.

The Uneasy Relationship

The preceding pages attempt to provide a picture of the uneasy relationship that has been maintained by developmental psychologists and Head Start since the onset of the program in 1965. Developmental psychologists have been useful to Head Start in offering representation, demonstration, idealization, and evaluation as essential aspects of policy planning and management of the program. Could those functions have been carried out without the participation of developmental psychologists? For the most part, yes. Such functions, however, were enriched, and made more accurate, complicated, and subtle through the contributions of researchers. Do such functions represent a central unifying principle? These functions converge on the problem of creating symbolic representations of Head Start's policies-in-practice. They make such policies more concrete and open to discussion and negotiation among the several parties whose interests and responsibilities center on Head Start.

Have the contributions of developmental psychologists created risks for, or done harm to, Head Start? Certainly, aspects of their activities have created problems for Head Start. Developmental psychologists have designed confusing pointillist representations of the needs and problems of the disadvantaged. Their mild obsession with cognitive development as the be-all and end-all of a child's life had a decided influence on the model programs that shaped public thinking about Head Start. They played a role in the creation and defense of the IQ story, and Westinghouse created genuine risks to the existence of Head Start.

Recently, Greenberg (1998) has criticized developmental psychologists, among other experts and professionals, for failing to recognize that the fundamental purpose of Head Start was the stimulation of community action and the empowerment of the poor through maximum feasible participation in community-based programs. Most members of the interdisciplinary Planning Committee could not, or would not, grasp this principle. While the staff of the Community Action Program "were talking about empowering Head Start parents to go after the agencies that were not servicing their children adequately and pressure them to do so" (59), members of the interdisciplinary Planning Committee "were talking about activating the expert academic community and everyday professionals—health, mental health, and so on—the focus was on providing services" (60). Greenberg takes particular note of the psychologists' unresponsiveness:

> To the few ivory tower developmental psychologists involved in early plans for Head Start, the prospect of "experimenting" with children was exotic and exciting. . . . Psychologists had researched their middle-class "lab rat" children down to the last finding and were exhilarated by the idea of a new "laboratory" (as some literally called it) of children from low-income families about whom to study, publish, and present. This is not to say that the academics did not want to help poor children do better in school and in life. I am simply pointing out professional priorities. University professors' brownie points do not come from the number of people they have helped out of poverty, but rather from research projects, books published by prestigious university presses, articles in scholarly journals, presentations at major academic conferences, and mentoring outstanding graduate students. (61)

Greenberg concedes in a backhanded way that elite academics were of help to Head Start, though she believes that this fact is indicative of serious deficiencies in the political system:

> And were it not for the elite academics who have advocated for Head Start since its inception, its values and virtues would not be heard. This is because, alas, due to the classism, masculinism, and adulation of pseudoscience in this country, nothing is believed by lawmakers and other decision-makers unless it is backed by the research—however flawed, tiny, and off-target the studies may be—of high-ranking, usually male, academics (or sometimes their female disciples). (62–63)

Committed as she is to community action, Greenberg (1998) does not mention that community action was an intensely problematic and controversial issue from the very beginning of the War on Poverty (Marris and Rein 1969; Moynihan 1969). The examination of congressional testimony, noted earlier, provides strong indications that most people consider and value Head

Start as a program dedicated to fostering the development of children. Lawmakers' attitudes toward research are neither submissive nor adulatory; rather, lawmakers have a healthy ability to ignore or disbelieve research. Greenberg is skeptical about the knowledge that developmental psychologists have brought into political deliberations regarding children, characterizing it as "flawed, tiny, and off-target studies." Indeed, as discussed later, some developmental psychologists with experience in the policy world have promoted systematic changes in the nature of research on children, perhaps resulting in more pertinent political and social deliberations regarding the needs and welfare of children.

However, the old and new methods of developmental psychologists do have merit. Their work focuses directly and clearly on children and issues of human development. To some degree, many people who bring images of children into the political world use those images for a variety of professional and political interests. Immensely appealing, not able to speak for themselves, children have their needs and wants "interpreted" in governmental processes by an astonishing variety of advocates with big or little political agendas. Developmental psychologists, however limited their research instruments, maintain a clear focus on the circumstances of children in various settings of our society.

The uneasy relationship between developmental psychologists and Head Start advocates and administrators is part of a long tradition of arm's-length interactions between researchers and practitioners. A case in point is the occasion, just before the turn of this century, when G. Stanley Hall stood up to address an audience of kindergartners in Chicago, and every single member of his audience walked out on him. In order to understand and deal with the relationship between disciplines such as developmental psychology and service programs such as Head Start, most likely we must go beyond the sociology of science, what the sociologist Znaniecki (1968) has explored in his classic work on the social role of the man of knowledge, and consider what might be called the politics of knowledge. We must recognize that parties such as developmental psychologists and Head Start administrators bring to knowledge-sharing enterprises issues of pride, prejudice, and conflicting professional and social responsibilities. Frequently, institutional change is required for simple and ostensibly technical forms of cooperation.

The Coevolution of Head Start and Developmental Psychology

Developmental psychology, as has been indicated, was a growing and changing discipline in the 1960s, when Head Start was coming to life. There is reasonably clear evidence that the experiences of two developmental psychologists active in Head Start led them to instigate fairly substantial changes in the work of the discipline. Urie Bronfenbrenner took exception to the limitations of developmental psychology's "normal science" for determination of real and meaningful social questions about the lives of children and parents. He characterized much of the research as "the science of children sitting in strange situations doing strange problems" and eventually projected an ecologically valid psychology, the study of children and parents in the natural and enduring environments in which they live. He has been a strong force, with Michael Cole, in the growing movement among developmental psychologists to study children in their everyday environments, and in efforts to create a cultural-historical approach to developmental psychology.

Edward Zigler was one of the designers of a series of Bush Centers on Child Development and Social Policy established at four universities around the country. The purpose of the centers was to train individuals in developmental psychology and social policy. The work of the Bush programs was not an unequivocal success; as is characteristic of cross-disciplinary programs, graduates often found that they were neither fish nor fowl, that in order to have reasonable careers, they had to commit themselves unequivocally to roles as either developmental psychologists or government administrators. But some Bush graduates are among the leaders in governmental activities on behalf of children today.

Head Start, on its side, has built an infrastructure designed to create a regular relationship with researchers in its activities. Grant programs have been deliberately designed to require partnerships between Head Start centers and nearby universities. A biennial series of conferences on research relevant to Head Start, sponsored jointly by the Administration on Children, Youth, and Families and the Society for Research in Child Development, has been well attended, has produced a good share of interesting papers, and is beginning to create a community of researchers with some depth of knowledge about Head Start's activities and effects. Perhaps it is this community of researchers that will, in the end, bring to life the Blueprint Committee's recommendations.

NOTES

We want to thank Edward Zigler for his many contributions to this chapter.

1. This description of the creation of Head Start for substantially political purposes echoes a remark in Greenberg's (1969/1990a) earlier book:

I understood that Head Start was a wedge made of appealing little children which would help the Administration wiggle itself into the hearts of the poor, minority groups, and liberals; that the purpose was more to win votes than to eliminate poverty. I understood that the poverty program as a whole was intended to reduce the restlessness and mounting anger of civil rights militants, partly by throwing them something to assuage the keenest edge of their hunger, partly by taking the wind out of their sails. (14)

2. A good description of CDGM Head Start, its communitarian philosophy, and its political setting is offered by Tom Levin (1967), the program's first director.

3. For example, George B. Brain, former Superintendent of Schools of the City of Baltimore, a member of the Planning Committee, remarks:

There were many points of view represented among the members of the Planning Committee. Some saw the program primarily as an effort to improve the health and physical well-being of children; some emphasized preparing youngsters for reading and academic success in later schooling; some stressed broader cognitive and intellectual development; others emphasized individualistic expression and social adjustment. However, as planning progressed the Committee agreed that emphasis on any single purpose to the exclusion of others would defeat the general goal of the continuous and full development of all children. (Zigler and Valentine 1979, 73)

4. Recommendations quoted in Zigler and Valentine 1979, 137, from a memorandum of R. Cooke to S. Shriver, "Improving the Opportunities and Achievement of the Children of the Poor," ca. February 1965.

5. One small sign of the distance is the fact that, until Head Start began to appear in the newspapers at the start of the Clinton administration, one of the authors (SHW) regularly met Harvard faculty colleagues who expressed surprise that Head Start still existed.

6. The dates of the citations antedate the beginnings of the programs, all of which were established before Head Start.

7. Those waves of activity may, in turn, have been stimulated by periodic bursts of public activity directed toward social welfare. Schlesinger (1990) is one of a number of commentators who have remarked on a periodicity to be found in American liberal initiatives:

History shows a fairly regular alternation in American politics between private gain and public good as the dominating motives of national policy. . . . As each conservative phase runs its course, the republic turns at 30-year intervals to public action— Theodore Roosevelt ushering in the Progressive era in 1901, Franklin Roosevelt the New Deal in 1933, John Kennedy the New Frontier in 1961—until each liberal phase runs its course too. (11)

It is interesting that Schlesinger's three dates—1901, 1933, 1961—fall close to the dates of peak activity in child study, close enough to suggest that the time relationships between federal initiatives for children and public support for child study ought to be looked at. Schlesinger describes the political periodicity as driven by oscillating motives and concerns for private gain alternating with concerns for public welfare. But the periodicity could conceivably have a structural aspect: periods of social reconstruction alternating with periods of equilibration and political stabilization.

8. The mixtures of the sacred and the profane in accounts of Head Start's creation would continue to make trouble for the program. At the beginning of the Clinton administration, when the president was seeking funds for an expansion of Head Start, a Washington report ("Project Rush-Rush" 1993) would claim that Shriver initiated Head Start to expend a first-year budget surplus in the War on Poverty. "I found out nobody could spend $300 million intelligently in one year," said Shriver. "So I wondered what the hell we were going to do with the rest of the money." A story like that, of course, would increase uncertainty about the program and discourage people from taking the program seriously.

9. Cravens's (1993) recent history of the Iowa Child Welfare Controversy provides a good account of the early nursery school controversies and suggests their linkage to the later controversies about Head Start. Interestingly, the earlier studies of nursery schools' effects on IQ were a diversion from the McMillans' conception of the meaning of their nursery school, just as the later studies of Head Start's effects on IQ would be a diversion from the goals and purposes envisioned by the program's early planners (White 1995).

10. (1) Flaxie M. Pinkett, President of the District of Columbia Citizens for Better Public Education; (2) James Banks, Executive Director of the United Planning Organization; (3) Norman Nickens, Head of Model Schools for the District of Columbia; (4) Roman C. Pucinski, U.S. Representative from Illinois; and (5) Dr. Carl Hansen, Superintendent of Schools of the District of Columbia, testifying before the Task Force on Antipoverty in the District of Columbia of the House Committee on Education and Labor in October 1965 and January 1966.

(6) Sam M. Gibbons, U.S. Representative from Florida; and (7) Ray J. Madden, U.S. Representative from Indiana, testifying before the House Committee on Rules on the Economic Opportunity Act Amendments of 1966 in June 1966.

(8) Sargent Shriver, Director of the Office of Economic Opportunity; (9) Hugh L. Carey, U.S. Representative from New York; (10) Charles E. Goodell, U.S. Representative from New York; and (11) Dr. Julius Richmond, Director of the Head Start Program, testifying before the Subcommittee on the War on Poverty Program of the House Committee on Education and Labor on the 1966 Amendments to the Economic Opportunity Act of 1964, in March 1966.

(12) Sargent Shriver, Director of the Office of Economic Opportunity; (13) Jule Sugarman, Associate Director of Head Start; (14) Lisle C. Carter Jr., Assistant Secretary for Individual and Family Services, Department of Health, Education, and Welfare; (15) Dr. Nolan Estes, Associate Commissioner of Elementary and Secondary Education; (16) William A. Steiger, U.S. Representative from Wisconsin; and (17) Charles A. Vanik, U.S. Representative from Ohio, testifying before the House Committee on Education and Labor on the Economic Opportunity Act Amendments of 1967 in June–July 1967.

(18) Robert Ezelle, President of the Mississippi Bedding Corporation and a member of the Jackson Head Start Advisory Board; (19) Priscilla Randall, first grade teacher; (20) Susan Valdez, first grade teacher; (21) Tom Lockwood, Coordinator of the Office of New Programs; (22) Jule Sugarman, Associate Director of Head Start; (23) Paul Martin, Executive Director of the Cambria County Community Action Council; (24) Elizabeth

Fee, kindergarten teacher; (25) John Burkhart, President of the College Life Insurance Company of America; and (26) Joseph S. Clark, U.S. Senator from Pennsylvania, testifying in a hearing examining the War on Poverty by the Subcommittee on Employment, Manpower, and Poverty of the Senate Committee on Labor and Public Welfare, in April–June 1967.

(27) William D. Ford, U.S. Representative from Michigan, and (28) E. C. Stimbert, Superintendent of the Memphis City Schools, testifying before the House Committee on Education and Labor on the Elementary and Secondary Education Amendments of 1967, in March 1967.

(29) Nathaniel H. Williams Jr., Director of the Metropolitan Action Commission in Nashville, testifying in a hearing on Riots, Civil and Criminal Disorders of the Permanent Subcommittee on Investigations of the Senate Committee on Government Operations in November 1967.

(30) Lawrence Feldman, Executive Director of the Day Care and Child Development Council of America; (31) Dr. William F. Brazziel, Member of the Education Committee of the National Urban League; (32) Cenoria Johnson, Washington Representative of the National Urban League; (33) Shirley Norris, Kansas State Director of Day Care Centers; (34) Dr. Lois B. Murphy, Director of the Division of Developmental Studies of the Menninger Foundation; (35) Dr. Robert McCloud from the Children's Clinic in Somerset, Kentucky; (36) Dr. Robert S. Mendelsohn, Medical Director of Head Start; (37) Dr. Hugh C. Thompson, President of the American Academy of Pediatrics; (38) Leo Desjarlais, Executive Director of Community Teamwork, Inc., in Lowell, Massachusetts; (39) Carl Wallace, Head of the California Division Community Action Program; and (40) Dr. Herman Marks, pediatrician, Providence, Rhode Island; testifying on the Economic Opportunity Amendments of 1969 before the Ad Hoc Hearing Task Force on Poverty of the House Committee on Education and Labor, in March–April 1969.

(41) Milton Akers, Executive Director of the National Association for Education of Young Children; (42) Pertina Scott, working mother; (43) LaVaughn DeHon, Director of a Head Start program in Vincennes, Indiana; and (44) Dr. Urie Bronfenbrenner, Professor of Psychology and Human Development at Cornell University, testifying in hearings on the Comprehensive Preschool Education and Child Day-Care Act of 1969 of the Select Subcommittee on Education of the House Committee on Education and Labor between November 1969 and February 1970.

(45) Christine Branche, Directing Supervisor of the Division of Early Childhood of the Cleveland Board of Education; (46) Walter F. Mondale, U.S. Representative from Minnesota; (47) Dr. Benjamin Bloom, Professor of Education at the University of Chicago; and (48) Dr. Robert Cooke, Chairman of the Planning Committee for Project Head Start, testifying in hearings on the Head Start Child Development Act of the Subcommittee on Employment, Manpower, and Poverty of the Senate Committee on Labor and Public Welfare in August 1969.

11. A more complete discussion of the Westinghouse Study and its findings can be found in White 1971, written by a member of the team that designed the Westinghouse Study.

12. A reasonable statement of Barbara Biber's outlook is found in Biber and Franklin 1967.

REFERENCES

Allport, G. W., and L. Postman. 1947. *The psychology of rumor.* New York: Holt.

Anderson, S., and S. Messick. 1974. Social competency in young children. *Developmental Psychology* 10:282–93.

Barnett, W. S. 1995. Long-term effects of early childhood programs on cognitive and school outcomes. *The Future of Children* 5 (3): 25–50.

———. 1998. Long-term effects on cognitive development and school success. In *Early care and education for children in poverty: Promises, programs, and long-term results,* ed. W. S. Barnett and S. S. Boocock. Albany: State University of New York Press.

Bereiter, C., and S. Englemann. 1966. *Teaching disadvantaged children in the preschool.* Englewood Cliffs, N.J.: Prentice-Hall.

Berruetta-Clement, J. R., L. J. Schweinhart, W. S. Barnett, A. S. Epstein, and D. P. Weikart. 1984. Changed lives: The effects of the Perry Preschool Program on youths through age 19. *Monographs of the High/Scope Educational Research Foundation* 8.

Biber, B., and M. B. Franklin. 1967. The relevance of developmental and psychodynamic concepts to the education of the preschool child. In *Disadvantaged child,* ed. J. Hellmuth, 305–23. New York: Brunner/Mazel.

Bloom, B. S. 1964. *Stability and change in human characteristics.* New York: Wiley.

Brazziel, W. F. 1969. Testimony before the Task Force on Poverty of the Committee on Education and Labor, U.S. Congress, May 8.

Caldwell, B. M., and J. B. Richmond. 1964. Programmed day care for the very young child—a preliminary report. *Journal of Marriage and the Family* 26:481–88.

Campbell, D. T. 1988. The experimenting society. In *Methodology and epistemology for social science: Selected papers,* ed. E. S. Overman, 290–314. Chicago: University of Chicago Press.

Cravens, H. 1993. *Before Head Start: The Iowa Station and America's children.* Chapel Hill: University of North Carolina Press.

Cunningham, H. 1991. *The children of the poor: Representations of childhood since the seventeenth century.* Oxford: Basil Blackwell.

Currie, J., and D. Thomas. 1995. Does Head Start make a difference? *American Economic Review* 85 (3): 341–64.

Deutsch, C. P., and M. Deutsch. 1968. Brief reflections on the theory of early childhood enrichment programs. In *Early education: Current research, theory, and action,* ed. R. D. Hess and R. M. Bear, 83–90. Chicago: Aldine.

Dombkowski, K., A. Smith, and M. Vinovskis. 1999. Social science research and early education: An historical analysis of developments in Head Start, kindergartens, and day care. Paper prepared for Policy History Conference, St. Louis, Mo., May 27–30.

Garces, E. 1999. Long-term effects of Head Start: Evidence from the PSID. Manuscript, University of California, Los Angeles.

Gomby, D. S., P. L. Culross, and R. E. Behrman. 1999. Home visiting: Recent program evaluations—Analysis and recommendations. *The Future of Children* 9. Los Altos, Calif.: The David and Lucile Packard Foundation.

Gray, S. W., and R. A. Klaus. 1965. An experimental preschool program for culturally deprived children. *Child Development* 36:887–98.

Greenberg, P. 1990a. *The devil has slippery shoes: A biased biography of the Child Development Group of Mississippi (CDGM): A story of maximum feasible poor parent participation.* Washington, D.C.: Youth Policy Institute. Original work published in 1969.

———. 1990b. Head Start—Part of a multi-pronged anti-poverty effort for children and their families . . . Before the beginning: A participant's view. *Young Children* 45:41–52.

———. 1998. The origins of Head Start and the two versions of parent involvement: How much parent participation in early childhood programs and services for children. In *Critical perspectives on Project Head Start: Revisioning the hope and challenge,* ed. J. Ellsworth and L. J. Ames, 49–72. Albany: State University of New York Press.

Haskins, R. 1989. Beyond metaphor: The efficacy of early childhood education. *American Psychologist* 44:274–82.

Himmelfarb, G. 1991. *Poverty and compassion: The moral imagination of the late Victorians.* New York: Vintage Books.

Hohmann, M., B. Banet, and D. P. Weikart. 1979. *Young children in action.* Ypsilanti, Mich.: High/Scope Press.

Hood, J. 1992. Caveat emptor: The Head Start scam. *Policy Analysis* 187. Washington, D.C.: Cato Institute.

Hunt, J. McV. 1961. *Intelligence and experience.* New York: Ronald Press.

Jensen, A. R. 1969. How much can we boost I.Q. and scholastic achievement? *Harvard Educational Review* 39:1–123.

Jones, H. E. 1954. The environment and mental development. In *Manual of child psychology,* 2d. ed., ed. L. Carmichael. New York: Wiley.

Lazar, I., and R. Darlington. 1982. Lasting effects of early education: A report from the Consortium for Longitudinal Studies. *Monographs of the Society for Research in Child Development* 47, Serial no. 195.

Levin, T. 1967. Preschool education and the communities of the poor. In *Disadvantaged child,* vol. 1, ed. J. Hellmuth, 349–406. New York: Brunner/Mazel.

Malakoff, M. E., J. M. Underhill, and E. Zigler. 1998. The effect of inner-city environment and Head Start experience on effectance motivation. *American Journal of Orthopsychiatry* 68:630–38.

March, J. G. 1979. Science, politics, and Mrs. Gruenberg. *Annals of the National Academy of Sciences,* 27–36. Washington, D.C.: National Academy of Sciences.

Masten, A. S., K. Best, and N. Garmezy. 1990. Resilience and development: Contributions from the study of children who overcome adversity. *Development and Psychopathology* 2:425–44.

Masten, A. S., and J. D. Coatesworth. 1998. The development of competence in favorable and unfavorable environments: Lessons from research on successful children. *American Psychologist* 53:205–20.

Oden, S., L. J. Schweinhart, and D. P. Weikart, with S. Marcus and Y. Xie. 1999. Into adulthood: A study of the effects of Head Start. Ypsilanti, Mich.: High/Scope Press.

Olsen, D. A. 1999. Universal preschool is no golden ticket: Why government should not enter the preschool business. *Policy Analysis,* no. 333. Washington, D.C.: Cato Institute.

Phillips, D. A., and N. J. Cabrera. 1996. *Beyond the blueprint: Directions for research on Head Start's families.* Washington, D.C.: National Research Council.

Project Rush-Rush. 1993. *CQ Researcher* 9 (April): 298–301.

Raver, C. C., and E. F. Zigler. 1997. Social competence: An untapped dimension in evaluating Head Start's success. *Early Childhood Research Quarterly* 12:363–85.

Rein, M., and S. H. White. 1977. Can policy research help policy? *Public Interest* 49:119–36.

Residents of Hull-House: A social settlement (at 335 South Halsted Street, Chicago, Ill.). 1895. *Hull-House maps and papers: A presentation of nationalities and waves in a congested district of Chicago, together with comments and essays on problems growing out of the social conditions.* New York: Thomas Y. Crowell.

Sameroff, A. J. 1995. General systems theories and developmental psychopathology. In *Manual of developmental psychopathology: Theory and methods,* ed. D. Cicchetti and D. Cohen, 1:659–95. New York: Wiley.

Schweinhart, L. J., H. V. Barnes, and D. P. Weikart. Significant benefits: The High/Scope Perry Preschool study through age 27. *Monographs of the High/Scope Educational Research Foundation,* no. 10.

Shriver, S. 1966. Testimony before the Subcommittee on the War on Poverty Program of the Committee on Education and Labor, House of Representatives, U.S. Congress, March 8.

———. 1967. Testimony before the Committee on Education and Labor, House of Representatives, U.S. Congress, June 19.

Siegel, A. W., and S. H. White. 1982. The child study movement: Early growth and development of the symbolized child. *Advances in Child Behavior and Development* 17:233–85.

Sroufe, L. A. 1997. Psychopathology as an outcome of development. *Development and Psychopathology* 9:251–68.

U.S. Department of Health and Human Services, Administration on Children, Youth and Families. 1990. *Head Start research and evaluation: A blueprint for the future. Recommendations of the Advisory Panel for Head Start Evaluation Design Project.* Washington, D.C.: Administration on Children, Youth and Families.

U.S. General Accounting Office. 1997. *Head Start: Research provides little information on impact of current program.* GAO/HEHS 97–59. Washington, D.C.: General Accounting Office.

Vinovskis, M. 1999a. Do federal compensatory education programs really work? A brief historical analysis of Title I and Head Start. *American Journal of Education* 107:187–209.

———. 1999b. *History and educational policymaking.* New Haven: Yale University Press.

Walker, D. K. 1973. *Socioemotional measures for preschool and kindergarten children: A handbook.* San Francisco: Jossey-Bass.

Weikart, D., D. Deloria, L. Lawser, and R. Wiegerink. 1970. Longitudinal results of the

Ypsilanti Perry preschool project. Monographs of the High/Scope Educational Research Foundation, no. 1.

Weikart, D., L. Rogers, C. Adcock, and D. McClelland. 1971. *The cognitively oriented curriculum: A framework for preschool teachers.* Washington, D.C.: National Association for the Education of Young Children.

Westinghouse Learning Corporation. 1969. *The impact of Head Start: An evaluation of the effects of Head Start on children's cognitive and affective development. Executive summary.* Ohio University report to the Office of Economic Opportunity. Washington, D.C.: Clearinghouse for Federal Scientific and Technical Information (ED036321).

White, S. H. 1971. The National Impact Study of Head Start. In *Disadvantaged child,* ed. J. Hellmuth. Vol. 3. New York: Brunner/Mazel.

———. 1978. Psychology in all sorts of places. In *Psychology and society: In search of symbiosis,* ed. R. Kasschau and F. S. Kessel, 105–31. New York: Holt, Rinehart, and Winston.

———. 1990. Child study at Clark University: 1894–1904. *Journal of the History of the Behavioral Sciences* 26:131–50.

———. 1991a. The rise of developmental psychology: Retrospective review of *Cognitive development in children: Five monographs of the Society for Research in Child Development. Contemporary Psychology* 36:469–73.

———. 1991b. Three visions of educational psychology. In *Culture, schooling, and psychological development,* ed. L. Tolchinsky-Landsmann, 1–38. Norwood, N.J.: Ablex.

———. 1995. Does Gutterella have an IQ problem? Invited address, American Psychological Association Convention, New York City, August 1995.

———. 1996. The relationships of developmental psychology to social policy. In *Children, families, and government: Preparing for the twenty-first century,* ed. E. Zigler, S. L. Kagan, and N. Hall, 409–26. New York: Cambridge University Press.

White, S. H., and S. Buka. 1987. Early education: Programs, traditions, and policies. In *Review of research in education,* ed. E. Z. Rothkopf, 14:43–91. Washington, D.C.: American Educational Research Association.

White, S. H., M. C. Day, P. A. Freeman, S. A. Hantman, and K. P. Messenger. 1973. *Federal programs for young children: Review and recommendations.* 3 vols. Washington, D.C.: U.S. Government Printing Office.

Zigler, E. 1999. Head Start is not child care. Comment. *American Psychologist* 54:142–43.

Zigler, E. F., and J. Freedman. 1987. Early experience, malleability, and Head Start. In *The malleability of children,* ed. J. J. Gallagher and C. T. Ramey, 85–95. Baltimore: Brookes.

Zigler, E. F., S. L. Kagan, and N. W. Hall, eds. 1996. *Children, families, and government: Preparing for the twenty-first century.* Cambridge: Cambridge University Press.

Zigler, E., and S. Muenchow. 1992. *Head Start: The inside story of America's most successful educational experiment.* New York: Basic Books.

Zigler, E., and S. J. Styfco. 1994. Is the Perry Preschool better than Head Start? Yes and no. *Early Childhood Research Quarterly* 9:269–87.

Zigler, E., and P. K. Trickett. 1978. IQ, social competence, and evaluation of early childhood intervention programs. *American Psychologist* 33:789–98.

Zigler, E., and J. Valentine, eds. 1979. *Project Head Start: A legacy of the War on Poverty.* New York: Free Press.

Znaniecki, F. 1968. *The social role of the man of knowledge.* New York: Harper and Row.

CHAPTER 5

Policy, Aging, and the Graying of Society

W. Andrew Achenbaum

Since the founding of the Republic, officials in Washington and various state governments have relied on social science researchers to produce knowledge useful to policy-making. The Lewis and Clark expedition (1804–6), subsidized by Thomas Jefferson and the American Philosophical Society, is one of the earliest examples. Some policy has revolved around the elderly's demographic, economic, and social characteristics, interest in which is first evident in the 1830 U.S. census.[1] This interest culminated in the original Social Security Act, which became the template upon which all subsequent population aging initiatives were crafted. Since that time, Americans have had difficulty designing policies that take account of aging, individual and societal, but new theoretical insights and empirical data regarding the potentials of the oldest old may provide the basis for bipartisan policies that resolve the generational-equity debate.

A century after census takers and labor officials began to monitor aspects of individual aging, a few demographers and social scientists began to take note of *societal aging*, the impact the increasing numbers of long-lived persons have on social structures that are themselves becoming older. Warren Thompson and P. K. Whelpton (1930, 394–95), for instance, forecast that the United States was becoming a "nation of elders in the making." In a larger report for Herbert Hoover's *Recent Social Trends,* the pair predicted that "such age changes are likely to produce significant consequences in our schools, in our business, in our politics and in our social structure" (Thompson and Whelpton 1933, 57). They speculated that population aging would also alter the country's productivity, consumption, and inheritance patterns.

By the end of the 1930s, some were warning that the trend might someday threaten America's growth and undermine its political institutions. In a major piece in the October 1939 issue of *Harper's,* Roy Helton offered a gloomy prognosis:

> The demands of the ageing are already becoming emphatic and the power of the ageing as a pressure group is recognized in politics everywhere. It is

a pressure group with a real problem: What is to be done for our growing population of ageing men and women who have not, because of economic changes, been able to provide for themselves. . . . It will not be a good national living, whether economically or politically, to allow those years to be years of increasing unhappiness and uselessness to our coming majority. It will not be safe for America to permit the present psychology of old age to dominate even a powerful minority of our citizens. (Helton 1939, 450–51)

Helton's ideas went beyond an age-old animus against an obsolescence associated with the debility and dependency of the elderly. He feared that the graying of America would imperil the current well-being and future options of rising cohorts. Helton's concern was grounded in the belief that chronological age in an industrial era determined one's worth. "No man should be made to retire unless he can find a better use for his time than to continue at some form of his life work" (457). The labor force favored youth. Shifts in the U.S. population structure, moreover, were altering the face of old-age dependency. "Poverty in old age can no longer be made impervious by mere hard work, frugality, and good habits. Our fortune has become dependent on altogether too many forces beyond our control" (Epstein 1929, 163). In short, there was mounting— although not yet compelling—evidence that "modern" conditions made the implications of societal aging as dire as the individual consequences of growing older.

The Great Depression underscored the plight of old Americans and the need for new ways to cope with adversity. Unemployment rates among workers over forty exceeded national averages. Pension funds folded; savings were lost. Charities and families could not provide sufficient resources for their elders. Some contributors to *Recent Social Trends* thought that hard times might encourage Americans to rehabilitate late life: Charles H. Judd (1933, 343) noted the advantages of expanding adult-education programs; Milbank's Edgar Sydenstricker urged greater efforts to conserve "vitality" among those over forty since "the search for these causes doubtless will go into the conditions of childhood and young adult life and, when successful, will result in further conservation of vitality throughout the entire life span" (1933, 660). But these were long-term goals. For the moment, the economic crisis underscored the flimsiness of the nation's safety net: the Great Depression, declared Paul Douglas (one of the few academics in the U.S. Senate), "increasingly convinced the majority of American people that individuals could not themselves provide adequately for their old age and that some sort of greater security should be provided by society" (Douglas 1936, 6–7).

Franklin Delano Roosevelt appointed five cabinet officers to form the Committee on Economic Security (CES) in 1934. FDR charged them to relieve

victims of the deepening economic catastrophe and to establish ways to miti-
gate risks in "modern" times. The policymakers relied heavily on scholars and
technocrats to develop a set of social-insurance initiatives. Assistant Secretary
of Labor Arthur Altmeyer, who had served as Wisconsin's chief statistician and
secretary of its industrial commission, headed a twenty-one-member technical
board. This panel of experts in turn was flanked by actuaries, physicians, medical administrators, social scientists, and professionals from the fields of child
welfare, public administration, and employment. A staff of eighty research
assistants was assembled under the direction of Edwin Witte, who chaired the
Economics Department at the University of Wisconsin. Within six months, the
committee issued nine major reports on unemployment, old age security, child
welfare, public relief, employment opportunities, and the relationship of health
to income security. In addition, CES produced memoranda on constitutional
issues and foreign experiences before it synthesized their findings into a fifty-
page report (Achenbaum 1988, 302–3).

The experts focused on several age-specific vicissitudes that caused hardships across every stage of life: "A program of economic security, as we vision
it, must have as its primary aim the assurance of an adequate income to each
human being in childhood, youth, middle age, or old age—in sickness or in
health. It must provide safeguards against all of the hazards leading to destitution and dependency" (Committee on Economic Security 1935, 3). Rather
than emulate European practices, the CES created a social-insurance scheme
that encouraged Americans to work and, at the same time, protected those
unable to do so. While legislative particulars were drafted in the Great Depression, lawmakers designed the Social Security Act to flourish in prosperous
times. They assumed that individual choices and family situations changed
amid the succession of generations. By capitalizing on past trends while
acknowledging future uncertainties, Social Security was meant to be adaptable
as U.S. society matured (Achenbaum 1986).

To wit: The federal-state formula for old-age assistance (Title I) operated
in tandem with an old-age insurance system (Title II) financed by equal contributions from employers and employees (Title VIII). As more and more
workers earned benefits in this pay-as-you-go system, CES projected that there
would be less need for relief. (Amendments enacted in 1939, before the original Title II went into effect, bolstered the welfare aspects of this measure.
Experts thought it possible to extend protection to cover workers' spouses and
children without raising taxes on earnings.) Provisions for the elderly were just
one way that Social Security assisted the young. Applicants who met certain age
criteria or suffered from particular conditions were eligible for special types of
categorical assistance. Under Titles III and IX, Congress established an unem-
ployment-compensation plan. Roughly $25 million was earmarked under Title
IV for "aid to dependent children." Title V allocated funds to crippled children,

rural public-health services, and rehabilitation. Title VI authorized $2 million for training new public health personnel. A three-member Social Security Board was created for "studying and making recommendations as to the most effective methods of providing economic security through social insurance" (Social Security Act 1935, sect. 702). Administrators needed hard data to run effectively a complex system that served very distinctive constituencies.

FDR was convinced that his program "to provide for the general welfare" linked aging to the graying of society. "This social security measure gives at least some protection to thirty millions of our citizens who will reap direct benefits through unemployment compensation, through old-age pensions and through increased services for the protection of children and the prevention of ill health," the president declared as he signed the measure into law on August 14, 1935. "It is, in short, a law that will take care of human needs and at the same time provide the United States an economic structure of vastly greater soundness" (reprinted in Pifer and Chisman 1985, 145). Roosevelt believed that addressing the current economic plight of the nation's aged cohort would allay the fears of rising generations. Increasing workers' stake in the common-weal was both shrewd politics and sound economics: according to the president, the promise of security strengthened the overall economy by boosting productivity.

Thus during the New Deal some strategic steps were taken to reallocate resources across the life course in order to anticipate some of the likely consequences of population aging—notably midlife unemployment and old-age dependency. The case for prescience should not be overstated: most lawmakers and researchers in the 1930s were not thinking primarily in terms of demographic challenges. Contributors to *Recent Social Trends,* after all, missed many opportunities to make policy-relevant connections between population aging and other trends that they were investigating. Thompson and Whelpton made no reference to "aging" in their concluding section on "population policy." Lawrence Frank wrote a chapter-long analysis of "childhood and youth," but there were few other references to the elderly. The question of old-age pensions merited two pages in the chapter on labor, two paragraphs in the one on social work, and one paragraph each in the chapters on public welfare, law, and family relations. By no means did every expert view the succession of generations as the catalyst that would result in a network of clients and agents linked through Social Security programs.

Indeed, establishing age-specific categories under Social Security caused tensions among the very constituencies targeted for relief. Princeton's J. Douglas Brown, who chaired the advisory council that crafted the 1939 Social Security amendments, warned that "the protection of the aged must not be at the expense of adequate protection of dependent children, the sick, the disabled, or the unemployed" ([1938] 1977, 18). Yet by emphasizing the societal risks associated with superannuation, policymakers probably downplayed the future burden of costs on younger wage earners. Public-opinion polls indicate that most Americans in the 1930s misunderstood differences between Title I and Title II. Respondents said that they wanted needs-based programs, but they rarely stated that it was in everyone's interest to care for the very young or the extremely old (Schlitz 1970, 44–49). Perhaps more seriously, accentuating age-specific hazards diverted attention from the issue of race. Few championed the plight of minority families who lacked access to minimal support for a decent standard of living.

The 1930s, in short, left a Janus-faced legacy for broad-scale policy-making in a graying society. The nation finally enacted a program aimed at relieving old-age dependency, but initiatives for elders still lagged behind those designed for younger citizens.[2] Piecemeal in development, there nonetheless was a theoretical, policy-relevant basis for integrating the country's diverse array of age-based measures into a coherent social-insurance scheme that covered the population from womb to tomb.

Social insurance ceased to be a priority, however, during the midst of World War II. The Social Security Board chairman wanted to liberalize the program: "A measure can be taken now which will provide the basis for a better society after the war and at the same time will serve the economic and fiscal needs of the moment" (Altmeyer 1942, 5). This position was consistent with FDR's so-called Second Bill of Rights (1944), which envisioned "a new basis of security and prosperity . . . regardless of station or race or creed." Alas, amendments to Social Security scheduled to go into effect in 1943 were tabled; no new welfare legislation was enacted. Dr. Win-the-War had replaced Dr. New Deal. Policymakers and academics lowered their profile, discussing only modest social welfare modifications. Nor could Harry S. Truman recapture momentum: a coalition of conservative Democrats and Republicans squelched his health-care reforms. Congress defeated attempts to liberalize Social Security. Incrementalism—a gradual expansion through technical adjustments—became policy analysts' prevailing modus operandi.

Limited Postwar Efforts to Situate the Aged in the Context of Societal Aging

Social gerontologists, especially those with demographic training, were among the pacesetters after World War II in writing about the manifold consequences of population aging. The University of Chicago's Philip Hauser, for example, contrasted "mature" and "young" nations in cold war terms: "If youth means vigor and age debility, the Western and free nations may be handicapped by the intense competition—economic, social, political, and perhaps military—

which seems to lie ahead. But youth has not always triumphed over age, and age has many virtues and strengths not possessed by youth." To Hauser (Hauser and Vargas 1960, 52; see also Hauser and Shanas 1952) such ruminations made "more clear and also more dramatic the need to learn about the consequences of the aging of nations." Several contributors to Clark Tibbitts's influential *Handbook of Social Gerontology* (1960) explored the impact of technology, social structure, and health programs on societal aging. Investigators wanted facts to illuminate "the basic foundations of any effective action program" for older Americans (Cottrell 1960, 119).

Medical researchers occasionally discussed the subject. In announcing a conference in 1949 on "the social and biological challenge of our aging population," the keynote speaker at the New York Academy of Medicine bluntly stated that the agenda was "to consider the problems proposed by the already large and growing group of the population who have 'outlived their usefulness to society.' . . . Because of complicated interacting economic forces a very serious problem of old age care and maintenance now exists" (Brown 1950, 3). Some participants opined that studying senescent individuals and societies offered wonderful opportunities for intellectual risk-taking: "Even discounting the pessimism, the challenge remains . . . we must first acquire a multidimensional comprehension of the problem" (Galdston 1950, vii). Few physicians, however, explored systematically the aged's place in postwar America.

Doctors were not alone. Researchers on aging liked to claim that they were working at the frontiers of knowledge, yet they generally did not roam too far from their disciplinary outposts. Specialization simultaneously sharpened and narrowed foci. Whereas authors in the first edition of Edmund Cowdry's *Problems of Ageing* (1939) referred to one another's work and speculated about future findings, subsequent compendiums offered more and more about less and less. Handbooks in the 1990s "provide no unifying themes, no compelling metaphors to tie the many excellent pieces together" (Achenbaum 1991, 133). The geometric growth in the gerontologic literature since 1945 has not fostered many venturesome cross-disciplinary explorations of societal aging. The exceptions to this generalization warrant examination.

The American Academy of Political and Social Science devoted its September 1974 *Annals* to the "political consequences of aging." In the first essay, "The Aging of Populations and Societies," Donald Cowgill devoted ten pages to rehearsing various demographic indicators. Then the social gerontologist turned to societal aging, which he equated with modernization. A construct used by social scientists to gauge progress in underdeveloped nations, "modernization" embraced the "transformation of a total society." Cowgill (1974) identified six salient aspects of modernization—aging and health technology, economic technology and aging, aging and urbanization, aging and education, aging and the work ethic, aging and the cult of youth—before alluding to future scenarios. Cowgill set an agenda that, if taken seriously, required volumes to execute. He did not specify, however, what might be excluded from consideration. Nor did Cowgill explain why thinking of modernization in terms of societal aging made more sense than, say, industrialization. The construct did not foment a paradigm shift in thinking.

Another article in the same journal *did* present lucid, practical insights into the societal ramifications of acknowledging longer-lived men and women in a population that was itself aging. After asserting that perceptions of the life cycle were changing, Bernice Neugarten hypothesized that a major shift was under way in the United States. With lower retirement ages and increasingly diverse life-styles, persons between the ages of fifty-five and seventy-five (who constituted 15 percent of the population) "might become major agents of social change in building the age-irrelevant society" (1974, 198). Those over seventy-five, whom she called the "old-old," would demand an increasingly larger share of the country's service budget. Neugarten feared that her twofold characterization would be misinterpreted, and it was. Yet, her focus on the "young-old" brilliantly demonstrated how rethinking relations across age categories raised new questions about how society allocated roles. As her article appeared, Neugarten embarked with her University of Chicago mentor, Robert Havighurst, on a three-year National Science Foundation project that probed the ethical dimensions of policy-making. In *Social Policy, Social Ethics, and the Aging Society,* the pair took a "conservatively optimistic position" in predicting the relative numbers and health status of young-old and old-old persons, and in envisioning their place in the labor force, intergenerational family structures, and the political arena. Neugarten and Havighurst asked economists, philosophers, health-care analysts, Social Security experts, priests, and political scientists to participate in "discussing some of the issues that policymakers are facing as they grapple with the fact that ours is an aging society" (Neugarten and Havighurst 1976, 121). Their emphasis on economic support and health care spurred a discussion, joined by lawyers and bench scientists, that became *Extending the Human Life Span: Social Policy and Social Ethics* (1977).

Neugarten soon had an opportunity to test her hunches about societal aging in the political arena. Jimmy Carter appointed her to the fifteen-member Federal Council on Aging for a three-year term (1980–83). Neugarten also served as deputy director of the 1981 White House Conference on Aging until her views displeased members of the Reagan administration. Nonetheless, her speeches and work in these highly visible positions justify my claim that Bernice Neugarten did more than any single scholar to turn an academic construct into a policy-relevant idea.

Once again, such a statement must be qualified. Neugarten was not the only scholar/policy analyst thinking along these lines. Wilbur Cohen (1980), a former secretary of Health, Education, and Welfare, discussed likely changes in economic well-being and income distribution in terms of historical changes he had witnessed since the 1930s. Several of Neugarten's colleagues, including Robert Binstock and George Maddox, participated in symposia with colleagues around the world to speculate about aging-based policies in the year 2000 (Selby and Schecter 1982). A Delphi poll of eighteen internationally renowned scientists referred to the consequences for human development of extending the human life span in the proximate future (Salomen 1983). Perhaps more important, publications that at first glance seemed to resonate with Neugarten's approach proved otherwise. For instance, the report of the President's Commission on a National Agenda for the Eighties (1980) merely recited familiar demographic patterns in discussing population aging. Little new appeared in an information paper by the U.S. Senate Special Committee on Aging on "Social Security in Europe: The Impact of an Aging Population" (1981).[3] And a publication from my own research center, *The Older Worker in an Aging Society* (Institute of Gerontology 1981), never defined what contributors meant by societal aging.

Neugarten advanced interest in societal aging in 1982 when she allied herself with an intellectual team being formed by Alan Pifer, president emeritus of the Carnegie Corporation. With a budget of several million dollars for three years, Pifer wanted to tie his long-standing commitment to promoting children's welfare with a more personal concern for ensuring that people like himself—healthy, bright and connected—would continue in retirement to have opportunities to contribute to the well-being of society. Pifer and his colleagues produced a special issue on "the Aging Society" for *Daedalus* (Pifer and Bronte 1986) and several publications on gender, race, and employment patterns (Aging Society Project 1984). There were other spin-offs: the Gerontological Society of America published *Higher Education and an Aging Society* (1989); Christine Cassel coauthored a paper with Neugarten about "the goals of medicine in an aging society" (1990). H. R. Moody, a member of the Carnegie project steering committee, edited an issue on "revisioning the aging society" for *In Depth* (1992).

Such contributions were positive steps. And yet, U.S. policymakers and academics were not at the forefront in reformulating ways to revamp social service, employment and income, and health-care programs to accommodate extensions in human longevity and alterations in the age structure. Consider publications issued during the 1980s in other advanced-industrial nations. A multidisciplinary group of London-based scholars published a series of reports focusing on the structured dependency of the elderly (Johnson 1987), the relationship between population aging and economic dependency (Falkingham 1987), and the economic consequences of population aging in advanced societies (Scott and Johnson 1988). They also monitored developments in Japan, which was in the vanguard in national planning for the consequences of societal aging.

Public and private leaders in Japan since 1960 had been tracking the impact of increases in life expectancy at birth and in middle age on traditional values and mores. In 1981 its Economic Council convened a group of 128 experts which met 182 times to weigh strategies to prepare their country "for an age of internationalization, the aging society and maturity." The panel concluded that all people, not just the aged, must be able to live in an enriched society; Japan had to be flexible, fair, tolerant, and cosmopolitan (Economic Council 1983, 139). In the 1980s, aging issues also took center stage in Australian political and policy-making circles. Amid new images of the life cycle, experts confronted unprecedented demands for public intervention. They had to reconcile past governmental action with the conflicting desires of various interest groups as they rethought housing policies and community services (Kendig and McCallum 1990). Meanwhile, David Thomson (1991) explored the aging of New Zealand's welfare state since the 1930s. He claimed that those who were young in the Depression had acquired entitlements that their children and grandchildren would not enjoy. Restoring equity became a major policy goal, one that would require sacrifices by every cohort.

Current Efforts to Think about Policy-Making in Terms of Societal Aging

During the past decade, there have been notable efforts to narrow the gap between "progressive" and "backward" thinking about societal aging. Some Americans have joined forces with experts in other countries to contemplate our collective future in global terms. For instance, Robert Butler, who won a Pulitzer Prize for *Why Survive?* and served as the first director of the National Institute on Aging, has forged partnerships with Japanese colleagues to study productive aging and longevity (Bass 1994). Other U.S. professional organizations have insinuated ideas about societal aging into their thinking. *The Prime Life Generation* (1985), issued by the American Council of Life Insurance and Health Insurance Association of America in conjunction with the National Council on the Aging and the National Council of Senior Citizens, built on Neugarten's concept of the young-old. The American Association of Retired Persons teamed with Resources for the Future in preparing *Aging of the U.S. Population: Economic and Environmental Implications* (1993). Congressional publications dealing respectively with veteran affairs, as well as Hispanic elders, incorporated ideas about societal aging circulating on campuses and in think tanks and lobbying groups along Connecticut Avenue (Select Committee on Aging 1986, 1988).

Three members of the steering committee of the Carnegie Corporation's Aging Society Project have sparked conversations between U.S. academics and policymakers. With support from the National Institute on Aging, Jack and Matilda Riley have assembled a multidisciplinary team of researchers for their Program on Age and Structural Change. The Rileys seize on the mismatch between the fact that people are living longer and the reality that essential structures (especially affecting family relations, job advancement, and institutional care) are resistant to affording them new roles.

> When the two dynamisms are far out of synchrony, as they are today, critical strains can eventuate—both for individuals and for society as a whole—and such strains continually press for still further changes.... We can discern a future society in which retirement as we know it today will be replaced by periods of leisure interspersed throughout the life course with periods of education and work; a society in which lifelong learning replaces the lockstep of traditional education; a society in which opportunities for paid work are spread more evenly across all ages; a society in which older people, as well as children, will be productive assets, not burdens; a society in which work is valued as much for its intrinsic satisfactions as for its economic returns; a society that can give new meanings not only to leisure but also to all of life—from birth to dying and death. (Riley and Riley 1994, 25, 33)

The Rileys and their collaborators endeavored to formulate a sound *theoretical* construct for understanding dynamic interactions between individual and societal aging—something in short supply in conversations thus far. Theory-building was imperative: Effecting profound societal change presupposed that people knew why they had to let go of prevailing notions of the human life course. They needed to embrace a set of values that empowered men and women alike to create their own futures as they aged.

Fernando Torres-Gil also investigated several forces—longevity, diversity, and sociopolitical generations—that he identified with an aging society. More than the Rileys, he was interested in redesigning policies for a new millennium. As the first Undersecretary of Health and Human Services for Aging (1992–96), Torres-Gil was well positioned to showcase his baby-boom cohort's vision. The gray lobby, he recommended, should eschew narrow interest group politics and help younger, disadvantaged groups. He wanted to forge a coalition between advocates for the disabled and the nation's elders. Indeed, he opposed age-segregated tactics: senior citizens, Torres-Gil urged, should be supporting public funding for public schools, fighting the war on drugs, and educating rising generations about the greater prospects for a ripe old age (1992, 89–90). The Clinton administration failed to achieve as much in the health-care and social-service arena as its partisans had hoped, but principal policymakers were basing policy recommendations on broad-gauged assumptions that took account of population aging and structural shifts. Emblematic was the decision of the policy institute of the Gerontological Society of America to change its name to the National Academy on an Aging Society to reflect its mission of focusing on "demographic changes and how they affect public and private institutions and families *of all ages,* today and tomorrow" (Friedland 1998).

Some recent scholarship continues to address the issues raised by Neugarten, the Rileys, and Torres-Gil. Major longitudinal studies—such as the Panel Study of Income Dynamics (PSID) and the Health and Retirement Study (HRS), conducted at the Institute for Social Research, University of Michigan—are quite relevant to discussions about societal aging. Even though the original design of the PSID in 1968 was not aimed at issues of aging, its key design features (following households longitudinally and following all branches from households) provide an unrivaled source of data for life-course and intergenerational behavior. For example, this design allows researchers to measure both income and wealth accumulation over the life cycle and the intergenerational transmission of income and wealth and to test theories of their determinants.

The Health and Retirement Study grew out of a set of discussions with the research community initiated by the National Institute on Aging beginning in the 1980s. Researchers discussed the need to develop a data base that could be used to study the health, economics, and demography of aging as the baby boomers entered retirement during the next century (Juster and Suzman 1995). The HRS, which originally focused on a longitudinal study of a preretirement cohort of 51–61-year-olds in 1992, was joined in 1993 by the AHEAD study, which followed a cohort of persons aged 70 and over (Soldo et al. 1997). In 1998, the HRS and AHEAD merged and added new cohorts to create a single longitudinal survey, which is cross-sectionally representative of the U.S. population over age 50 (Willis 1999). This sample will be followed longitudinally every two years, and a new cohort representing the leading edge of the baby boomers will be added in 2004.

The Health and Retirement Study provides detailed measures of physical and mental health, economic status, family structure and transfers, and participation in public programs such as Social Security and Medicare. Other study advantages include linked administrative data from Social Security earnings and benefit histories, Medicare linkages, and linkages to employer pension-plan information. The HRS collects data that cuts across domains that have previously been the specialties of individual disciplines. For this reason, the HRS is beginning to support new types of interdisciplinary research in aging, much of which is highly relevant to policy.

Once again, however, certain caveats must be issued. Politics on the Potomac remains incremental in scope. Commissions on Social Security financing rarely tackle health-care reforms. Despite the clamor for needs-based measures, many U.S., state-level, and corporate employment and welfare programs still use age as an eligibility criterion.

Conclusion: Why Has It Been So Difficult to Think in Terms of Societal Aging?

Since the Great Depression, scholars have been identifying essential elements for formulating theories of societal aging. Most experts agree that extensions in human longevity and alterations in the nation's population structure will affect American values and institutional life. Conversely, few U.S. lawmakers would scrap Social Security or any program that satisfied the needs of millions of voters. Yet conversations about societal aging remain more advanced among academics and policymakers in western Europe and the Pacific Basin than in North America. Let me suggest six reasons why this is so.

1. *There remains a gap between basic and applied research.* "Contemporary social science contains within itself two types of orientation that divide it into two blocks of workers: the scholars and the technicians," observed Robert S. Lynd in *Knowledge for What?* (1939, 1). Both camps in the 1930s acknowledged the relevance of each other's work in making sense of present-day problems and in exploring the unknown. Yet two research cultures still exist today. Most scholars belong to academic tribes with their own disciplinary conventions. Those who serve power must deliver pertinent facts in a timely manner mindful of political exigencies. "Important problems tend to fall into oblivion between the two groups of workers; and the strains generated by current institutional breakdowns are prompting sharp and preemptory scrutiny of the roles and adequacy of social sciences" (1). The graying of America is simply too *big* a problem to be handled in most seminars and legislative corridors.

2. *Reductionist analyses count for more than bold syntheses in the academy.* Scholarly advancement basically hinges on producing and presenting ideas that fit colleagues' expectations. Most researchers try to build on existing paradigms. Universities and funding agencies justify support for interdisciplinary programs by calling them antidotes to the allegedly stultifying effects of narrow disciplinarity. Yet few social scientists, after satisfying their peers, have the energy or inclination to commit the time and investment to work with investigators trained in different ways to tackle problems that require multiple perspectives and a combination of methods to explicate. This is particularly true in gerontology, where much of the interest in societal aging has arisen. The field is "a land of many islands of data with few bridges between them," observes James Birren, a psychologist who *has* collaborated effectively with bench scientists and humanists. "We do not have an adequate scientific language or theory

to address the interactions of the experientially organized functions with the biologically oriented ones . . . We are nowhere near understanding the full significance of the consequences of learning and practice in relation to age" (1989, 144–45).

3. *The politics of interest-group liberalism rarely pays more than lip service to the big picture.*   A two-party system has long dominated American political history, but factions, voluntary associations, and charismatic leaders have also played critical roles in shaping the national agenda. So have interest groups, especially in the twentieth century. The late Jack Walker reported that two-thirds of the national citizen sector organizations on the scene in the mid-1980s were founded since Dr. King's march on Washington. Their aims and ecology vary greatly. Some groups advance professional careers; others respond to threats to recent or anticipated gains in a "mobilization-countermobiliza-tion cycle"; still others advocate on behalf of their clients, to protect benefits or to demand more; still others lobby for environmental or economic issues that transcend any demographic constituency (Walker 1991, 55). Interest groups proliferate. As markets become more refined, there is less chance that an issue such as the possible consequences of longevity on major institutions will electrify voters.

4. *Generational warfare attracts more attention than the ties that bind.* Commentators since Aristotle have been highlighting the contrast between youth and age. Fights between fathers and sons, daughters and mothers fill court dockets and sell books. A debate over "generational equity" made headlines in the United States during the 1980s. For some conservative groups, pandering to the anxieties of baby boomers worried about their inheritance and their parents' health provided a way to attack entitlement programs. The children of the Great Depression, who had fought on two fronts and then paid all those bills, suddenly were denounced as "greedy geezers." Generational rifts became a surrogate for class, long a taboo topic in the United States. But not for long. Americans for Generational Equity collapsed. Nor was there compelling evidence to corroborate the proposition that intergenerational differences had displaced the economic and cultural wellsprings for cross-generational solidarity (Bengtson and Achenbaum 1993). The issue fizzled, but suspicions remained. Can lawmakers reform Medicare? Would Generation X collect its rightful Social Security? Missing in the rhetoric was a central theme of those concerned with societal aging: the status quo could not be sustained, but would the future be worse? Did opportunity or disaster lie ahead?

5. *America can no longer rely on its allies to take the lead in thinking through the consequences of societal aging.*   Demographically, the United States has never had the oldest population. France took pride of place earlier in the century, followed in turn by Scandinavian countries. Now Japan is the most longevous nation. Americans in the past, moreover, had the luxury of seeing

how workers' compensation, unemployment insurance, social security, child-care credits, and health-care measures played out in Europe before developing their own distinctive set of policy initiatives. Yet according to Daniel Patrick Moynihan, the Senate's leading social scientist, "there is no industrial democracy with as much social dysfunction as the United States today. . . . We are at the point of knowing a fair amount about what we don't know. The past quarter-century has been on the whole productive in this regard. On the other hand, our social situation is considerably worse" (1996, 222, 225). In U.S. policy-making, unlike that of our peers, race remains the wild card. Morbidity and mortality rates among African Americans differ from whites. Recent influxes of Muslims, southeast Asians, and Spanish-speaking peoples with distinctive customs have made this pluralist nation more heterogeneous than ever before in terms of values and infrastructures. The trajectories of population aging, never monolithic historical vectors, are harder than ever to project.

6. *Societal aging requires a steady, patient gaze at a future in which the young will not be the only actors worth watching.*   Although the United States is the world's oldest republic, as a nation we remain obsessed with youth. "She starts old, old, wrinkled and writhing in an old skin," noted D. H. Lawrence. "And there is a gradual sloughing of the old skin, towards a new youth. It is a myth of America" (1923, 54). Obsolescent myths are harder to shed than skin. Regardless of age, most of us doubt that men and women over fifty can really renew us. Ageism is as pervasive as racism and sexism—perhaps this is why so few graduate students pursue topics in gerontology, and most legislative aides leave the Hill before they reach forty. It is hard to imagine our future selves living in a world inhabited by people whose joys and suffering we have not ourselves experienced. We fear that "mature" organizations will shape our destinies in ways that we cannot control. So we escape into nostalgia and science fiction, into genres that represent yesterdays and tomorrows that never really existed. That milieu is comforting, but its solace usually is short-lived.

Getting older, Art Linkletter warned us, is not for sissies. The prospect of society having to change basic institutions and values sounds grim—if only because few of us like to change the way things are unless (and until) it is absolutely necessary. Toffler's *Future Shock* no longer scares us. George Orwell's *Animal Farm*, Aldous Huxley's *Brave New World*, and Ayn Rand's *Atlas Shrugged*, great fun to read in college, lose their capacity to spark our imagination on dark nights in middle age. Even I dread academics who speculate about the future of aging. "The prophets of prolongevity taken pride in their ability to confront forbidding questions. Would society stagnate if death lost its sting? Would people avoid risk, devoting all their energies merely to staying alive? Would old people, still young in mind and body, refuse to make room for new arrivals? Would society become indifferent to the future?" Christopher Lasch wondered in *The Culture of Narcissism*. "Devoid of historical perspective, it has no way of recognizing the future when the future has become the here and now" (1978, 215–16). There are bound to be distressing elements associated with any social transformation. But history also indicates that human beings are remarkably adaptable, quite capable of realizing (for better and worse) future choices. So we need facts and policies *now* with which to build on what we have accomplished in order to create the sorts of pathways we imagine are within our collective reach.

NOTES

1. Carroll Wright's surveys of Massachusetts household incomes in the 1870s and Charles Booth's analyses *Pauperism and the Endowment of Old Age* and *The Aged Poor in England and Wales,* both published two decades later, became models for analysts. The U.S. Bureau of Labor and more than a dozen state legislatures between 1910 and 1940 gauged studies of the causes and extent of old-age dependency (see Achenbaum 1978; DeBow 1854; Gratton 1986; and Haber 1983).

2. Federal officials demonstrated their intent to promote infant and maternal health through the Sheppard-Towner Act (1921); the Smith-Hughes Act (1917) spurred vocational education. Veterans' benefits, which were increasingly generous after the 1880s, protected many middle-aged men and their dependents. In the years before World War I, debates over workers' compensation moved from the state house to the Capitol (Berkowitz and McQuaid 1988; Skocpol 1992).

3. More imaginative was that body's "Investing in America's Families: The Common Bond of Generations" (1986), though its emphasis on maintaining equity across age lines did not lead to a broader discussion of the ramifications of societal aging in meting out justice.

REFERENCES

Achenbaum, W. Andrew. 1978. *Old age in the new land: The American experience since 1790.* Baltimore: Johns Hopkins University Press.
———. 1986. *Social Security: Visions and revisions.* New York: Cambridge University Press.
———. 1988. The place of researchers in Social Security policy making. *Journal of Aging Studies* 2:301–10.
———. 1991. The state of the handbooks, 1990. *Gerontologist* 31:131–33.
Aging Society Project. 1984. *Human resource implications of an aging work force.* New York: Carnegie Corporation and Manpower Demonstration Research Corporation.
Altmeyer, Arthur J. 1942. The desirability of expanding the social insurance program now. *Social Security Bulletin* 5 (November): 3–8.

American Association of Retired Persons and Resources for the Future. 1993. *Aging of the U.S. population.* Washington, D.C.: AARP.

American Council of Life Insurance, et al. 1985. *The prime life generation.* New York: American Council of Life Insurance.

Bass, Scott A. 1994. *Productive aging and the role of older people in Japan: New approaches for the United States.* New York: Japan Society.

Bengtson, Vern L., and W. Andrew Achenbaum, eds. 1993. *The changing contract across generations.* New York: Aldine de Gruyter.

Berkowitz, Edward, and Kim McQuaid. 1988. *Creating the welfare state.* New York: Praeger.

Birren, James E. 1989. My perspectives on research on aging. In *The course of later life,* ed. Vern L. Bengtson and K. Warner Schaie, 135–50. New York: Springer.

Brown, J. Douglas. 1977. *Essays on Social Security.* Including his foreword to the *Final report of the advisory council on Social Security,* December 10, 1938. Princeton: Industrial Relations Section.

Brown, Norton. 1950. Orientation. In *The social and biological challenge of our aging population,* 3–6. New York: Columbia University Press.

Cassel, Christine K., and Bernice L. Neugarten. 1990. The goals of medicine in an aging society. In *"Too old" for health care?* ed. Robert H. Binstock and Stephen G. Post. Glenview: Scott Foresman.

Cohen, Wilbur J. 1980. Economic well-being and income distribution. In *The American economy in transition,* ed. Martin Feldstein, 486–93. Chicago: National Bureau of Economic Research.

Committee on Economic Security. 1935. *Report of the Committee on Economic Security.* Reprinted in a 50th anniversary edition by Alan Pifer and Forrest Chisman for the National Conference on Social Welfare, Washington, D.C.

Cottrell, Leonard. 1960. The technological and societal basis of aging. In *Handbook of social gerontology,* ed. Clark Tibbitts, 92–119. Chicago: University of Chicago Press.

Cowdry, Edmund, ed. 1939. *Problems of ageing.* Baltimore, Md.: Williams and Wilkins.

Cowgill, Donald. 1974. The aging of populations and societies. *Annals of the American Academy of Political and Social Science* 415:1–18.

DeBow, J. B. D. 1854. *Statistical view of the United States . . . being a compendium of the seventh census.* Washington, D.C.: A. O. P. Anderson.

Douglas, Paul H. 1936. *Social Security in the United States.* New York: McGraw-Hill.

Economic Council. 1983. *Japan in the year 2000.* Tokyo: Japan Times, Ltd.

Epstein, Abraham. 1929. Facing old age. *Commonweal* 11:163.

Falkingham, Jane. 1987. Britain's ageing population: The engine behind increased dependency? London: London School of Economics.

Friedland, Robert. 1998. Changes at the National Academy on Aging. Newsletter.

Galdston, Iago, M.D. 1950. Introduction. In *The social and biological challenge of our aging population.* New York: Columbia University Press.

Gerontological Society of America. 1989. *Higher education and an aging society.* Washington, D.C.: GSA.

Gratton, Brian. 1986. *Urban elders.* Philadelphia: Temple University Press.

Haber, Carole. 1983. *Beyond sixty-five.* New York: Cambridge University Press.

Hauser, Philip M., and Ethel Shanas. 1952. Trends in the ageing population. In *Cowdry's problems of ageing,* 3d ed., ed. Albert I. Lansing, 965–92. Baltimore, Md.: Williams and Wilkins.

Hauser, Philip M., and Raul Vargas. 1960. Population structure and trends. In *Aging in Western societies,* ed. Ernest W. Burgess, 29–53. Chicago: University of Chicago Press.

Helton, Roy. 1939. A nation of elders in the making. *Harper's* 259:450–51.

Hoover, Herbert. 1933. Foreword. In *Recent social trends,* by the President's Research Committee on Social Trends. New York: McGraw-Hill.

Institute of Gerontology, University of Michigan. 1981. *The older worker in an aging society.* Ann Arbor: Institute of Gerontology.

Johnson, Paul. 1987. The structured dependency of the elderly: A critical note. London: Centre for Economic Policy Research.

Judd, Charles H. 1933. Education. In *Recent social trends,* by the President's Research Committee on Social Trends, 325–81. New York: McGraw-Hill.

Juster, F. T., and Richard Suzman. 1995. An overview of the Health and Retirement Study. *Journal of Human Resources* 30 (Suppl.): S7-S56.

Kendig, Hal L., and John McCallum, eds. 1990. *Grey policy: Australian policies for an ageing society.* North Sydney: Allen and Unwin.

Kennedy, Paul. 1987. *The rise and fall of the great powers.* New York: Random House.

Lasch, Christopher. 1978. *The culture of narcissism.* New York: W. W. Norton

Lawrence, D. H. 1923. *Studies in classic American literature.* New York: Viking.

Lynd, Robert S. 1939. *Knowledge for what?* Princeton: Princeton University Press.

Moody, Harry R., ed. 1992. Revisioning the aging society. *In Depth* 2.

Moynihan, Daniel Patrick. 1996. *Miles to go: A personal history of social policy.* Cambridge: Harvard University Press.

Neugarten, Bernice L. 1974. Age groups in American society and the rise of the young old. *Annals of the American Academy of Political and Social Science* 415:187–98.

Neugarten, Bernice L., and Robert J. Havighurst, eds. 1976. *Social policy, social ethics, and the aging society.* Washington, D.C.: Government Printing Office.

———. 1977. *Extending the human life span: Social policy and social ethics.* Washington, D.C.: Government Printing Office.

Pifer, Alan, and Lydia Bronte, eds. 1986. The aging society. *Daedalus* 115. Also published as Our aging society. New York: W. W. Norton.

Pifer, Alan, and Forrest Chisman, eds. 1985. *The report of the Committee of Economic Security of 1935,* 50th anniversary edition. Washington, D.C.: National Conference on Social Welfare.

President's Commission on a National Agenda for the Eighties. 1980. *A national agenda for the eighties.* Washington, D.C.

Riley, Matilda White, and John W. Riley Jr. 1994. Structural lag: Past and present. In *Age and structural lag,* ed. Matilda White Riley, Robert L. Kahn, and Anne Foner, 15–36. New York: Wiley-Interscience.

Salomen, Michel. 1983. *Future life.* New York: Macmillan.

Schlitz, Michael. 1970. *Public attitudes toward Social Security, 1935–1965.* Research Report 33. Washington, D.C.: Department of Health, Education and Welfare.

Scott, Peter, and Paul Johnson. 1988. The economic consequences of population ageing in advanced societies. London: Centre for Economic Policy Research.

Selby, Philip, and Mal Schecter. 1982. *Aging 2000.* Lancaster: MTP Press.

Skocpol, Theda. 1992. *Protecting soldiers and mothers.* Cambridge: Harvard University Press.

Social Security Act. 1935. 74th Congress, H.R. 7260.

Soldo, B. J., M. D. Hurd, W. L. Rodgers, and R. B. Wallace. 1997. Asset and health dynamics among the oldest old: An overview of the AHEAD study. *Journal of Gerontology: Social Sciences* (Special Issue) 52B:2–20.

Sydenstricker, Edgar. 1933. The vitality of the American people. In *Recent social trends,* by the President's Research Committee on Social Trends, 602–60. New York: McGraw-Hill.

Thompson, Warren S., and P. K. Whelpton. 1930. A nation of elders in the making. *American Mercury* 19:394–95.

———. 1933. Population. In *Recent social trends,* by the President's Research Committee on Social Trends, 1–58. New York: McGraw-Hill.

Thomson, David. 1991. *Selfish generations?* Wellington: Bridget Williams Books.

Tibbitts, Clark, ed. 1960. *Handbook of social gerontology.* Chicago: University of Chicago Press.

Torres-Gil, Fernando. 1992. *The new aging.* Westport, Conn.: Auburn House.

U.S. House of Representatives, Select Committee on Aging. 1986. Aging veterans in an aging society: Public policy at a crossroads. Washington, D.C.: Government Printing Office.

———. 1988. Demographic characteristics of the older Hispanic population. Washington, D.C.: Government Printing Office.

U.S. Senate, Special Committee on Aging. 1981. Social Security in Europe: The impact of an aging population. Washington, D.C.: Government Printing Office.

———. 1986. Investing in America's families: The common bond of generations. Washington, D.C.: Government Printing Office.

Walker, Jack L., Jr. 1991. *Mobilizing interest groups in America: Patrons, professions, and social movements.* Ann Arbor: University of Michigan Press.

Willis, R. J. 1999. Theory confronts data: How the HRS is shaped by the economics of aging and how the economics of aging will be shaped by the HRS. *Labour Economics* 6 (2): 119–45.

CHAPTER 6

Welfare Reform Policy from Nixon to Clinton: What Role for Social Science?

Sheldon Danziger

Social scientists have conducted hundreds of empirical studies related to various aspects of welfare policies in the thirty-five years since the War on Poverty was declared. Major findings of this research and their policy implications were virtually ignored, however, in the welfare reform debates leading up to President Clinton's signing of the Personal Responsibility and Work Opportunity Reconciliation Act of 1996 (the PRWORA). This act, the most significant welfare reform since the 1930s, ended the entitlement to cash assistance and dramatically changed the nature of the social safety net. The welfare program the act created—the Temporary Assistance to Needy Families Program (TANF)—implicitly assumes that almost everyone who is willing to search for a job will get hired and be able to attain self-sufficiency before the new time limit on the receipt of cash assistance becomes effective.

This assumption ignores numerous studies that document how employer demand for less-skilled workers has declined over the past quarter century (e.g., Freeman and Gottschalk 1998; Levy and Murnane 1992). Policymakers should have known that declines in employer demand make it very difficult for many welfare recipients to get a job and earn enough to support their families without continuing supplementation from welfare or other forms of government assistance.

Whereas politicians ignored available research on changes in labor demand for less-skilled workers, social scientists should be faulted for not having pursued research on an important aspect of labor supply—the labor market capabilities of welfare recipients. For the most part, little research prior to the mid-1990s focused on the extent to which welfare recipients have an array of personal barriers—for example, physical and mental health, substance abuse, and domestic violence problems—that make their labor market prospects even more problematic than those of other less-skilled workers.

Welfare reform was "put into play" by candidate Clinton's 1992 promise to "end welfare as we know it." This promise drew on social science research, especially analyses by the Michigan Panel Study of Income Dynamics (Duncan et al. 1984; Bane and Ellwood 1986) and evaluations of randomized welfare-to-work demonstrations (Gueron, this vol.; Gueron and Pauly 1991). These analyses and evaluations had been widely discussed during the welfare debates of the late 1980s (Baum 1991; Haskins 1991; Wiseman 1991), and they influenced the development of the president's own 1994 welfare reform proposal (Ellwood 1987, 1988). Yet the rejection of the Clinton administration proposal and the debates that culminated in the 1996 act are notable for their inattention to social science findings that conflicted with the primary goal of the act's proponents—reducing the welfare caseload.

In the first section, I review the evolution of welfare reform proposals from the War on Poverty through President Nixon's Family Assistance Plan, President Carter's Program for Better Jobs and Income, the workfare demonstration projects encouraged by the Omnibus Budget Reconciliation Act of 1981, the Family Support Act of 1988, and the 1996 PRWORA. Over this quarter century, expectations for work on the part of single mothers steadily increased, whereas support for their entitlement to cash assistance and the inflation-adjusted value of welfare benefits steadily declined. At the same time, as I discuss in the second section, the labor market prospects of less-skilled workers were declining. The third section reviews recent evidence comparing welfare recipients to nonrecipients across a range of labor market experiences and personal attributes, and makes the case that recipients have employment and earnings prospects that are inferior to those of the typical less-skilled worker. The essay concludes that, because of declining employer demand for less-skilled workers in general and because of the personal and labor market disadvantages of long-term welfare recipients in particular, even though the 1996 welfare reform has contributed to dramatic declines in the welfare caseload, it has also contributed to increased economic hardship for some former recipients.

A Brief History of Welfare Reform Policy

Welfare reform proposals in the late 1960s sought to reduce poverty by extending welfare eligibility and raising benefit levels, even though these provisions would have increased total welfare spending. Later, as public dissatisfaction with rising welfare rolls and spending increased, greater attention was paid to constraining budgetary costs and to promoting work incentives, work opportunities, and work requirements, all of which came to be applied to mothers with children at increasingly younger ages. Research techniques have become more sophisticated since the 1960s and research findings have accumulated as social scientists carried out the negative income tax experiments in the 1970s and the welfare-to-work demonstrations and analyses of panel data on welfare spells in the 1980s and 1990s. From this research emerged a consensus that any shift from a cash-based to a work-based safety net was feasible but would be difficult (Gueron, this vol.; Bane and Ellwood 1994).

In a brief interlude following passage of the Family Support Act of 1988, expectations for the personal responsibilities of recipients and the mutual responsibilities of government were both increased. Although the Family Support Act drew heavily on research evidence and was passed with strong bipartisan support, its lessons were set aside when President Clinton made further welfare reform one of his most visible campaign priorities. In the mid-1990s, Congress and President Clinton followed a different path—one that neglected much of what social scientists had documented. They increased expectations of personal responsibility on the part of recipients even further and diminished government's responsibility for the economic well-being of the poor.

In late 2000, four years after passage of PRWORA, the entitlement to cash assistance has ended, and welfare rolls have declined more dramatically than almost any analyst had predicted when the act was passed. This is due, in part, to the rapid growth of the economy and, in part, to the states' aggressive pursuit of caseload-reduction strategies (Danziger 1999b). However, an effective work-based safety net is not yet in place—there is no guarantee that a welfare recipient or former recipient who seeks work but cannot find a job will receive any cash assistance or any opportunity to work in return for assistance.

I now turn to discussion of the major welfare reform proposals of the last quarter century. I focus on the rise and fall of poverty reduction as a welfare reform goal and then show how "ending welfare as we know it" came to focus primarily on the goal of caseload reduction.

The War on Poverty

War on Poverty was declared by President Johnson in 1964. The strategy proposed included a broad range of policy instruments but did not include either a public jobs program or an increase in cash welfare (except for the aged and disabled), although these were advocated by several policymakers at the time. Little attention was paid to the issues of welfare dependency or public-sector jobs of last resort because the president's economic advisers thought that if stable economic growth could be maintained, as it had been since the end of World War II, government programs and policies could eliminate income poverty if sufficient resources were devoted to the task.

The most important components of the initial War on Poverty proposals emphasized labor-supply policies to raise the low labor-market productivity of the poor (Lampman 1959, 1971; U.S. Council of Economic Advisors 1964).

Poverty was high, according to the administration, because the poor did not work enough or because their skills were insufficient even if they worked hard. Thus, employment and training programs were established or expanded to enhance individual skills, especially for young people, through classroom education and on-the-job training. Graduates were given job search assistance and launched into the labor market with little concern about the public provision of postprogram jobs, since unemployment rates were at historically low levels, even for less-skilled workers.

Little attention was focused on welfare dependency during this period because the total caseload was quite small, about 4 million recipients in the mid-1960s. However, in the aftermath of program liberalizations fostered by the War on Poverty, caseloads increased to about 6 million by 1969, leading to proposals for welfare reform.

The Family Assistance Plan

In 1969, President Nixon proposed the Family Assistance Plan (FAP) as a replacement for the Aid to Families with Dependent Children Program (AFDC) (Burke and Burke 1974). FAP included a national minimum welfare benefit coupled with a work requirement. However, the president stated, "a welfare mother with pre-school children should not face benefit reductions if she decides to stay home. It is not our intent that mothers of pre-school children must accept work" (Nixon 1969). The president's view was consistent with both the original goal of AFDC and the conventional wisdom of the 1960s that mothers of young children should stay home and care for them. FAP and other contemporary negative income tax (NIT) or guaranteed income plans (Lampman 1965; Tobin 1966) emphasized the extension of welfare to two-parent families, the establishment of a national minimum welfare benefit, the reduction of work disincentives arising from AFDC's high marginal tax rate on earnings, and the decoupling of cash assistance and social services.[1] The view that welfare recipients needed assistance from social workers was replaced by the view that their primary needs were economic.

Welfare reform continued as a focus of federal policy debates after the legislative defeat of FAP. Even though a cash NIT for all poor persons never passed, the Food Stamp program evolved into one—by the mid-1970s it provided a national benefit in food coupons that varied by family size, regardless of state of residence or living arrangements or marital status. The income maintenance system continued to expand between the late 1960s and the mid-1970s as new programs were introduced, benefit levels were increased, and eligibility requirements were liberalized. The number of AFDC recipients increased from about 6 million to 11 million, and the number of food stamp recipients, from about 1 million to 19 million over this period. As higher cash and in-kind benefits became available to a larger percentage of poor people, the work disincentives and high budgetary costs of welfare programs were increasingly challenged. The public and policymakers (but not most social researchers) came to view increased welfare recipiency as evidence that the programs were subsidizing dependency and encouraging idleness (Anderson 1978; Murray 1984).

Because income maintenance policies cannot both increase work effort and reduce the number of people receiving welfare, renewed attention was focused on raising the employment and earnings of the poor via labor market policies. In addition, higher unemployment rates—particularly those of youth, women, and minorities—brought on by recession in the early 1970s shifted concerns from augmenting the labor market skills of the disadvantaged to increasing their employment opportunities.

The first public service employment (PSE) program since the Great Depression was enacted as part of the Emergency Employment Act in 1971, primarily as a countercyclical device to fund about 100,000 jobs with state and local governments. PSE slots were increased by the Comprehensive Employment and Training Act of 1973 (CETA) and became the largest component of the employment and training budget at that time. Amendments to this act in 1976 targeted a greater percentage of the PSE jobs to the disadvantaged, particularly the long-term unemployed and welfare recipients. Even though concerns about structural unemployment increased, relatively few AFDC recipients participated in CETA, since it was still considered appropriate for the mothers of young children to remain at home and care for them. Nonetheless, CETA represents the most extensive recent public response to inadequate labor demand for the disadvantaged. In 1978 there were more than 750,000 PSE participants (Mirengoff et al. 1980).

The Program for Better Jobs and Income

The negative income tax developments in income maintenance policy and the PSE jobs emphasis in employment and training policy were integrated in President Carter's 1977 proposal, the Program for Better Jobs and Income (PBJI) (Lynn and Whitman 1981). PBJI proposed a universal NIT with one income guarantee for those not expected to work and a lower income guarantee for those expected to work. Because those expected to work would also have been eligible for a PSE job of last resort, PBJI represents the first welfare reform proposal to guarantee jobs for recipients.

Whereas the welfare reform debates of the 1990s emphasized time-limiting welfare benefits and work requirements, PBJI would have both expanded the welfare rolls and provided work opportunities for recipients who could not find an employer who would hire them. It would have created up to 1.4 million minimum-wage public service jobs at an estimated cost of $8.8 billion in 1980 (about $17 billion in 1998 dollars). As was the case with Nixon's FAP a decade earlier, a single mother with a child of age six or younger would have been exempted from the work requirement. Those whose youngest child was between the ages of seven and fourteen would have been expected to work part-time; those whose youngest child was over age fourteen would have been expected to work full-time.

By providing jobs of last resort and supplementing low earnings, PBJI would have raised the family income of welfare recipients working at low wages, regardless of family composition or state of residence and, in many cases, would have taken them out of poverty. PBJI is thus a precursor to proposals formally articulated in the late 1980s, "to make work pay." Of course, the plan would have increased total federal welfare spending substantially, which was a key reason for its failure to become law. The Congressional Budget Office estimated a cost increase for all of PBJI's provisions of $14 billion for 1982 (about $24 billion in 1998 dollars).

PBJI also provides an important benchmark against which subsequent welfare reform developments can be evaluated because it called attention to insufficient employer demand for less-skilled workers. It recognized that some welfare recipients would want to work but would not be able to find a regular job in the private or public sectors, and that a minimum wage job of last resort would be needed to address their involuntary unemployment and provide an alternative to welfare receipt. As I suggest below, the 1996 act neglected the demand side of the labor market when it ended the entitlement to cash assistance without implementing any work opportunity, such as an entitlement to work in exchange for welfare benefits. Second, PBJI's welfare benefit would have supplemented wages for families with low earnings, addressing the issue of falling real wages for the less skilled, a trend that was just then emerging.[2]

PBJI also marked the first time that welfare policy would have imposed a sanction on a family head who was expected to work but refused to do so. The welfare benefit for such a family would have been reduced to about one-half of that of a similar family where the head was not expected to work. For example, a single mother of three children, the youngest of whom was age six, would have received $4,200 per year in 1980. In 1981 she would have been expected to work part-time because her youngest child had turned seven. If she did not find a part-time job on her own or refused the part-time job of last resort offered by PBJI, she would have lost her share of the family's welfare benefit—the family would have received $2,300, representing benefits only for the children. As discussed below, after PRWORA, partial sanctions such as this one, and full-family sanctions, which terminate all benefits when a family head does not comply with work requirements, became federal mandates.[3]

From the War on Poverty through PBJI and into the early 1980s, many social scientists, economists in particular, favored a cash negative income tax as an antipoverty and welfare reform strategy. An NIT, such as FAP or PBJI, provides recipients greater freedom of choice than in-kind transfers, such as food stamps; does not interfere directly in labor markets; and has relatively modest administrative costs and work disincentives compared to AFDC. Congress and the public never shared economists' enthusiasm, especially in light of the research results of the negative income tax experiments (Watts and Rees 1977). Whereas many NIT proponents considered the documented negative work and family effects of the experiments to be quite modest, critics used them to generate further dissatisfaction with such plans (e.g., Anderson 1978).

Carter's PBJI offered a combination of a cash NIT (for those not expected to work) with a work requirement/work opportunity (for those expected to work). Like FAP, it fared better with policy analysts than with policymakers. Its failure, due in large part to its higher budgetary costs, marked the end of the era of expansive welfare reform proposals. What followed was an era of welfare retrenchment.

The Reagan Years

The Reagan presidency marked a profound change in welfare policy because the administration was "rare if not unique in American politics—truly an ideological one" (Glazer 1984). It sought to roll back the welfare system that had expanded so much since the War on Poverty. Reducing welfare caseloads replaced poverty reduction as the primary goal of welfare reform. Reducing spending replaced controlling costs as a priority; the emphasis on work requirements intensified, replacing concern with a lack of work incentives and work opportunities.

Policies to aid the working poor were no longer seen as an integral part of welfare reform. Rather, the Reagan administration thought eligibility for welfare benefits had increased so much that many persons who were not "truly needy" were receiving benefits. Work effort, according to this view, was best promoted by strict work requirements (proposed by the president, but not enacted by Congress), not by work incentives.[4] The Reagan administration opposed what had been a key goal of both FAP and PBJI—simultaneous receipt of wages and welfare benefits. Rather, it proposed that welfare become a safety net, providing cash assistance only for those unable to secure jobs. Public employment was considered an unnecessary intrusion into the labor market, and CETA was abolished.

The Omnibus Budget Reconciliation Act of 1981 fostered these goals through several changes in benefit calculations and eligibility criteria. The "30 and a third rule," originally introduced as a work incentive in 1967, was eliminated. This rule allowed recipients to earn $30 per month before losing any benefits and then reduced benefits by $2 for every $3 earned beyond the first $30. After 1981, once a recipient had received welfare for four months, benefits were reduced by one dollar for every dollar earned. As a result, by early 1983 nearly 14 percent of all beneficiaries had been removed from the AFDC rolls.[5] OBRA's reforms actually contributed to increased public dissatisfaction with welfare because it removed most working recipients from the caseload. As a result, the percentage of welfare recipients who did not work increased. Non-work would become the key focus of welfare reform in the ensuing decade (Mead 1992).

Although real spending on and eligibility for cash welfare were cut back in the 1980s, spending on the working poor increased. The Earned Income Tax Credit (EITC), enacted in 1975, provides families of the working poor with a refundable income tax credit (i.e., the family receives a payment from the Internal Revenue Service if the credit due exceeds the income tax owed). The EITC raises the effective wage of low-income families, is available to both one- and two-parent families, and does not require them to apply for welfare. The maximum EITC for a poor family was $400 in 1975 and rose to $550 by 1986.

The 1986 Tax Reform Act increased the EITC so that by 1990 a low-income working parent received a maximum credit of $953. The number of families receiving credits increased from between 5 and 7.5 million families a year between 1975 and 1986 to more than 11 million by 1988.[6] Because the expanded EITC supplements low earnings, it became easier for policymakers to emphasize welfare reform policies that could place recipients into any job, rather than training them for "good jobs." If a nonworking recipient took a low-wage job, a substantial EITC could make work pay as much as a higher-wage job would have paid in the absence of an EITC. For example, by the mid-1990s, the income of a single mother with two children working half-time at the minimum wage plus her EITC exceeded welfare benefit levels in most states (Ellwood 1999).

The Family Support Act

The Family Support Act (FSA) of 1988 reflected a bipartisan consensus in which liberals achieved a broader safety net and conservatives achieved stronger work requirements (Baum 1991; Haskins 1991; Mead 1992). The act expanded the scope of the AFDC program for two-parent families, instituted transitional child care and Medicaid for recipients leaving welfare for work, and added funds and required states to establish programs to move greater numbers of welfare recipients into employment. Custodial and absent parents were required to take more responsibility for supporting their children. Custodial parents were required to participate in programs designed to increase their attachment to the labor force. A greater percentage of absent parents were required to pay more child support. The state was required to provide additional training and support services through a new training and education program for AFDC recipients—the Job Opportunities and Basic Skills Training Program (JOBS). The federal government was to provide modest additional matching funds (about $1 billion) to cover most of the additional costs of JOBS incurred by the states.

JOBS was based on the experiences of many states with the welfare-to-work demonstration programs that were undertaken in response to the Community Work Experience Programs enacted as part of OBRA 1981. The Manpower Demonstration Research Corporation (MDRC) evaluated many of these programs and found them modestly successful in reducing dependence on welfare and increasing earnings (Gueron, this vol.; Friedlander and Burtless 1995). For many liberals, who had opposed workfare prior to these evaluations, an important finding was the fact that many participants judged the programs fair and helpful in connecting them to the work force. The evaluations were promising enough that, by the late 1980s, support for moving welfare recipients into employment had become bipartisan and widespread among both policymakers and social scientists (Novak et al. 1987; Ellwood 1988).

Liberals and conservatives still disagreed on other goals of welfare-to-work programs. Liberals thought welfare reform should expand opportunities for welfare mothers to receive training and work experiences that would help them raise their families' living standards by working more and at higher wages. Conservatives emphasized work requirements, obligations welfare mothers owed in return for government support whether or not their families' incomes increased (Mead 1986, 1992).

Results from the MDRC evaluations satisfied each group. Gueron and Pauley (1991) showed that successful programs modestly reduced welfare dependence and encouraged some recipients to leave the welfare rolls.[7] The typical welfare-to-work program participant earned about 15 to 30 percent more during the first two years than the typical control group member. While these were substantial percentage gains, monthly earnings remained low on average, and most participants remained poor. Employment rates for participants and controls were about 34 and 30 percent, respectively, after two years. AFDC participation and state welfare spending also declined modestly. After three years, 39.2 percent of the participants and 42.6 percent of controls remained on welfare.

The Family Support Act incorporated many lessons from the MDRC demonstrations and sought to improve on the previous program results.[8] States were required to implement welfare-to-work programs, extend them to a greater proportion of the caseload, and offer a range of education, skills training, job placement, and support services for such items as child care and transportation. By the time of the 1996 welfare debate, however, support for state requirements to provide many services had diminished, as had support for the view that a mother should move from welfare to paid employment only if she could achieve a net improvement in her economic situation. This shift in attitudes was due, in part, to the fact that one of the most successful JOBS programs, in terms of getting recipients into employment (Riverside, California), implemented a "work first" program. Work First programs adopt the philosophy "that any job is a good job and that the best way to succeed in the labor market is to join it, developing work habits and skills on the job rather than in a classroom" (Brown 1997, 2). This reduces the need for states to provide funds for education, training, or expanded support services, and allows them to serve a greater percentage of recipients with a fixed budget.

The FSA took effect just as the economic expansion of the 1980s ended. State governments faced falling tax revenues and increasing costs in many social programs, especially Medicaid, and few were inclined to begin or expand major social initiatives. In addition, FSA had a long start-up period as states initially required few recipients to participate. This fiscal situation encouraged states to avoid experimenting with programs that involved increased expenditures in the initial years, even innovative ones that promised to save more money in future years.[9] When the welfare rolls jumped in the late 1980s and early 1990s from about 11 to about 14 million recipients, dissatisfaction with welfare again increased. Even though JOBS had not yet been fully implemented, it had come under enough criticism that candidate Clinton saw political gain in placing welfare reform at the top of his policy agenda.

JOBS also raised work expectations and provided sanctions for recipients who did not cooperate. It lowered the child's age at which a welfare recipient was expected to participate. Once her youngest child reached age three, she was required to participate for up to twenty hours per week; once that child reached age six, she could be required to participate for up to forty hours per week. Participating meant agreeing to a reasonable "employability plan" the state devised, as long as the state provided child care, transportation, and other work-related expenses. Any recipient who complied with JOBS requirements continued to receive welfare; any failing to comply without good cause could reduce the recipient's monthly grant to reflect a family with one fewer person (i.e., the type of partial sanction proposed by PBJI).

Time limits, which came to dominate the welfare reform debates of the 1990s, were not part of the Family Support Act. Recipients could enter AFDC, enroll in JOBS, find a job, lose that job, return to the rolls, and re-enroll in JOBS. JOBS reflected a commitment to mutual responsibility: recipients were required to exercise personal responsibility and take advantage of education, training, and work opportunities that the government had the responsibility to provide. If the state did not appropriate sufficient funds to provide a JOBS slot (and many states did not), the recipient was not sanctioned for the state's failure. Within a few years, however, personal responsibility would take center stage, and such requirements on the states would be greatly reduced.

Welfare as We Have Come to Know It

PRWORA replaced AFDC with Temporary Assistance for Needy Families (TANF) and ended the entitlement to cash assistance. Each state can now decide which families to assist, subject only to a requirement that they receive "fair and equitable treatment." PRWORA also reduced the total amount of spending required from the federal and state governments. The federal contribution changed from a matching grant to a block grant that is essentially capped for each state at its FY1994 spending level. Increased welfare costs associated with population growth or economic downturns or inflation will be borne by the states or else by the poor. Moreover, states now are required only to expend 75 percent of their 1994 level of expenditures on AFDC, JOBS, child care, and emergency assistance. Any state could, for example, impose a 25 percent cut in welfare benefits without any loss of federal funds, and it could freeze expenditures at 75 percent of the 1994 level for the foreseeable future.[10]

States that have both the funds and the inclination can choose to provide an even more supportive safety net than existed before. Each state can pursue whatever kind of reform it chooses, including mutual responsibility reforms that would increase the state's commitment to help recipients find jobs. In practice, however, most states have worked harder to cut welfare caseloads than they have to provide work opportunities and services to current recipients or those who have left the rolls, including those who have been unable to find work.

The centerpiece of the new reform is its time limit—states may not use federal block grant funds to provide more than a cumulative lifetime total of sixty months of cash assistance to any welfare recipient, no matter how willing she might be to work for her benefits, and they have the option to set shorter time limits. States can grant exceptions to the lifetime limit and continue to use federal funds for up to 20 percent of the caseload. As discussed below, however, given declining employer demand for less-skilled workers, and given the labor market capabilities of recipients, more than 20 percent of the current caseload is likely to have great difficulty leaving welfare for work before reaching the time limit.

The extent of work expectations has also been increased. Single-parent recipients with no children under age one will be expected to work at least thirty hours per week by FY2002 in order to maintain eligibility for cash assistance. States can require participation in work or work-related activities regardless of the age of the youngest child. Whereas President Nixon called for work exemptions for mothers of children under age six, some states now exempt a mother for only thirteen weeks following childbirth.

It is ironic that the intellectual foundations of PRWORA emerged from research that sought to reduce both poverty and welfare dependency. Bane and Ellwood's (1986) analyses of longitudinal data, from the Panel Study of Income Dynamics (PSID) conducted by the Institute for Social Research, University of Michigan, challenged earlier PSID studies. For example, Duncan et al. (1984) emphasized that during a ten-year time span as much as a quarter of the total population used welfare at least once. They concluded that "dependency is the exception rather than the rule" because only about 2 percent of persons were persistently dependent on welfare during the late 1960s and 1970s (91). Ellwood and Bane, using a more sophisticated methodology, showed that even though many people used AFDC at some point in their lives, a small percentage of new entrants, comprising almost half of the caseload at any point in time, was in the midst of a welfare spell lasting ten or more years.

These findings led Ellwood to propose a "divide and conquer" strategy for welfare recipients (Ellwood 1987). Time-limiting AFDC benefits could provide a way to distinguish between the needs of short-term and long-term recipients. A two-year or three-year time limit would have little effect on the larger number of short-term recipients who used welfare at some point in their lives—their welfare spells were already shorter than the time limit, and they did not need extensive services to get them into jobs. Time limits were intended to target long-term welfare recipients and provide more extensive services to reduce the length of their welfare spells.

Garfinkel and McLanahan's (1986) discussion of how AFDC might be changed from a cash-relief to a work-relief program is the first reference (of which I am aware) to a time limit for cash assistance. "The first step would be to limit the amount of time that the heads of AFDC families could receive cash benefits without either working or progressing satisfactorily in an education or training program" (185).

Their thought experiment became a central proposal in Ellwood's widely cited *Poor Support: Poverty and the American Family* (1988), which recommended converting welfare into a transitional system. Cash support would be provided for a limited period of time; when this limit was reached, a recipient would be expected to earn wages in a regular job or in a work opportunity program. Low wages would be supplemented by expanded tax credits, access to subsidized child care and health insurance, and guaranteed child support. Ellwood's proposal captured the attention of candidate Clinton and provided the basis for the campaign promise to "end welfare as we know it." Once elected, Clinton appointed Ellwood and Bane as two of the three cochairs of his Welfare Reform Task Force.[11]

Ellwood elaborated his proposal in "Reducing Poverty by Replacing Welfare" (Bane and Ellwood 1994, chap. 5), written just before he joined the Clinton administration.

But if we had an effective child support enforcement and insurance system, if we ensured that people got medical protection, if we made work pay, there would be far less need for welfare. Single parents could realistically support themselves at the poverty line if they were willing to work half time, even at a job paying little more than the minimum wage. If they were willing to work full-time, they could move well above the poverty line . . .

If people can realistically support themselves, then the notion of a time-limited, transitional assistance program for both single-parent and two-parent families makes sense. A rich set of training and support services ought to be included as part of the benefits. But the cash program would be of limited duration . . .

The duration of assistance might be allowed to vary with the age of the youngest child. Generally it might last eighteen months to three years, depending on how old the youngest child is. But the key is that this assistance would be *transitional*. One could not requalify for much more transitional assistance by having another baby or by claiming that no jobs were available . . .

When benefits were used up, one would have to work for some period to requalify for more. Many support services—certainly child care and some training—might continue past the transitional period, but cash benefits would end. After benefits ran out, the only alternative for support would be to supplement child support with work.

. . . If government is not willing to provide cash support forever, it must provide full- or part-time jobs for those who exhaust transitional support. (157–58)

In hindsight, Ellwood and most social scientists (including me) who supported this plan to "make work pay, and end welfare as we know it" should have been more concerned about how it was likely to be scaled back by the political process. It was obvious to analysts that the plan, which was based on social science research including the MDRC evaluations, would have cost a substantial amount more than the programs it would have replaced or modified, probably an additional $25 billion per year. Analysts should have recalled that previous ambitious welfare reform plans, like FAP and PBJI, had not fared well in Congress. Carter's PBJI, which, like Ellwood's Plan, emphasized both poverty reductions and work opportunities of last resort, was defeated without leaving any public policy legacy, in part because of its added costs and in part because it also would have greatly expanded the scope of the welfare system.

Nixon's Family Assistance Plan for the able-bodied, labeled *Nixon's Good Deed* by Burke and Burke (1974), was also rejected by Congress in two legislative sessions. But Congress subsequently established the Supplemental Security

Income Program (SSI) for the elderly, blind, and disabled, which incorporated a number of FAP's features, including a national minimum welfare benefit. SSI is a cash negative income tax that is less expensive than FAP would have been because it targets a narrower group of recipients. SSI also proved more politically popular than AFDC because it focused on the "deserving" poor for whom work and family disincentives were of less concern.[12]

When candidate Clinton first announced his welfare reform goal, he reflected the broad nature of Ellwood's plan:

> It's time to honor and reward people who work hard and play by the rules. That means ending welfare as we know it—not by punishing the poor or preaching to them, but by empowering Americans to take care of their children and improve their lives. No one who works full-time and has children at home should be poor anymore. No one who can work should be able to stay on welfare forever. (Clinton 1992)

However, the notion of time-limiting welfare was so popular that the early sound bite from this quote, "make work pay and end welfare as we know it" quickly became "end welfare as we know it." Within a short period of time, there was little discussion of providing jobs for those reaching the time limit or of reducing poverty for workers. Intense discussion of the goal of caseload reduction took center stage.

In the aftermath of the 1994 congressional elections, it became clear that government would prove both unwilling to provide cash support forever and unwilling to take any responsibility for providing jobs for those who exhaust transitional support. The Republican majority embraced the time limit but rejected most other aspects of the welfare reform plan that had been presented by the Clinton administration in June 1994. Thus, PRWORA might be labeled "Clinton's Bad Deed" or, according to Peter Edelman (1997), "The Worst Thing Bill Clinton Has Done."

The PRWORA offers no opportunity to work in exchange for welfare benefits when a recipient reaches her lifetime limit of sixty months of federally supported cash assistance.[13] Although there is substantial evidence, reviewed below, that the labor market prospects for less-skilled workers have greatly eroded since early 1970s, the government is no longer responsible for providing a cash safety net. Although states can exempt up to 20 percent of the caseload from the time limit, as discussed below, more than 20 percent of recipients who remain on the postreform caseloads are likely to need extended cash assistance or a last resort work-for-welfare opportunity. This follows because the personal attributes of many long-term recipients make their employment prospects even more precarious than those of the typical less-skilled worker.

The Relationship between Welfare Reform Policy and Welfare
Reform Research

This review of federal welfare reform proposals from 1969 to 1996 reveals a pattern by which government increased demands on recipients to work and decreased resources for training and public employment programs. Over this period, with the exception of the Family Support Act, social science research on welfare tended to be one cycle behind the welfare reform policy debate and to have had little impact on policy outcomes. Instead, policies, once they have been implemented, have influenced the nature of subsequent welfare reform research.[14]

In the decade following the declaration of War on Poverty, spending on cash assistance increased rapidly, reform proposals emphasized the reduction of income poverty, and few demands and expectations were placed on welfare recipients. Negative income tax proposals were put forward, and while they did not become law, they led to a series of negative income tax experiments that furthered social science research techniques (Haveman 1987). By the time researchers had fully digested the results of the NIT experiment, however, welfare reform policy had moved away from income guarantees toward work requirements.

In hindsight, the increase in the extent of work expected from recipients, which began with PBJI and accelerated in the 1980s, together with the accumulating research on the difficulties of low-skilled workers in the changing labor market (reviewed in the next section), should have focused the attention of policymakers on the need for labor demand policies, such as employer subsidies or minimum wage public jobs of last resort. However, after the Reagan administration eliminated the CETA program, researchers turned away from studying public employment programs. While they may have been able to further their understanding by studying such programs and labor demand policies in other countries or by analyzing them at a conceptual level, it is easy to see how attractive it became to evaluate the welfare-to-work demonstration projects that the states had begun to implement. These demonstrations provided an opportunity for social scientists to study the substance and methodology of randomized experiments. Thus, the research agenda shifted to the evaluation of policies that were being implemented rather than focusing on alternative policies that might be implemented.[15]

In the mid-1980s, researchers sought to distinguish between short-term and long-term welfare recipients and to identify which services might help reduce the length of welfare spells. The Family Support Act marked the high point of the influence of social science research on welfare reform policies, as its provisions reflected the recently evaluated experiences of the states with welfare-to-work programs. The FSA guidelines, which mandated services states had to offer, reflected these contemporary studies—more work was to be expected from welfare recipients, but more government resources were to be devoted to helping them. This was the only time in the last three decades when welfare policies and welfare reform research were in sync.

In the 1990s, following Clinton's call to "end welfare as we know it," policymakers escalated their demands for recipients to work and reduced government obligations toward and funds to serve them. In the aftermath of PRWORA, policymakers have acted as if there were no need for researchers to study long-term welfare recipients—time limits mean that new welfare entrants no longer have the option to become long-term recipients. Policymakers are implicitly assuming that there is no longer a need to study which services ought to be provided before single mothers are expected to work—single mothers are expected to work, regardless of which services, if any, the state chooses to provide.

Now, welfare reform research is once again following policy as numerous studies are analyzing the effects of PRWORA. For example, welfare reform is proceeding on the assumption that welfare recipients (with few exceptions), like the population at large, can work and earn enough to support their families. In response to this policy, researchers have begun to study the relative levels of health, mental health, and other capacities of recipients, which suggest that they are more disadvantaged than their nonwelfare peers and hence less able to work (e.g., S. K. Danziger et al. 2000; Zedlewski 1999).

Reductions in Employer Demands for Less-Skilled Workers

Ample research evidence was available to policymakers documenting how adverse changes in employer demands for less-skilled workers make it difficult for many welfare recipients to get jobs and keep them. In *America Unequal,* Peter Gottschalk and I (Danziger and Gottschalk 1995) show that the period from the early 1970s to the mid-1990s was an era of "uneven tides," characterized by slow economic growth and increasing inequality in earnings and family incomes. The economic experience of the period differs dramatically from that of the quarter century following World War II, when a "rising tide lifted all boats" and earnings gains and income gains were rapid and widely shared—by the poor, the middle class, and the rich, and by less-skilled as well as by skilled workers. It was this economic experience of rising living standards and falling poverty that shaped the optimism of the planners on the War on Poverty. But antipoverty efforts and welfare reform policies today must operate in a very different context.

Structural changes in the labor market since the early 1970s have made it harder for less-educated workers to secure employment that can lead to economic independence. Many factors moved the labor market in the same direction (Danziger and Gottschalk 1995). The decline in union membership, reductions in manufacturing employment, increased global competition, and the consequent expansion of the import and export sectors all lowered the wages of less-skilled workers. The automation that accompanied the introduction and widespread use of computers and other technological innovations also increased demand for skilled personnel who could run more sophisticated equipment. Simultaneously, demand declined for less-skilled workers, who were either displaced by the automated systems or had to compete with overseas workers producing the rising volume of imports. Despite the long economic recovery and falling unemployment rate of the 1990s, many less-skilled workers, especially welfare recipients, continue to face economic difficulty.

These changes in the nature of the labor market have important implications for less-skilled workers. For example, consider the labor market prospects of a group of workers who are more advantaged in the labor market than the typical welfare recipient—male high school graduates with some earnings, between the ages of twenty-five and thirty-four. Whereas these young men are similar in age to the typical welfare recipient, they have more education (about half of current recipients lack a high school degree), more labor-force experience, less responsibility for child care, and fewer other family demands on their time. Because of differences in their human capital characteristics and because they may also experience gender discrimination, labor market outcomes for welfare recipients are likely to be worse than those of these young men.

Median earnings (in constant dollars) for young male high school graduates increased rapidly during the post–World War II boom, rising by more than 70 percent in real terms between 1949 and 1969. Since the early 1970s, however, their real median earnings have declined and in 1997 were still below the 1969 levels. Consider the percentage of these young men whose annual earnings fall below the poverty line for a family of four ($16,400 in 1997 dollars). In 1997, about one-quarter of young, white, non-Hispanic high school graduates who were in the labor force and about two-fifths of comparable black, non-Hispanic men earned less than $16,400. The percentage of low-earnings males was, in 1997, about 2.5 and 3.5 times higher than in 1969, when almost all young male high school graduates could support a family on their own earnings. And the 1997 percentages were almost as high as they had been in 1949 (Danziger 1999a).[16]

Thus, as public demands for welfare recipients to work and become self-sufficient increased over the past quarter century, culminating in the time-limiting of welfare benefits by PRWORA, the ability of male high school graduates to do so was declining. Although policymakers have neglected these trends in reforming welfare, they did respond to the deterioration in earnings by expanding the Earned Income Tax Credit several times, most recently in 1993.[17] As a result, the maximum EITC benefit level had increased by 1997 to $3,556 for a low earner with two children and to $2,152 for a low earner with one child.

If men have fared so badly in the labor market, what can we expect single mothers to earn? The typical welfare recipient is likely to fare worse than even the typical single mother who does not receive welfare, because she has less education, is younger, has more children, and is more likely to have never married. For example, 1990 census data (Danziger and Lehman 1996) show that about one-quarter of nonrecipients, but half of recipients, were never married; about one-fifth of nonrecipients, but more than two-fifths of recipients, lacked a high school degree; about one-sixth of nonrecipients, but one-quarter of recipients, were below twenty-five years of age; about one-sixth of all nonrecipients, but one-third of recipients, had three or more children. These differences in observed characteristics suggest that welfare recipients, ceteris paribus, are likely to have lower earnings capacities than nonrecipient single mothers.

Danziger and Lehman (1996) estimated that in 1989 only 41.5 percent of welfare mothers could have earned more than the poverty line for a family of three if they had not received welfare and had worked as much as working single mothers. In contrast, 64.3 percent of the nonrecipient single mothers earned this much. These estimates, while showing that welfare recipients have a high probability of being poor based on their own earnings, overstate their labor market prospects because they assume that welfare recipients differ from nonrecipients only in terms of observed demographic characteristics. But, as I discuss in the next section, many welfare recipients have a much greater prevalence of health, mental health, and other unmeasured personal problems that pose barriers to their employment (S. K. Danziger et al. 2000).

It is simply not the case that most welfare recipients can obtain stable employment that would allow them to escape poverty, if only they would try harder. Fear of destitution is a powerful incentive to survive, but it will not guarantee that an unskilled worker who actively seeks work will be able to support her family. PRWORA's increased pressures on welfare mothers to search for work are likely to make only modest differences in their family incomes unless they are accompanied by policies to expand their labor market opportunities, especially if the national unemployment rate moves above 6 percent.

If declining employer demand for less-skilled workers means that many welfare mothers will have difficulty maintaining employment in the regular labor market, by how much would their prospects improve if they were guaranteed access to a job? Danziger and Jakubson's (1982) analysis of the Supported Work Demonstration provides suggestive evidence, although it is based on a randomized experiment from the mid-1970s. Supported Work, a public employment demonstration program for persons with labor market disadvantages, sought to improve work skills and attitudes to increase employment and earnings. Participants worked in small groups under close and supportive supervision; demands for punctuality, attendance, and productivity were initially low and slowly increased until normal labor market standards were reached. Participants were required to leave Supported Work after a specified period (usually twelve months) whether or not they had found another job. Job placement efforts were provided, and in some instances a worker moved from a Supported Work job to a regular job in the same firm or agency. Participants had characteristics similar to those of today's long-term welfare recipients.

Data gathered during the ninth month of the demonstration exemplify a situation in which any recipient can work at a public job of last resort; data gathered during the twenty-seventh month exemplify the situation of a woman who was, but is no longer, eligible for a transitional job. These later estimates suggest what we might expect from the kind of transitional access offered by some current welfare-to-work programs.

At nine months, only 3 percent of women participating in supported work, but 64 percent of those in the control group, reported no earnings or hours of work. Thus, the provision of public jobs greatly increased work. At twenty-seven months, 52 percent of women who had participated and 60 percent of the control group reported no earnings or hours work. Supported Work was beneficial—at twenty-seven months the former participants worked and earned more than the control group. Nonetheless, the dramatic reduction in the postprogram work effort of the participants when they had to compete for regular jobs suggests that disadvantaged welfare recipients have great difficulty maintaining employment when they do not have access to a job of last resort.

How Different Are Welfare Recipients from Other Less-Skilled Workers?

The estimates in the previous section concerning the labor market prospects of welfare recipients are likely to be biased upward because recent research suggests that they have unobserved characteristics that negatively affect employment and earnings. While we know much about how the labor market has changed for less-skilled workers, we know relatively little about how the skills and abilities of recipients differ from those of other less-skilled workers. Social scientists have avoided studying the personal attributes of recipients out of a concern that to do so is to blame the victim. They have tended to assume that recipients are similar to other poor persons, and either faced different constraints or made different choices. Liberals tended to argue that long welfare spells were due primarily to structural labor market constraints (skills mismatch, spatial mismatch, discrimination) and recipients' need for further education and training. Conservatives tended to argue that dependency was due to recipients' unwillingness to take available jobs, not to structural constraints or personal barriers to work.

Numerous studies, for example, examine how demographic characteristics, schooling, training, and work experiences affect a welfare recipient's employment and wages. They have largely ignored factors such as physical and mental health, alcohol and drug problems, experiences of domestic violence, and other personal problems that are likely to be more common among welfare mothers than among other women. Some recent evidence, however, indicates both that employers are demanding specific labor market skills that many recipients do not have and also that some recipients have multiple personal problems that pose barriers to their employment.

Harry Holzer (1996) provides evidence on specific skill deficiencies of welfare recipients that have not been measured in most studies. He surveyed 3,200 employers in four metropolitan areas about entry-level jobs available to workers without a college degree. He asked what skills were required, how employers screened workers, and what the demographic characteristics of recent hires were. He measured skill requirements by the frequency with which a set of tasks was performed—dealing with customers either in person or on the phone, reading and writing paragraphs, doing arithmetic and using computers.

Most entry-level jobs required several skills, educational credentials, and work experience. Each task about which Holzer asked (with the exception of writing paragraphs) was performed daily in half or more of the entry-level jobs. Employers used several credentials to screen applicants—about three-fourths required a high school diploma, general experience, and references; two-thirds required specific experience; two-fifths, training; over half required applicants to pass a test. Employers who required vocational experience or reading and writing skills were significantly less likely to hire women, particularly black women.

Holzer and I (2000) conducted simulations that attempt to bring employer demands and worker skills together by "matching" workers to jobs on the basis of skill and spatial and racial characteristics of each. We found that only 10 percent of welfare recipients without a high school degree or GED (about one-half of all recipients) had worked in jobs where they had to read and write paragraphs and do arithmetic on a regular basis. In contrast, employers required these skills for about one-third of all newly filled jobs. Even in the simulations, which assumed no shortage of jobs relative to the number of applicants, from 20 to 30 percent of all welfare recipients were not matched with a job.

The skill deficiencies and other barriers to employment for welfare recipients have been documented in several recent studies. Barton and Jenkins (1995), using data from the 1992 National Adult Literacy Survey, find that 70 percent of AFDC recipients, compared to 48 percent of the total population, scored in the two lowest prose literacy levels. They also show that average weeks worked during the year and average weekly wages increase as the prose literacy level increases for all persons and for recipients. For example, for AFDC recipients, average weeks worked were 11, 16, 20, and 24 for recipients at literacy levels 1, 2, 3, and 4 respectively. Welfare recipients between the ages of seventeen and twenty-one read, on average, at the sixth-grade level (National Institute for Literacy 1996), and 70 percent of recipients scored in the bottom quartile of the Armed Forces Qualification Test (AFQT) (Burtless 1995).

Health problems are also quite common. Among participants in California's Greater Avenues to Independence (GAIN) program who had received welfare for more than two years, almost 30 percent had been deferred at some point for a medically verified illness and 27 percent had been deferred for a severe family crisis (Riccio and Freedman 1995). Health problems accounted for 9 to 13 percent of all job losses in several welfare-to-work programs (Hershey and Pavetti 1997).

Substance abuse and mental health problems also can restrict a woman's ability to participate effectively in training programs, to leave welfare for work, or to perform adequately on the job. For example, major depression, which is quite high among welfare recipients, interferes with daily functioning and productive activity. Substance abuse and mental health problems, by adversely affecting social functioning, may partially explain why some welfare spells are so long and why many women leaving welfare for work have difficulty maintaining employment.

Jayakody, Danziger, and Pollack (2000) use the 1994 and 1995 National Household Survey of Drug Abuse (NHSDA) and analyze a sample of about 2,700 single mothers eighteen years of age and older. The NHSDA collected information on four psychiatric disorders (major depression, generalized anxiety disorder, panic attack, and agoraphobia), as well as information on the use of illegal substances. Welfare recipients are significantly more likely than nonrecipients to have major depression (12 vs. 8 percent), and to have at least one of the four psychiatric disorders (19 vs. 13 percent). Welfare recipients have a significantly higher prevalence of cocaine and crack use (5 percent of recipients had used cocaine or crack in the past year compared to 3 percent of nonrecipients) and of alcohol dependence (9 vs. 5 percent).

Jayakody et al. estimated logistic regression models to examine how psychiatric disorders and substance use affect welfare receipt. Sociodemographic control variables included marital status, education, race, health status, number of children, urbanicity, and region. Controlling for these variables, single mothers with a psychiatric disorder have a likelihood of receiving welfare that is 39 percent higher than women without a disorder; having used cocaine or crack in the past year doubles those odds.

S. K. Danziger et al. (2000), in a study of women who had been welfare recipients in February 1997, document both a high prevalence of personal problems and a strong association between these problems and employment in fall 1998. These characteristics include human capital and skills (education, number and type of prior job skills, work experience), physical and mental health (mother's self-rated health status, health-related limitations in physical activities, and meeting the diagnostic criteria for major depression), transportation problems, and self-reported discrimination in the workplace. One woman in four, for example, had experienced a major depression within the past year, and 15 percent met the criteria for posttraumatic stress disorder, much higher than the national rates. Respondents were twice as likely as the general population of adult women to report physical limitations, and three to five times as likely to describe their general health as "poor" or "fair."

Danziger and colleagues estimated a regression model that expresses employment of more than twenty hours per week as a function of fourteen potential barriers to employment and a series of demographic control variables. The number of barriers that a woman faces was significantly associated with the likelihood of work. The 21 percent of women with only one work barrier had a 71 percent probability of work. Thereafter, the likelihood that a woman works decreases steadily as her number of potential barriers increases. The 24 percent of respondents with four to six potential barriers to work had about a 40 percent chance of working, whereas for the 3 percent of respondents with seven or more barriers, the likelihood of employment was below 6 percent.

States may exempt 20 percent of the Temporary Assistance to Needy Families (TANF) caseload from the five-year limit on federally funded cash aid. This exemption is intended to protect the most disadvantaged recipients from severe hardship. However, given the rapid reduction in caseloads, to about 5.8 million in mid-2000, it is quite likely that more than 20 percent of current recipients experience health, mental health, or substance abuse problems. If these problems limit women's ability to maintain stable employment (as recent research suggests), and if efforts to detect and treat these problems are not greatly expanded, then benefits for many recipients who are not very employable are likely to be terminated (although they may be quite willing to work).

Conclusion

Any welfare system will produce errors of commission and omission. The pre-1996 welfare system was biased toward false positives by providing cash assistance to some recipients who could have made it on their own in the labor market. Some of these false positives might have been unwilling to look for a job; others might have been offered jobs and turned them down because the wages were low or because they did not provide health insurance. It is not unreasonable for taxpayers to expect that welfare recipients who are offered jobs accept them, especially if mothers leaving welfare for a low-wage job have access to subsidized child care and health care.

The PRWORA has virtually eliminated false positives by cutting off people who will not search for work or cooperate with the welfare agency. But the labor market experiences in recent years for millions of low-skilled workers who do not receive welfare suggest that PRWORA will generate many false negatives. Many recipients who reach the time limits or who are sanctioned for not finding a job will be denied cash assistance even though they are willing to work, simply because they cannot find any employer to hire them. This labor demand problem will increase during recessions when states are strapped for funds and will remain even in good economic times if employer demands for a skilled work force continue to escalate. If many recipients have the kinds of personal problems discussed above, and if these problems continue to go undetected and untreated, the number of false negatives will rise even further.

Because I support a work-oriented safety net, I am not suggesting we return to the welfare system that operated prior to 1996. That system did need to be reformed. But PRWORA's "time limit and out" differs markedly from the "time limit followed by a work-for-welfare opportunity of last resort" originally proposed by Ellwood and endorsed by candidate Clinton. Welfare recipients who have no serious impairments should have the personal responsibility to look for work, but if they diligently search for work without finding a job, their cash assistance should not be terminated. At a minimum, they should be offered an opportunity to perform community service in return for continued cash assistance. A more costly option, but one that would have a greater antipoverty impact, would be to provide them with low-wage public service jobs of last resort. Welfare recipients who were willing to work could then combine wages with the Earned Income Tax Credit and support their families even when there was little employer demand for their skills.

The best way to reduce welfare dependency without harming recipients who are willing to "work hard and play by the rules" is to reform PRWORA to incorporate the lessons of the research reviewed here. Now that PRWORA has increased work expectations and demands for personal responsibility on the part of welfare recipients, it is time to increase demands on government for mutual responsibility. If we are to reduce poverty as well as the welfare caseload, we must demonstrate greater willingness to spend public funds to complete the task of turning a cash-based safety net into a work-oriented safety net. For recipients with the most extensive personal problems, this requires an expansion of social service and treatment programs, experimentation with sheltered workshops, and increased exemptions or extensions of time limits. For employable recipients, government must ensure that labor demand expands to keep pace with the labor supply increases brought about by welfare reform.

NOTES

1. A negative income tax provides a certain payment, "the guaranteed income," for a family with no other income. This amount is then reduced as the family's income increases until the "break-even point" is reached and the family no longer receives any negative income tax payments.

2. The Earned Income Tax Credit, enacted in 1975, now serves this earnings-sup-plementation function.

3. By 1998, fourteen states had full-benefit sanctions as their initial sanction; thirty-six states had them as their most severe sanction (Gallagher et al. 1998).

4. Congress did give states the option to require some recipients to participate in Community Work Experience Programs (CWEP) in exchange for benefit receipt. Many states implemented such programs in the 1980s (Gueron and Pauly 1991), and state experimentation with these programs paved the way for both the Family Support Act of 1988 and PRWORA.

5. In 1980 forty-two states, but by 1984 only seven states, provided some AFDC benefits to a woman with two children who had earnings at 75 percent of her poverty line (U.S. House of Representatives 1993, 1242).

6. The EITC was substantially expanded again in 1990 and 1993. By 1997, total spending on the EITC, about $27 billion, exceeded federal cash welfare payments, about $17 billion. The number of families benefiting from the EITC increased to more than 18 million in the late 1990s (U.S. House of Representatives 1998).

7. The early state programs consisted primarily of employment counseling and assistance in searching for jobs. By the end of the 1980s, some programs also provided such services as subsidized child care and transportation, follow-up counseling after employment began, and education and training services.

8. Senator Moynihan provided this jacket quote for the Gueron and Pauly book: "Above all others, Judy Gueron and her colleagues at MDRC did the research that led Congress to pass the Family Support Act. . . . As a result, we now have a historic oppor-tunity to help welfare recipients become self-sufficient."

9. Lurie (1996) reports that, in 1994, most states did not spend enough to get their full federal matching funds from JOBS, and all states together spent enough to use only about 75 percent of available funds.

10. Because caseloads fell so rapidly between 1996 and 2000, states have found them-selves with more funds than they have chosen to spend. A few states have even raised benefit levels. It remains to be seen how states will respond in a recession when case-loads increase.

11. The third task force cochair, Bruce Reed, a White House political operative, had no research background and was opposed to aspects of Ellwood's proposal that would have required additional funds.

12. Complaints about SSI increased in the 1990s because of controversies regarding an increased number of child disability cases and the use of SSI by elderly immigrants and substance abusers. PRWORA restricted SSI eligibility for these groups.

13. The limit has been set at as little as eighteen months in some states, as the act provides this state option; twenty-two states have set limits of less than sixty months (Gallagher et al. 1998).

14. For example, PRWORA was crafted in Congress with little reliance on social science research. Now, however, there are dozens of large social science research teams conducting research on the act's effects on caseloads, recipient well-being, and other topics.

15. One exception to the pattern of research following policy involves child support. Irwin Garfinkel (Garfinkel and McLanahan 1992, 1986), his colleagues, and others began analyzing issues related to child support in the late 1970s. This research has strongly influenced the evolution of child support policy. However, it is also the case here, as with welfare reform, that the reforms that have been implemented have been those that sought to reduce government spending by increasing child support collections from absent fathers. Garfinkel's proposal to require the government to fund a national minimum child support benefit for all children living in single-parent families has not been adopted and was rarely discussed by policymakers.

16. Official poverty rates for men are lower than these for several reasons. First, many of these men have working wives; second, many live in families with fewer than four persons.

17. The 1993 act both raised the maximum EITC benefit levels and indexed them to rise at the rate of inflation.

REFERENCES

Anderson, Martin. 1978. *Welfare: The political economy of welfare reform in the United States.* Stanford: Hoover Institution Press.
Bane, Mary Jo, and David T. Ellwood. 1986. Slipping into and out of poverty: The dynamics of spells. *Journal of Human Resources* 21 (1) (winter): 1–23.
———. 1994. *Welfare realities: From rhetoric to reform.* Cambridge: Harvard University Press.
Barton, Paul E., and Lynn Jenkins. 1995. *Literacy and dependency.* Princeton: Policy Information Center, Educational Testing Service.
Baum, Erica B. 1991. When the witch doctors agree: The Family Support Act and social science research. *Journal of Policy Analysis and Management* 10 (fall): 603–15.
Brown, Amy. 1997. *Work First: How to implement an employment-focused approach to welfare reform.* New York: Manpower Demonstration Research Corporation.
Burke, Vincent J., and Vee Burke. 1974. *Nixon's good deed: Welfare reform.* New York: Columbia University Press.

Burtless, Gary. 1995. The employment prospects of welfare recipients. In *The work alter-native: Welfare reform and the realities of the job market,* ed. Demetra Nightingale and Robert H. Haveman. Washington, D.C.: Urban Institute Press.

Clinton, Bill. 1992. *Putting people first: How we can all change America.* New York: Times Books.

Danziger, Sandra K., et al. 2000. Barriers to the employment of welfare recipients. In *Prosperity for all? The economic boom and African Americans,* ed. R. Cherry and W. Rodgers. New York: Russell Sage Foundation.

Danziger, Sheldon. 1999a. In pursuit of Robert J. Lampman's "modest goal": Antipoverty policy after welfare reform. *Focus* 20 (spring): 8–12. Madison, Wis.: Institute for Research on Poverty.

Danziger, Sheldon, ed. 1999b. *Economic conditions and welfare reform.* Kalamazoo, Mich.: Upjohn Institute for Employment Research.

Danziger, Sheldon, and Peter Gottschalk. 1995. *America unequal.* Cambridge: Harvard University Press.

Danziger, Sheldon, and George Jakubson. 1982. The distributional impacts of targeted public employment programs. In *Public finance and public employment,* ed. Robert H. Haveman. Detroit: Wayne State University Press.

Danziger, Sheldon, and Jeffrey Lehman. 1996. How will welfare recipients fare in the labor market? *Challenge Magazine* 39 (March/April): 30–35.

Duncan, Greg J., et al. 1984. *Years of poverty, years of plenty: The changing economic for-tunes of American workers and families.* Ann Arbor: Survey Research Center, Insti-tute for Social Research, University of Michigan.

Edelman, Peter. 1997. The worst thing Bill Clinton has done. *Atlantic Monthly* 297 (March): 43–58.

Ellwood, David T. 1987. *Divide and conquer: Responsible security for America's poor.* Ford Foundation Project on Social Welfare and the American Future. Occasional Paper Series, no. 1. New York: Ford Foundation.

———. 1988. *Poor support: Poverty in the American family.* New York: Basic Books.

———. 1999. The impact of the Earned Income Tax Credit and other social policy changes on work and marriage in the United States. Cambridge: Harvard Univer-sity, Mimeo.

Freeman, Richard B., and Peter Gottschalk, eds. 1998. *Generating jobs: How to increase demand for less-skilled workers.* New York: Russell Sage Foundation.

Friedlander, David, and Gary Burtless. 1995. *Five years after: The long-term effects of wel-fare-to-work programs.* New York: Russell Sage Foundation.

Gallagher, L. J., et al. 1998. One year after federal welfare reform: A description of state temporary assistance for needy families decisions as of October 1997. Occasional Paper No. 6. Washington, D.C.: Urban Institute.

Garfinkel, Irwin, and Sara McLanahan. 1986. *Single mothers and their children: A new American dilemma.* Washington, D.C.: Urban Institute Press.

———. 1992. *Assuring child support: An extension of social security.* New York: Russell Sage Foundation.

Glazer, Nathan. 1984. The social policy of the Reagan administration. In *The social con-tract revisited: Aims and outcomes of President Reagan's social welfare policy,* ed. D. Lee Bawden. Washington, D.C.: Urban Institute Press.

Gueron, Judith, and Edward Pauly. 1991. *From welfare to work.* New York: Russell Sage Foundation.

Haskins, Ron. 1991. Congress writes a law: Research and welfare reform. *Journal of Policy Analysis and Management* 10 (fall): 616–32.

Haveman, Robert H. 1987. *Poverty policy and poverty research: The Great Society and the social sciences.* Madison: University of Wisconsin Press.

Hershey, A. M., and L. Pavetti. 1997. Turning job finders into job keepers: The challenge of sustaining employment. *Future of Children* 7 (1): 74–86.

Holzer, Harry J. 1996. *What employers want: Job prospects for less-educated workers.* New York: Russell Sage Foundation.

Holzer, Harry J., and Sheldon Danziger. 2000. Are jobs available for disadvantaged workers in urban areas? In *Urban inequality: Evidence from four cities,* ed. Alice O'Connor, Chris Tilly, and Lawrence Bobo. New York: Russell Sage Foundation.

Jayakody, Rukmalie, Sheldon Danziger, and Harold Pollack. 2000. Welfare reform, substance use, and mental health. *Journal of Health Politics, Policy, and Law* 25 (4): 623–51.

Lampman, Robert. 1959. *The low-income population and economic growth.* U.S. Congress, Joint Economic Committee, Study Paper no. 12. Washington, D.C.: Government Printing Office.

———. 1965. Approaches to the reduction of poverty. *American Economic Review* 55 (2): 521–29.

———. 1971. *Ends and means of reducing income poverty.* Chicago: Markham.

Levy, Frank, and Richard J. Murnane. 1992. U.S. earnings levels and earnings inequality: A review of recent trends and proposed explanations. *Journal of Economic Literature* 30 (September): 1333–81.

Lurie, Irene. 1996. A lesson from the JOBS program: Reforming welfare must be both dazzling and dull. *Journal of Policy Analysis and Management* 15 (fall): 572–86.

Lynn, Laurence E., and David Whitman. 1981. *The president as policymaker: Jimmy Carter and welfare reform.* Philadelphia: Temple University Press.

Mead, Lawrence M. 1986. *Beyond entitlement: The social obligations of citizenship.* New York: Free Press.

———. 1992. *The new politics of poverty: The non working poor in America.* New York: Basic Books.

Mirengoff, William, Lester Rindler, Harry Greenspan, and Scott Seablom. 1980. *CETA: Assessment of public service employment programs.* Washington, D.C.: National Academy of Sciences.

Murray, Charles. 1984. *Losing ground: American social policy, 1950–1980.* New York: Basic Books.

National Institute for Literacy. 1996. *Policy update.* August.

Nightingale, Demetra, and Robert H. Haveman, eds. 1995. *The work alternative: Welfare reform and the realities of the job market.* Washington, D.C.: Urban Institute Press.

Nixon, Richard M. 1969. Welfare reform: A message from the President of the United States. House Document No. 91–146, *Congressional Record,* vol. 115, no. 136, The House of Representatives, 91st Congress, First Session, H7239–7241.

Novak, Michael, et al. 1987. *The new consensus on family and welfare: A community of self-reliance.* Milwaukee: Marquette University.

Riccio, James, and Stephen Freedman. 1995. Can they all work? A study of the employment potential of welfare recipients in a welfare-to-work program. Manpower Demonstration Research Corporation Working Paper, New York.

Tobin, James. 1966. The case for an income guarantee. *Public Interest* 4 (summer): 31–41.

U.S. Council of Economic Advisors. 1964. *Economic report of the president.* Washington, D.C.: Government Printing Office.

U.S. House of Representatives, Committee on Ways and Means. 1993, 1998. *Background material and data on programs within the jurisdiction of the Committee on Ways and Means: Green book.* Washington, D.C.: Government Printing Office.

Watts, Harold W., and Albert Rees, eds. 1977. *The New Jersey income maintenance experiment, volume II: Labor supply responses.* New York: Academic Press.

Wiseman, Michael. 1991. Research and policy: An afterword for the symposium on the Family Support Act of 1988. *Journal of Policy Analysis and Management* 10 (fall): 657–66.

Zedlewski, Sheila. 1999. Work activity and obstacles to work among TANF recipients. *Assessing the new federalism: National survey of America's families,* Series B, no. B-2, September. Washington, D.C.: Urban Institute.

CHAPTER 7

Welfare Reform at the State Level: The Role of Social Experiments and Demonstrations

Judith M. Gueron

Rigorous evaluation of the past twenty years of work-focused welfare reform strategies produced a large body of reliable information that played a significant role in shaping social policy and program practice. From the start, this research has proven unusually real-world in two senses: It was designed to answer questions posed by policymakers and program operators, and it resulted from field tests conducted in actual operating welfare offices throughout the country. Today America faces a new world of welfare in which variation among state welfare programs will increase greatly, creating both greater opportunity for progress and heightened risk of unintended consequences. Therefore, the need for hard data on the effects of different approaches to reweaving the safety net is more acute than ever.

This chapter summarizes the origin, context, and main themes of some major studies conducted during the past twenty years and looks ahead to likely challenges and opportunities for further evaluation within work-focused welfare reform strategies. The chapter centers on the Manpower Demonstration Research Corporation (MDRC) story: how it launched rigorous, state-based studies and why these studies impacted state and federal policy. Limited in scope, this chapter provides an incomplete picture of lessons learned during this period (for example, the influential work on welfare dynamics [Bane and Ellwood 1983] is not discussed). In addition, the reader is cautioned that, although she sought to be objective, the author was a direct actor in MDRC work.

Step One: Recognizing the Need

In 1974, the Ford Foundation together with six federal agencies established MDRC with the goal of improving public policy for low-income people by identifying and strengthening effective programs. The intent was to provide policymakers and practitioners with reliable evidence on effective and ineffective programs, and to obtain this evidence by field-testing new ideas in real-world operating environments.

MDRC grew out of a concern with government implementation and assessment of initiatives for the poor. Too often, new ideas developed into national programs that then terminated, leaving no record of what they had or had not accomplished. Policy was made by hunch and discredited by anecdote. Indeed, the same approaches and questions were visited and revisited by policymakers, in part because available evidence was not wholly believed. MDRC endeavored to assist in building such a record by test-marketing new social program ideas in much the same way companies test a new product. MDRC would not administer programs but would work with communities and organizations operating the programs and would manage the process to produce reliable data. In their research, MDRC staff would ask tough questions: Is it feasible to implement the innovation? Does it make a difference, and for whom? Is it a worthwhile investment? Is it replicable, and under what conditions? If it works, what explains success? If it does not work, why not, and what does this suggest for future policy?

Fundamental to our approach were correct diagnosis of the problem, the use of a reasonable treatment, a reliable method to measure success, and the independence to publish insights gathered through the research. Since the goal was to affect policy—not to fill libraries—we took an active approach to information dissemination.

Our experience suggests the value of rigorous research stemming from a source viewed by the intended audience as objective. Social policy operates in an environment rich in opinion and acrimony and short on generally agreed-upon facts. One is often challenged to dispel the view that nothing works, that a new program represents good money being thrown after bad. To counter this view, rock-solid evidence of a program's effectiveness is needed. When MDRC was created, the problem was not a lack of studies. Many federally funded demonstrations and initiatives existed, but they often ended with a conference at which a group of experts argued about what had been learned—not what the findings meant for policy, but what the findings actually were. No body of extant evidence was widely believed across the political spectrum.

Commenting on this state of affairs, Henry Aaron, in his influential book *Politics and the Professors,* addressed the conservative force created by academic, jargon-filled disputes over arcane techniques. He called such conflict "self-canceling research" and argued that it paralyzes policy and undercuts the "simple faiths" that make action possible. "What is an ordinary member of the tribe [i.e., the public] to do," he asked, "when the witch doctors [the scientists and scholars] disagree?" (1978, 158–59).

MDRC was established to overcome the "tribe and witch doctor" conflict.

A key factor in attaining this goal was pioneering the use of random-assignment field experiments to test operating social programs. This approach was undertaken neither out of stubbornness nor from some mystical conviction, but out of the belief that the simplicity and credibility of random assignment would matter in the policy process—that it would reduce the conflict and jargon and sell itself. MDRC's enthusiasm for random assignment also developed from an ethical concern that in large-scale field studies that involve primary data collection and that would be costly whether or not they used random assignment, first-order questions must be answered clearly.

Step Two: Testing Social Policies in a Laboratory Environment

MDRC's first project, the National Supported Work Demonstration, was the first instance in which an operating employment program was tested in multiple sites as a social experiment while using random assignment (Supported Work offered twelve to eighteen months of paid employment to former drug abusers, ex-offenders, long-term welfare recipients, and disadvantaged youth). In those early years, most experts felt that it would be impossible to persuade program operators—who, quite naturally, believed they were doing good—to agree to a random intake process. Just as doctors would refuse to deny service to a patient, program administrators, it was argued, would refuse to turn people away just because those people had lost a research-based intake lottery (see, e.g., MDRC 1980, 42–43; Gueron 1980, 1984).

MDRC staff carefully explained that the whole reason for the experiment was that we did not know whether the program actually would help people—and that, moreover, there were resources to enroll only a small number of those likely to be interested in Supported Work jobs. Ultimately, ten pioneering community-based Supported Work programs joined the demonstration, convinced that valuable, policy-impacting knowledge would be gained through the experiment, and became allies of the project in the process. The result was the first definitive study of an employment program and the first convincing evidence that work programs have a positive effect on welfare recipients.

Step Three: Moving out of the Laboratory and into the States

The next critical step in learning came in 1981, when President Reagan came to office with the controversial goal of changing welfare into workfare—the idea that aid recipients would have to work in exchange for their benefits. (The specific approach proposed in 1981, formally called Community Work Experience Programs—CWEP—required welfare recipients to work each month for the number of hours that would equal the amount of their grant divided by the minimum wage.) Due to the many unanswered questions and high political stakes surrounding the workfare concept, Congress did *not* enact national workfare, but instead gave states, for the first time, the option to require workfare for Aid to Families with Dependent Children (AFDC) recipients. Congress also offered state governments new flexibility to reshape the Work Incentive (WIN) Program and use welfare funds to subsidize private employers who hired welfare recipients.

The 1981 legislation was passed in a highly charged environment, in which some people in the new administration viewed evaluation as a tool of left-leaning professors. Despite some initial plans to assess workfare implementation, the federal government chose not to study the states' responses to the legislation. This inaction on the part of the federal government prompted the staff of MDRC to perceive the critical need for an independent, objective evaluation. Key questions for evaluation included the following: What would the states do in response to the new flexibility? Would states implement large-scale workfare programs or opt for other welfare-to-work strategies (such as job search, or education and training)? Where implemented, would workfare be "make-work" or would it produce useful services for communities? Would mandates be widely enforced? Would they lead to increased employment and reduced reliance on welfare? Who would gain and who would lose: welfare recipients, government budgets, or both?

To address these and other questions, MDRC sought and received a substantial challenge grant (i.e., a grant requiring a match from other sources) from the Ford Foundation. MDRC used this grant to create the eleven-state Demonstration of State Work/Welfare Initiatives, in which random-assignment studies were embedded in operating welfare offices in multiple locations within eight of the participating states. MDRC endeavored to leverage the necessary funds from mainstream sources, creating major new opportunities to learn about the nature and effectiveness of state innovations.

To translate this vision into reality, MDRC staff met with welfare commissioners in more than thirty states, searching for a combination of innovation, scale, quality administrative data (to track outcomes over time), matching funds, and a willingness to implement the random-assignment concept. The project was presented to states as an opportunity to answer the questions that they cared about—an argument that carried much weight (for a discussion of the process of gaining states' participation in these experiments, see Gueron 1985; Gueron and Nathan 1985). Key state staff often agreed to use random assignment because none of them possessed the resources or capacity to implement their reform program—whether workfare, job search, private sector subsidies, or a combination of these and other elements—for *all* welfare recipients statewide. Because of the inaccessibility of these programs on a large scale, MDRC argued that random assignment remained a fair way to ration scarce social services.

State-level administrators also recognized that data on program *outcomes* (e.g., the number of job placements or welfare departures) would not tell them how much *difference* or *impact* a new program made. Initially, this point was illustrated with data from the control groups in the Supported Work and other random-assignment studies. Later, Mary Jo Bane and David Ellwood's influential study of welfare caseload dynamics showed that people frequently moved onto and off of welfare without assistance, further calling into question the validity of using high scores on typical job placement measures to calculate the "value added" (from program participation) without comparing it to what people would have accomplished independently (Bane and Ellwood 1983). Armed with these results, MDRC argued that a random-assignment test could provide uniquely convincing evidence of the change brought about by a state's planned initiative. A further argument for this research approach was the clear evidence that it could be implemented within the regular welfare intake processes. The evidence for this assertion was provided by a number of studies MDRC conducted in several WIN offices during the late 1970s (Goldman 1981; Wolfhagen 1983).

Administrators also had less obvious reasons to join the studies: some were under conflicting pressure from legislatures and advocates and hoped to test specific approaches on a modest scale and to obtain objective evidence on which to base their broader decisions. Most saw political and substantive advantages in belonging to a small group of states at the forefront of innovation. All saw participation in these studies as an opportunity to obtain higher-quality information than they could finance with their own budget. But states also raised concerns: Would the studies place undue burdens on hard-pressed staff? Would they undercut the states' ability to meet ongoing performance requirements? What "treatment" would be offered to people in the control group?

After much negotiation, a series of studies and a new method of learning about state innovations resulted that ultimately inspired a large number of rigorous evaluations of state welfare reforms (Greenberg and Wiseman 1992; Gueron and Pauly 1991). While the Ford Foundation's grant and MDRC's efforts were the catalysts for change, in some sense the real heroes were in state capitals across the country and at the U.S. Department of Health and Human Services (HHS) in Washington. At the state level the welfare commissioners opened up their programs to objective scrutiny, and the key staff in state agencies and legislatures cooperated with the research protocols, provided the data, used the findings, and often became fans of high-quality evaluations. At HHS, the heroes were those much-maligned bureaucrats who, for the past twenty years, through Republican and Democratic administrations, took seriously the language Congress had put in Section 1115 of the Social Security Act, which allowed states to waive provisions of the AFDC law in order to test out welfare reform ideas, but only if the states assessed their innovations.

Throughout 1995, the governors often railed against the waiver process and the need to go to Washington "on bended knee" to request federal approval for changing the AFDC program. Although the process was cumbersome and did limit state flexibility, it produced a strong knowledge base about welfare reform options—the envy of many people working in related domains—largely because of the bureaucrats who insisted on rigorous evaluations. The 1996 federal welfare law ends this waiver process at the very time that the replacement of AFDC by block grants to states makes information on the effects of different strategies even more critical; there is no comparable mechanism for assuring that the nation learns the achievements and drawbacks of the myriad state policies likely to result from the legislation.

The research approach described in this chapter has been used to test different areas of reform: various types of welfare-to-work programs, changed financial incentives, subsidized wages in the private sector, programs in which welfare recipients are required to work in order to receive public assistance, and time limits on welfare (see Bloom 1997 for a summary of these studies). Most of the completed studies assess mandatory welfare-to-work programs. After briefly discussing why work programs have been at the center of welfare reform for thirty years, this chapter summarizes knowledge gained about the success of various strategies and then describes the techniques that MDRC has used to bring that knowledge to policymakers. The conclusion presents the lessons drawn from that final experience.

The Emphasis on Work

Before it was replaced by block grants, AFDC was the nation's largest cash welfare program. It was created in 1935 explicitly to help a group of poor single mothers (primarily widows) remain *out* of the labor force and stay home to care for their children. The goal was to reduce child poverty, and the possibility of long-term welfare for this group was accepted and considered fair. Since then, much has changed. Most important, women have flooded into the labor market (often not by choice), and most mothers on welfare are now unmarried. Providing long-term support seems less equitable and is clearly much less popular with the American public than it once was.

The public wanted change within the AFDC program, but—and this is where the challenge of reform comes in—it has historically called for change that would satisfy two often conflicting goals: provide a safety net for children (no one wants children to starve or to be homeless) and require that their parents work (the public does not think government should substitute for parents). The problem arises because parents and their children are a package: One set cannot be helped without helping the other.

Starting in the late 1960s, and notably in 1988 with the creation of the Job Opportunities and Basic Skills Training (JOBS) program (WIN's successor, under the Family Support Act), Congress and the states crafted a new basic compromise in an effort to reconcile those goals. The concept seemed simple: Welfare should be transformed from a no-strings-attached entitlement (if poor, one received money from the federal or state government) to a program where families would continue to get support, but parents would have to participate in some work-directed activity (such as looking for a job, or participating in training or education) or work for their benefits.

There have been several visions of how to make this mandate real. One vision included work-promoting, welfare-to-work programs: using mandates to involve welfare recipients in activities that would move them off welfare into unsubsidized jobs. Some who shared this vision advocated programs emphasizing education and training, with the hope that these activities would earn the participants better and longer-lasting jobs and help to move families out of poverty. Others, however, argued that any job was a good job, stressing the importance of conserving taxpayers' money by reducing welfare receipt.

A second vision—a work-for-benefits strategy—focused on the importance of an ongoing quid pro quo, even if this path did not directly lead to unsubsidized work. Under this approach, those who were unsuccessful in finding regular jobs would have to work in government-created positions in order to receive continued support. Whether called workfare, Community Work Experience Programs, or community service jobs, the program endeavored to deliver on the public's expectation that children be supported, but that able-bodied parents be required to work—in the bargain, also producing useful public services (see, e.g., Mead 1986).

Architects of the plan hoped that participation in work-related activities and work requirements themselves would simultaneously change the values conveyed by the welfare system, make welfare less attractive, and require participation in services that themselves would speed the transition to self-support.

This idea was the thrust of all major reform proposals until the presidential election of 1992, when candidate Bill Clinton called for a limit on the length of time people could receive work-promoting services, after which their only option for continuing public support would be a community service job. Although President Clinton described a plan that would have required welfare recipients to work after they had received assistance for two years, his language about "ending welfare as we know it"—and the fact that a work-based safety net would probably cost more than just providing cash—started the country down the path toward the new law that allows states to end all cash support.

The 1996 Personal Responsibility and Work Opportunity Reconciliation Act (PL 104–93), which substituted Temporary Assistance for Needy Families (TANF) block grants for AFDC, put the United States at a historic crossroads. Under the new system, states receive a fixed amount of federal funds, ending the sixty-year-old federal-state partnership that funded and structured the welfare entitlement. Although there are new restrictions on the use of federal funds (e.g., with some exceptions, they cannot be used to support anyone for more than five years), states have gained great flexibility in the use of their own funds (funds that formerly were used to match federal AFDC funds and that the new law requires states to continue spending) and thus in the overall design of the state safety nets.

The law is in many ways a statement of faith or hope: If the rules of the game change dramatically, poor people will alter their behavior. If welfare is time-limited or not available at all, more people will go to work and avoid having more children, and some women will be deterred from becoming single mothers in the first place. If states receive block grants, they will make wise decisions and run more efficient systems. Previous efforts to reform welfare have been cautious, incremental, and knowledge-based, as officials balanced their fears of hurting vulnerable people and burdening budgets against their desire to move the system in new directions. In contrast, the legislation signed in 1996 was a radical leap into the unknown. It assumed that changes in government programs would ultimately lead to major shifts in very personal behavior such as childbearing and marriage. Past research showed that changes in government policy could affect some types of behavior, but that the effects were usually modest. While those advocating the elimination of AFDC hoped that more dramatic change would result, opponents of this idea pointed to the high-stakes gamble as well as the risk for children and poor communities.

Mandatory Welfare-to-Work Programs

An unusually lengthy and reliable record of studies on the effect of mandatory welfare-to-work programs in the pre-TANF environment points to four broad conclusions.

1. There are clear positive results.   Many studies show that programs requiring welfare recipients to participate in welfare-to-work activities increase employment, reduce dependency on public assistance, and ultimately save taxpayers' money.

Welfare-to-work programs can prove fourfold winners by providing money for children, substituting work for welfare, generating eventual budget savings, and making welfare more consistent with public values (Gueron and Pauly 1991; Riccio, Friedlander, and Freedman 1994; Friedlander and Burtless 1995; Freedman and Friedlander 1995; Gueron 1996). The most widely cited evidence of this fact comes from an MDRC study of California's JOBS program, called Greater Avenues for Independence (GAIN). At its most successful, in Riverside County, GAIN raised employment rates by 10 percentage points, increased five-year earnings by 42 percent, and led to a 15 percent decline in welfare outlays, thereby (over five years) returning taxpayers almost $3 for every $1 spent to run the program (Knab and Freedman 1997). This and other studies show that welfare-to-work programs require an up-front investment, but that the investment may be more than repaid in future budget savings—an unusual and positive occurrence for a social program.

2. There are also clear limitations.   Although changes may be substantial, they are typically more modest: Many people remain on welfare, and participation in the programs does not usually leave people much better off, since earnings gains are largely offset by welfare reductions.

Even skeptics have called the Riverside results "dramatic" (Murray 1994, 28), but the impacts in other parts of California, although improving over time, were approximately half those of Riverside (Freedman et al. 1996). Findings also reveal another limitation. Mandatory welfare-to-work strategies may encourage more people to work, but they seldom affect average income or move many families out of poverty. This results in part from low skill levels but also from the incentive structure within the welfare system, where benefits are cut (often dollar for dollar) when people go to work. When the added expenses of working (child care, transportation, etc.) are considered, people may be financially worse off employed than on welfare. This is one reason why many subsequently return to the rolls. A final limitation relates to the new context of time-limited welfare. Two years ago, the Riverside findings appeared to indicate success, but now program administrators must reckon with the fact that, even in this very successful county, 30 percent of single mothers with school-aged children (the group targeted) remained on welfare at the end of five years, the maximum time limit set for federal cash assistance under TANF.

3. Different approaches achieve different results.   Much information is available concerning "job clubs," structured efforts to teach the unemployed how to find a job. Job clubs and other job search activities do enable more people to enter into employment quickly, thereby saving taxpayers' money. However, these programs do not appear to enable people to obtain jobs offering higher wages than positions that most would have found independently, nor do they succeed with the most disadvantaged populations. Also, the results, though positive, are modest. Typically, these programs raise the percentage of people who find a job by 5 percentage points—for example, from 30 to 35 percent (that is, 30 percent would have found a job anyway). Vocational skills training costs more but can lead to better jobs and may make a greater long-term difference in earnings. The problem with this approach, however, is that results are not consistent. Some programs—such as the Center for Employment Training (CET) program in San Jose—have proven very successful; others have not surpassed the results for a control group.

The research record is less encouraging on the approach of adult education (remedial English and math, preparation for the GED test, and instruction in English as a second language). Many welfare recipients indicated no inclination to return to the classroom, and earnings gains did not seem to warrant the added monetary investment. Some programs, such as Riverside's, employ a mixed strategy: they emphasize getting people into jobs quickly but also include training or education services. These multilevel programs are able to provide the benefits of different strategies: increased income level for welfare recipients, conservation of taxpayers' money, and a change in the employment behavior of some more disadvantaged recipients (these findings are discussed in Bloom 1997; Brown 1997; Freedman and Friedlander 1995; Friedlander and Burtless 1995; Gueron and Pauly 1991; Hamilton and Brock 1994; Hamilton et al. 1997; Riccio, Friedlander, and Freedman 1994; Zambrowski and Gordon 1993).

4. Management and resources matter.   The extent to which a program succeeds and is cost-effective depends not only on the mix of services but also on the quality of implementation. A large expenditure does not assure success while a small one does not assure savings. Wise management of resources and a strong focus on program goals are central to a successful program. A number of studies (Riccio, Friedlander, and Freedman 1994; Bardach 1993; Brown 1997; Riccio and Orenstein 1996) suggest that many superior programs

1. set high expectations;
2. establish demanding standards and enforce the participation requirement;
3. maintain a strong employment focus;
4. provide supports for work once people enter the work force;
5. involve the private sector in job placement and in the development of training programs;
6. target a wide group of welfare recipients, not merely the motivated and employable, who are likely to locate employment independently;
7. maintain good data and management systems.

Financial Incentives

Because wages for the low-skilled have declined significantly over the past twenty years, moving people from welfare to work and ending poverty have become two separate tasks (Blank 1997). A fundamental choice facing welfare reformers is how much money to invest in operating large-scale welfare-to-work programs of demonstrated effectiveness, and how much to invest in making work pay—for example, by changing the extent to which welfare is cut when people go to work or by offering earnings supplements, child care, medical care, and other supports for the working poor. More than thirty states have acted to change the economics of work for welfare recipients. This shift is motivated by a strongly held conviction that the state cannot successfully promote work if families will be less financially stable at work than they were on welfare.

The research record here is thinner and less clear, and the potential budget costs higher. Several ongoing studies are examining how financial incentives affect job-taking, job-holding, and income (Brock et al. 1997; Miller et al. 1997; SRDC 1996). One vital question in this investigation is which of two possible effects will be the more significant: more people going to work or more income flowing to people who would have located work independently (and who, as a result, may actually reduce the number of hours they work). A second key question is whether such programs can increase work and reduce poverty simultaneously, a goal that has eluded reformers.

Early findings are available from two quite different programs focused on long-term welfare recipients. Results from a study of the Minnesota Family Investment Program show that a combination of mandatory welfare-to-work services and intense promotion of incentives permitting people to keep more of their AFDC benefits when they returned to work produced a large gain in employment and a sizable reduction in poverty (over eighteen months, a 27 percent increase in earnings and a 16 percent reduction in poverty), at the cost of a relatively modest (8 percent) increase in welfare outlays. In contrast, simply informing welfare recipients of the financial incentive and not requiring participation in the services led frequently to the second type of effect noted above: a rise in income (primarily from a substantial increase in welfare outlays) for people who would have gone to work anyway (Miller et al. 1997). Findings from Canada's Self-Sufficiency Project indicate that a generous, time-limited, earnings supplement, payable to long-term recipients who work full-time and leave welfare, sharply increased earnings, employment, and total income—at fifteen months, it produced a 58 percent increase in earnings, a doubling of full-time employment, and a 23 percent increase in income (Card and Robins 1996; SRDC 1996).

These results are encouraging but raise complex trade-off questions in the new TANF context. Increasing welfare benefits to the working poor (if implemented as in Minnesota) may encourage work, but it will also keep them on the rolls longer, particularly during months when they receive reduced grants. If the state places a time limit on welfare receipt (as many now do) and does not stop the clock for people who combine work and welfare (as only a few do), welfare recipients will use precious months during which they may receive very limited assistance at the risk of no aid in a future time of crisis.

Private Sector Subsidies

During the 1980s a number of states tested the feasibility and results of encouraging large numbers of private sector employers to hire welfare recipients by subsidizing wages for a fixed period of time (usually less than six months). The positive finding was that these on-the-job training programs usually provided welfare recipients with somewhat better jobs, with longer hours or higher wages, than they would have located independently. (They also seemed to target more employable recipients, however, many of whom would have moved off of welfare in the absence of the program.) The main drawback to the program was that the aforementioned initiatives rarely reached any substantial scale. Despite considerable effort and subsidies ranging from 25 to 83 percent of wages, only a relatively small number of employers responded, suggesting that employers are more interested in qualified job candidates than in government subsidies (see Bangser, Healy, and Ivry 1986; Orr et al. 1996; Auspos, Cave, and Long 1988; Freedman, Bryant, and Cave 1988).

Community Work Experience Programs

Even the most successful welfare-to-work programs, incentives, and employer subsidies leave many welfare recipients on the rolls and unemployed. Mandatory community service work is an attractive policy option because it meets the public's desire to support children but require parents to work. In the past, the high cost of large-scale, subsidized work programs together with implementation challenges constrained program size, but the 1996 law requires all states to meet participation rates that will dramatically increase the number of welfare recipients working at either subsidized or unsubsidized jobs.

Research on work programs for welfare recipients is primarily about workfare, unpaid work experience in which people are required to work a certain number of hours to earn their welfare check. The research record is thin and mixed (see Brock, Butler, and Long 1993; Gueron and Pauly 1991). On the positive side, studies from the 1980s show that it is feasible to convince people to work for grants, that they often view short-term work assignments as fair, and that they do real work. Furthermore, under reasonable assumptions, the value to the local community of the work produced usually offsets the cost (approximately $2,000 to $4,000 a year per slot filled, plus the cost of child care). Thus, such programs can provide an alternative way to maintain a safety net for children while sending a pro-work signal to parents.

On the other hand, officials as diverse as Governor Reagan of California and Mayor Koch of New York City experienced difficulty in developing large numbers of work sites and found some welfare recipients unable to work. As a result, programs were almost always smaller than anticipated. Even the currently very large New York City workfare program is small relative to the size of the TANF and general assistance caseloads.

Because the number of studies is limited, the research is inconclusive regarding whether mandatory workfare programs actually speed the eventual transition to unsubsidized work. Therefore, it appears that, in strictly budgetary terms—that is, ignoring the value of the work performed—sending people a small welfare check is probably cheaper than providing them with a non-market way to earn it. The reason lies in the fact that free labor is not really free: Time and money are required to develop, manage, and monitor work sites, and to provide child care for the children of workfare participants.

In summary, mandatory work programs meet the public's desire to link support to work, but past efforts have never reached the scale needed to project the outcome of work-based support. Given the tough work requirements in the new welfare law, it will be critical to determine the feasibility and cost of larger-scale work programs, as well the success rate of states in transitioning people from workfare programs into unsubsidized work.

Time Limits

The findings discussed above are drawn from studies launched prior to the introduction, in some states, of time-limited cash benefits. A number of current studies focus specifically on the design and implementation of time limits, their effect on work behavior, and a range of outcomes for families and children. Guiding questions in these studies include the following: What forms do time limits take? What are the major operational challenges of time-limit programs? Will they lead to dramatic increases in employment, either before or after welfare recipients reach the time limit? Will many people be cut off from welfare benefits with no work, or will states "blink" and grant extensions or exemptions? How will families survive without welfare? Will there be long-term effects on childbearing, family formation, or the well-being of children?

Early findings point to the challenges in implementing such programs: for example, gearing up and strengthening welfare-to-work programs to maximize pre–time-limit employment; balancing flexibility and discretion (to reflect the diversity in the caseload) against firmness (to send a clear message); communicating the message that the time limit is real; and helping recipients manage their use of welfare within the time limit (see Bloom 1997; Bloom and Butler 1995; Bloom, Kemple, and Rogers-Dillion 1997; Brown, Dan, and Butler 1997). Preliminary results are available for the more advantaged recipients of the Escambia County caseload in Florida—one of the first states to implement a time limit, and one that combined the time limit with increased services and more generous financial incentives. Researchers found that the program did not prompt people to leave the rolls more quickly *before* reaching the time limit (i.e., they did not "bank" their eligible months), but did reduce welfare receipt *after* the limit (at which point almost everyone had her or his benefits canceled). The program also seems to have increased earnings and income, but it is not yet clear what role the time limit (as opposed to the incentives or services) played in that result (Bloom et al. 1998).

Lessons on Running Social Experiments

The studies described above are credited with exerting an unusually large influence on policy. This was particularly true during the mid-1980s, in the California debate preceding the passage of GAIN legislation and the congressional debate culminating in the Family Support Act (see, e.g., Baum 1991; Haskins 1991; Greenberg and Mandell 1991; Szanton 1991; Wiseman 1991; Wallace and Long 1987). This series of studies suggests twelve lessons about implementing a successful social experiment.

Lesson 1: Diagnose the problem correctly.   The life cycle of a major experiment or evaluation is often five or more years. To succeed, the study must be rooted in issues of consequence—concerns that will outlive the tenure of an assistant secretary or a state commissioner and that will still be of interest when the results are compiled and published—and it must be rooted where there are important unanswered questions.

Lesson 2: Devise a reasonable treatment.   An experiment should test an approach that appears both operationally and politically feasible—where, for example, it is likely that the relevant delivery systems will cooperate, that the subjects will participate enough for the intervention to engender a positive difference, and that the costs of the experiment will not be so high as to rule out replication.

Lesson 3: Design a real-world test.   The program should be tested fairly (e.g., not during a chaotic start-up period) and, if possible, in multiple sites. It is uniquely powerful to be able to say that similar results emerged in Little Rock,

San Diego, and Baltimore. Replicating success in diverse environments is highly convincing to both Congress and state officials (Rikki Baum stresses this point in Baum 1991).

Lesson 4: Address the questions about which the public cares.   In welfare reform, the American people care about a range of questions: Does the new approach work? For whom? Under what conditions? Can it be replicated? How do benefits compare with costs? It is important not only to calculate hard numbers, but also to build on the social experiment in order to understand how to make programs function more efficiently and to address some qualitative concerns underlying public attitudes.

Lesson 5: Determine a reliable method of evaluating whether the program works. Here the unique strength of conducting a social experiment is evident. Policymakers flee from technical debates among experts. They do not want to take a public stand only to find that evidence has evaporated in the course of obscure debates on methodology. The key in large-scale projects is to answer a few questions well. Failure is not in determining that an approach does not work, but rather arriving at the end of a large investigation only to say, "I don't know." The cost of disagreement among the witch doctors is indeed paralysis. Ultimately, such altercations threaten to discredit social policy research.

The social experiments of the past twenty years illustrate the possibility of producing a data base widely accepted by congressional staff, federal agencies, the Congressional Budget Office, the General Accounting Office, state agencies, and state legislatures. When these studies began, ambiguity surrounded knowledge of the cost, impacts, and feasibility of welfare-to-work programs. Now this uncertainty has been narrowed dramatically.

Random assignment alone does not assure success, however. Large samples, adequate follow-up, quality data collection, and isolation of the control group from the spillover effects of the treatment are also essential ingredients to a successful experiment. Moreover, rigor in research has its drawbacks. Peter Rossi once formulated several laws about policy research, one of which was the following: The better the study, the smaller the likely net impact (see Baum 1991). Quality policy research must continually compete with the claims of greater success based on weaker evidence.

Lesson 6: Contextualize the results.   To impact policy, social scientists must often do more than carry out a good project and report the lessons. The audience needs assistance in assessing the relative value of the approach tested versus the relative value of other comparable investigations. A useful way of accomplishing this task is to lodge the results of the experiment in the broader context of what is known about effective and ineffective programs.

Lesson 7: Simplify.   If an advanced degree is required in order to understand the lessons, they are unlikely to impact policymakers. One of the beauties of a social experiment is that anyone can understand what was done and what was learned. In the 1980s, MDRC developed a standard way to present research results and adhered to that pattern. Thus, the public learned to read MDRC studies and understand the results.

Lesson 8: Actively disseminate results.   It is important to design the project so that it will have intermediate products and to share results with federal and state officials, congressional staff and Congress, public interest groups, advocates, and the press. At the same time, the pressure to produce early results—at the risk of later having to reverse conclusions—must be resisted.

Lesson 9: Do not confuse dissemination with advocacy.   The key to long-term successful communication is trust. If an organization overstates findings or distorts them to fit an agenda, the audience will ultimately discern this and reject the message.

Lesson 10: Be honest about failures.   Although many of our studies have produced positive findings, the results are often mixed, and at times clearly negative. State officials and program administrators share the human fondness for good news. To their credit, however, most officials seek to learn from disappointing results, which often prove as valuable as successful results when shaping policy.

Lesson 11: Dramatic results are not necessary to impact policy.   Many have said that the Family Support Act was based on, and passed on, the strength of research—and it was research about modest changes. Reliable results usually suggest that social programs (at least the relatively modest ones usually tested in this country) are not panaceas, but that they can improve current conditions. Based on the twenty years of MDRC work, one can observe that modest changes have often been enough to make a program cost-effective and to convince policymakers to act. However, while this was true in the mid-1980s, it was certainly not true in the mid-1990s. In the last round of federal welfare debates, modest improvements were often cast as failures.

Lesson 12: Solicit partners and buy-in from the beginning.   In conceptualizing and launching a project, allow the major delivery systems, public interest groups, and advocates to own the project and the lessons. If research organizations take this step, they will not have to promote their results forcefully; rather, others will do it.

One reason MDRC research impacted policy was the change in the scale, structure, and funding of social experiments described at the beginning of this chapter. The Supported Work and negative income tax experiments of the 1970s were relatively small-scale tests conducted outside mainstream delivery systems (in laboratory-like or controlled environments) and supported with generous federal funds. This situation shifted dramatically in 1981, with the virtual elimination of federal funds to operate field tests of new initiatives. Every MDRC social experiment conducted since then used the regular, mainstream delivery systems to operate the program. There has been very little special funding.

The clear downside of this new mode was a limit on the boldness of what could be tested. We had to build on what could be funded through the normal channels, which may partly explain the modest nature of the program impacts. The upside was the immediate state and/or local ownership, since we were by definition evaluating real-world state or local initiatives, not projects made in Washington or at a think tank. In order to randomly assign 10,000 people in welfare offices in a large urban area, state or county employees have to have a reason to cooperate. When researchers are relying on state welfare and unemployment insurance earnings records to track outcomes, state officials have to have a reason to provide these data. In seeking cooperation, we argued that these were *their* studies, addressing *their* questions, and conducted under state contracts. In the end, state officials had a greater sense of ownership for the studies: they were paying some of the freight, and thus they had a commitment to making the research succeed. Their commitment was aided by the fact that such evaluations also could satisfy the Section 1115 research requirements imposed by HHS (see the previous discussion).

Through this process, MDRC leveraged state welfare-reform demonstration ideas into social experiments. We involved the key institutions as partners all along. For the major actors and funding streams, relevance was clear from the outset. This buy-in was critical to success. The state–research organization partnership also had a positive effect on the researchers, forcing them to consider both the audience and their questions. In this process, during the 1980s and 1990s, social experiments moved out of the laboratory and into welfare and job training offices. Studies no longer involved a thousand people, but tens of thousands. Researchers did not have to convince policymakers and program administrators that the findings were relevant; the tests were not the prelude to a large-scale test but instead informed states directly what major legislation was delivering (see Greenberg and Mandell 1991; Blum 1990). Because of the studies' methodological rigor, the results were widely believed. But the limited funding narrowed the outcomes that could be measured and the boldness of what was tested.

Four years ago, I might have argued that these twelve factors explained why MDRC studies had such a large impact on state and federal policy in the

1980s and early 1990s. But they were less important in 1996. In contrast to the Family Support Act, TANF is very much a leap into the unknown. While not necessarily pleasant, it is always useful for researchers to remember that their work is only one ingredient in the policy process and that politics trumps research when the political stakes are high enough. The past thirty years have also shown, however, that legislation (particularly federal legislation) has played only a small part of the welfare reform process. Welfare reform researchers should carefully observe how states use their new flexibility, including the extent to which research findings inform state choices and appetite for continuing to learn from the reform process. Early evidence suggests a hunger (particularly at the county level) for evidence regarding effective programs and shows some state enthusiasm for continuing the pre-TANF evaluations (e.g., thirty states applied to HHS to continue or to modify waiver evaluations launched prior to 1996).

Conclusion

Over the past twenty years, policy researchers have built a solid foundation of high-quality studies on the effectiveness of various welfare reform approaches. This knowledge base has proven the envy of other fields. In the early 1970s it was not known whether social experiments could be used to test real-world operating programs. Researchers now know, however, that social experiments are successful, that the results are positive and convincing, and that the studies have mattered. But this success is no reason for complacency. The combination of block grants and the termination of the Section 1115 waiver process puts this approach at risk. States will surely innovate, but simply because a thousand flowers bloom does not indicate that researchers will learn whether they bloom well. In the new climate, less money is available for research, states have the option to neglect evaluation of important innovations, and policy-making will likely be influenced more by politics than by research. The stakes are high for states, which, under the new law, will bear the full financial risk of welfare changes. This reality creates pressure on states to acquire reliable and objective data (i.e., to learn early about unintended consequences and costs of state reforms), but politicization of the welfare debate pushes states in the opposite direction. Not-in-my-backyard arguments may be applied to the world of social policy research: Studies are a good thing, but for the neighbors, not for me.

Beyond the political challenges, the magnitude of change—and the likelihood that it will affect the full welfare caseload—makes the random-assignment paradigm less feasible and appropriate. Fortunately, a number of states have chosen to complete (and in some cases even expand) major random-assignment studies launched under the 1990s waivers. This commitment to learning is impressive and important, since these studies will provide critical, early information on alternative approaches to time limits, work incentives, welfare-to-work strategies, broad antipoverty efforts, programs to increase the employment and child support payments of noncustodial fathers of children on welfare, learnfare, family caps, and other building blocks of state TANF policies. In addition, a number of major studies will monitor states' actions under the 1996 legislation and assess the impact of the new policies on families and communities. A number of new initiatives are also targeted at particularly disadvantaged populations and communities (see, for example, Riccio 1997). Finally, while it may prove impossible to use random assignment to assess the total system that replaces AFDC, it will remain possible to use this approach to compare key policy alternatives that are central to state design choices and program costs. The impressive record from past research—and the early evidence of some state interest in continuing to learn—sets a challenge for those in this field to develop research strategies that provide convincing lessons and respond to the new policy framework.

NOTE

This chapter is based upon a paper published in a slightly altered version in *Progress and future directions in evaluation,* ed. Debra J. Rog and Deborah Fournier (San Francisco: Jossey-Bass, 1997). Grateful acknowledgment is made to Jossey-Bass Publishers for permission to reprint this work.

REFERENCES

Aaron, Henry J. 1978. *Politics and the professors: The Great Society in perspective.* Washington, D.C.: Brookings Institution.

Auspos, Patricia, George Cave, and David Long. 1988. *Maine: Final report on the training opportunities in the private sector program.* New York: MDRC.

Bane, Mary Jo, and David T. Ellwood. 1983. *The dynamics of dependence: The routes to self-sufficiency.* Cambridge, Mass.: Urban Systems Research and Engineering, Inc.

Bangser, Michael, James Healy, and Robert Ivry. 1986. *Welfare grant diversion: Lessons and prospects.* New York: MDRC.

Bardach, Eugene. 1993. *Improving the productivity of JOBS programs.* Papers for Practitioners. New York: MDRC.

Baum, Erica B. 1991. When the witch doctors agree: The Family Support Act and social science research. *Journal of Policy Analysis and Management* 10 (4): 603–15.

Blank, Rebecca M. 1997. *It takes a nation: A new agenda for fighting poverty.* Princeton: Princeton University Press (with the Russell Sage Foundation, New York).

Bloom, Dan. 1997. *After AFDC: Welfare-to-work choices and challenges for states.* ReWORKing Welfare: Technical Assistance for States and Localities. New York: MDRC.

Bloom, Dan, and David Butler. 1995. *Implementing time-limited welfare: Early experiences in three states.* Cross-State Study of Time-Limited Welfare. New York: MDRC.

Bloom, Dan, Mary Farrell, James J. Kemple, and Nandita Verma. 1998. *FTP: The Family Transition Program—Implementation and interim impacts of Florida's initial time-limited welfare program.* New York: MDRC.

Bloom, Dan, James J. Kemple, and Robin Rogers-Dillon. 1997. *FTP: The Family Transition Program—Implementation and early impacts of Florida's initial time-limited welfare program.* New York: MDRC.

Blum, Barbara B. 1990. Bringing administrators into the process. *Public Welfare* 3:4–12.

Brock, Thomas, David Butler, and David Long. 1993. *Unpaid work experience for welfare recipients: Findings and lessons from MDRC research.* MDRC Working Paper. New York: MDRC.

Brock, Thomas, Fred Doolittle, Veronica Fellerath, and Michael Wiseman. 1997. *Creating new hope: Implementation of a program to reduce poverty and reform welfare.* New York: MDRC.

Brown, Amy. 1997. *Work First: How to implement an employment-focused approach to welfare reform.* ReWORKing Welfare: Technical Assistance for States and Localities. New York: MDRC.

Brown, Amy, Dan Bloom, and David Butler. 1997. *The view from the field: As time limits approach, welfare recipients and staff talk about their attitudes and expectations.* Cross-State Study of Time-Limited Welfare. New York: MDRC.

Card, David, and Philip Robins. 1996. *Do financial incentives encourage welfare recipients to work? Initial 18-month findings from the self-sufficiency project.* Ottawa, Ontario: Social Research and Demonstration Corporation.

Freedman, Stephen, J. Bryant, and George Cave. 1988. *New Jersey: Final report on the grant diversion project.* New York: MDRC.

Freedman, Stephen, and Daniel Friedlander. 1995. *Early findings on program impacts in three sites.* The JOBS Evaluation. Washington, D.C.: U.S. Department of Health and Human Services, Office of the Assistant Secretary for Planning and Evaluation.

Freedman, Stephen, Daniel Friedlander, Winston Lin, and Amanda Schweder. 1996. *The GAIN evaluation: Five-year impacts on employment, earnings, and AFDC receipt.* The GAIN Evaluation, Working Paper 96.1. New York: MDRC.

Friedlander, Daniel, and Gary Burtless. 1995. *Five years after: The long-term effects of welfare-to-work programs.* New York: Russell Sage Foundation.

Goldman, Barbara. 1981. *Impacts of the immediate job search assistance experiment: Louisville WIN research project.* New York: MDRC.

Greenberg, David H., and Marvin B. Mandell. 1991. Research utilization in policymaking: A tale of two series (of social experiments). *Journal of Policy Analysis and Management* 10 (4): 633–56.

Greenberg, David, and Michael Wiseman. 1992. What did the OBRA demonstrations do? In *Evaluating Employment and Training Programs*, ed. Charles Manski and E. Garfinkel. Cambridge: Harvard University Press.

Gueron, Judith M. 1980. The supported work experiment. In *Employing the Unemployed*, ed. Eli Ginzberg. New York: Basic Books.

———. 1984. Lessons from managing the supported work demonstration. In *The National Supported Work Demonstration*, ed. Robinson G. Hollister Jr. and P. Kemper. Madison: University of Wisconsin Press.

———. 1985. The demonstration of state/work welfare initiatives. In *Randomization and Field Experimentation*, ed. Robert F. Boruch and Werner Wothke. San Francisco and London: Jossey-Bass; special issue, *New Directions for Program Evaluation* 28:5–14.

———. 1996. A research context for welfare reform. *Journal of Policy Analysis and Management* 15:547–61.

Gueron, Judith M., and Richard P. Nathan. 1985. The MDRC work/welfare project: Objectives, status, significance. *Policy Studies Review* 4:417–32.

Gueron, Judith M., and Edward Pauly. 1991. *From welfare to work.* New York: Russell Sage Foundation.

Hamilton, Gayle, and Thomas Brock. 1994. *Early lessons from seven sites.* National Evaluation of Welfare-to-Work Strategies (formerly called the JOBS Evaluation). Washington, D.C.: U.S. Department of Health and Human Services.

Hamilton, Gayle, Thomas Brock, Mary Farrell, Daniel Friedlander, and Kristen Harknett. 1997. *Evaluating two welfare-to-work program approaches: Two-year findings on the labor force attachment and human capital development programs in three sites.* National Evaluation of Welfare-to-Work Strategies. Washington, D.C.: U.S. Department of Health and Human Services, Administration for Children and Families and Office of the Assistant Secretary for Planning and Evaluation.

Haskins, Ron. 1991. Congress Writes a Law: Research and Welfare Reform. *Journal of Policy Analysis and Management* 10 (4): 616–32.

Knab, Jean Tansey, and Stephen Freedman. 1997. *The GAIN evaluation: Five-year benefit-cost analysis of California's GAIN program.* The GAIN Evaluation, Working Paper 97.1. New York: MDRC.

Manpower Demonstration Research Corporation (MDRC) Board of Directors. 1980. *Summary and findings of the national supported work demonstration.* Cambridge, Mass.: Ballinger.

Mead, Lawrence M. 1986. *Beyond entitlement: The social obligations of citizenship.* New York: Free Press.

Miller, Cynthia, Virginia W. Knox, Patricia Auspos, Jo Anna Hunter-Manns, and Alan Orenstein. 1997. *MFIP: Making welfare work and work pay—Implementation and 18-month impacts of Minnesota's family investment program.* New York: MDRC.

Murray, Charles. 1994. What to do about welfare. *Commentary* 98 (6): 26–34.

Orr, Larry L., Howard S. Bloom, Stephen H. Bell, Fred Doolittle, Winston Lin, and George Cave. 1996. *Does training for the disadvantaged work? Evidence from the national JTPA study.* Washington, D.C.: Urban Institute Press.

Riccio, James. 1997. A research framework for evaluating the Jobs-Plus demonstration, A saturation place-based employment initiative for public housing residents.

Paper presented at the annual meeting of the Association for Public Policy and Management (APPAM), New York City, November 6–7.

Riccio, James, Daniel Friedlander, and Stephen Freedman. 1994. *GAIN: Benefits, costs, and three-year impacts of a welfare-to-work program.* New York: MDRC.

Riccio, James A., and A. Orenstein. 1996. Understanding best practices for operating welfare-to-work programs. *Evaluation Review* 20 (1): 3–28.

Social Research and Demonstration Corporation (SRDC). 1996. *When work pays better than welfare: A summary of the self-sufficiency project's implementation, focus group, and initial 18-month impact reports.* Ottawa, Ontario: Social Research and Demonstration Corporation.

Szanton, Peter L. 1991. The Remarkable "Quango": Knowledge, politics, and welfare reform. *Journal of Policy Analysis and Management* 10 (4): 590–602.

Wallace, John, and David Long. 1987. *GAIN: Planning and early implementation.* New York: MDRC.

Wiseman, Michael. 1991. Research and policy: An afterword for the symposium on the Family Support Act of 1988. *Journal of Policy Analysis and Management* 10 (4): 657–66.

Wolfhagen, C. 1983. *Job search strategies: Lessons from the Louisville WIN laboratory project.* New York: MDRC.

Zambrowski, Amy, and Anne Gordon. 1993. *Evaluation of the minority female single parent demonstration: Fifth-year impacts at CET.* New York: Rockefeller Foundation.

CHAPTER 8

The Making and Analysis of Public Policy:
A Perspective on the Role of Social Science

Laurence E. Lynn Jr.

In the 1960s and early 1970s the policy analysis "movement" irrupted into American political life. Opportunistically assembling rudiments of authority, knowledge, technical skill, and application that began to accumulate with the emergence of the modern administrative state, a well-positioned group of federal executives succeeded in forging new structural links between research-based knowledge and policy-making. The legacies of their efforts are still evident in social science scholarship; in undergraduate, graduate, and professional training; and in administrative institutions, technologies, and practices at all levels of government. These legacies remain controversial, however. The role of social science in democratic governance and the mediating contributions of policy analysts are vigorously contested, raising issues concerning the future of policy analysis training and practice.

The advent of policy analysis as an administrative technology[1] marked a watershed in public administration: both a culmination of trends toward governance by qualified managers, initiated in the nineteenth century, and, in view of the movement's tendency to centralize political power, a stimulus to late-twentieth-century efforts to democratize policy-making influence and expertise. Public policy scholarship, textbooks, curricula, and folklore, however, still tend to idealize executive-oriented policy analysis. Thus a relatively young profession has seemed slow to adapt to the post–cold war, "third way," communication-based politics that appears to call for changes in policy analysis methods and applications.

This apparent inertia in policy analysis training and practice may appear to vindicate its most recent and strident critics, who see positive social science and its applications as inimical to democracy, community, truth seeking, and constructive change. I shall argue that both supporters and critics of contemporary research- and analysis-based policy-making inadequately appreciate the extent to which tendencies toward rationalizing public action on the basis of expertise are tightly woven into our political-legal-bureaucratic institutions. These tendencies antedate the policy analysis movement, and they will survive its severest critics. The issue is not whether but how social science–based policy analysis will inform state action in ways that are both constructive and consistent with evolving American political values.

Scholars concerned with such matters have demonstrated two rather distinct tendencies. In the first, social scientists as interested parties, in other words, experts who view the public sector as a source of resources and opportunity, are preoccupied with the question "Are we making a difference?" They produce what may be termed a "knowledge and power" literature. In the second, social scientists as relatively disinterested scholars consider policy-making as a social process from a variety of disciplinary and epistemological perspectives, addressing the question "What is the role and influence of expertise?" They produce a critical "science and society" literature. This essay adopts the second orientation to address the first.

The discussion is organized as follows: The next section is concerned with the power side of knowledge and power, addressing administrative developments that have enlarged opportunities for expert influence. I will argue that the power of policymakers, whether executive, legislative, or judicial, and their need for knowledge derive from their discretionary authority, that is, their formal and actual authority to propose and to design actions to be taken by others. The issue of how and why policymakers should act has grown in importance, inspiring important innovations in administrative technology, among them policy analysis.

The following section discusses the knowledge side of knowledge and power. The argument is that an important stimulant to the acquisition of social science knowledge has been its potential value to policymakers, especially as these officials are compelled to argue for the legitimacy of their discretionary actions before partisan legislators, stakeholders, and an often skeptical judiciary.

With these sections as foundation, I take up the controversies that have been associated with policy analysis when viewed as an administrative technology mediating between social science scholarship and policy-making. Do experts and their mediators produce enlightenment or distortion? I then consider the implications for the role of policy analysts and for policy-relevant research of recent tendencies toward the diffusion throughout the polity of influence over public policy. The concluding argument is that policy analysts and the researchers that inform them must diversify their focus, de-emphasizing executive decision making in favor of addressing the varied needs for enlightenment of other influential actors enmeshed within complex processes of political communication.[2]

An "Active, Originating, Inventing, Contriving Element"

The United States is a representative democracy founded on governmental power that is checked, balanced, and limited by the Constitution and by the rule of law. Its public administrators must in the first instance fulfill legal obligations imposed by legislatures, courts, and formal executive orders. It now seems self-evident that making and managing public policy in such a system requires human agency: judgment and discretion by officials with legitimate authority to act. While administrative discretion occurred in practice from the beginning of the Republic, the concept of administrative discretion in public administration theory and the existence of administrative law that formally recognizes it are distinctly twentieth-century developments, features of the modern administrative state and, in particular, of the post–New Deal welfare state.[3] The delegation of power to public managers for the accomplishment of public mandates, moreover, has been controversial from the time the modern state began to emerge. Unreviewable authority to act has been regarded, especially in our governmental system, as a potential danger to democracy. For this reason, the incorporation of doctrines of administrative discretion into jurisprudence, political theory, and administrative practice is far from complete.

Prior to the twentieth century, the law governing public administration in the United States was assumed to be indistinguishable from private law.[4] With the emergence of the administrative state, the courts had to decide how to rule on issues involving the exercise of discretion by administrative officers in a wide range of matters. The law governing executive authority in the administrative state evolved as courts tried to reconcile the dramatically increased lawmaking authority of the executive branch with a constitutional system that made no provision for it.[5] Further, the courts had to resolve contentious issues involving the separation of powers and the nondelegation doctrine, which pitted legal formalism against reasonable interpretation. A milestone was the 1946 enactment of the Administrative Procedures Act, but the high-water mark of deference to administrative discretion was reached when the Supreme Court issued its 1984 decision in the case of *Chevron USA v. Natural Resources Defense Council.* In this case, federal district judges were directed to defer to agency decision making (a) if agency action is in clear conformity with legislative intent and (b) if, in the absence of clear legislative intent, the agency's actions are reasonable.

Administration by Professionals

The need for discretionary action by administrators within a constitutional regime that does not actually provide for it gives rise to the enduring issues of policy-making and implementation. The study of policy-making can be viewed as the study of administrative discretion, its location, and its uses. Among the branches, levels, and agencies of government, who shall define the goals of public policy? In whose hands shall its execution be placed, and how much discretion shall the executors be allowed to exercise? To whom and how shall those with delegated authority be accountable? How shall conflicts over authority and performance be resolved?

The institution of professional administrative roles, formally insulated from political rewards and reprisals, introduced the idea of qualifications, tenure, and neutral competence into governance. The creation of a professional civil service beginning late in the nineteenth century enabled the large complex organizations of government. Policymakers were able to delegate responsibility for program administration to subordinates through an employment contract while remaining generally accountable to the public for the activities of their employees. In the meantime, these subordinates would have the authority to do what was needed to implement public law. They would need training and expertise to do their work well, stimulating the emergence of public administration as a profession to replace public officeholding as an extension of legislative politics.

Administrative discretion might seem to be intrinsically an executive function. This idea was given scientific support by Frederick Taylor's (1911) concept of "scientific management," which divided formal responsibility for administration between a managerial group and a group that performed the work. This division of labor became popular in both business and public administration (Rainey 1991). But, as Justice Holmes recognized, there are no intrinsic legislative, judicial, or administrative actions. The courts were consistently hostile to administrative discretion, believing it to be inherently arbitrary, and they assumed responsibility for addressing the kinds of questions listed above. As Marshall Dimock saw it,

> The general rule which the courts have laid down is that, before administrative officials will be permitted to exercise a discretionary power affecting an individual's rights, the legislature must have created a standard. . . . [However], the law on the subject [of standards] is elusive. (1936b, 53–54)

Over time, "personnel" and "procedural elements" came to be recognized as the best safeguards against the arbitrary exercise of administrative discretion. Are public managers qualified, and have they followed procedures that preclude the abuse of power? Early public administration doctrine came to emphasize an "institutional" approach to administration where "the emphasis is shifted from legal rules and cases to the formal framework and procedures of the administrative machine" (Dimock 1936a, 7). Judicial rules and decisions, statutory and constitutional limitations and requirements, and, later, executive orders and administrative rules having the force of law were thought to govern administration.

Excluded from the foundation of administrative action by public law and institutional traditions were concrete experience and the "human side of administration" (Dimock 1936b). Laski (1923) argued, "Administrative discretion is the essence of the modern State." More fully developed notions concerning executive discretion with respect to policy-making began to take shape with the first attempts to institutionalize social planning in the United States. "Heretofore," said Dimock, "discretion has been viewed through the lawyer's eyes; let us try to observe it from the perspective of the administrator as well" (47). His argument was that administrative discretion had been hostage to judges as yet unable to grasp the requirements of the modern administrative state and instinctively disposed to view administrative discretion as essentially arbitrary and subject to abuse. This, Dimock believed, was a fundamental misconception.

Theory and Invention

Following this line of thinking, Dimock (1936a), foreshadowing the policy analysis movement, identified an alternative approach he called "theory and invention." Its purpose "is largely to uncover false assumptions and to invent new ideas and ways of doing things for the administrator" (8). He pointed out that practicing administrators tend to emphasize experience and "the practical approach." They are prone to denigrate theoretical or technical approaches even though they themselves are influenced by "ideas and researches." The pragmatism associated with John Dewey contributed to the idea that administration is "a tool by which the problems of society may be solved" (8). "The law related to the subject must, of course, be considered, but in addition the economic situation, the pressure of political parties, and vested interests must be given consideration" as well since they constitute "influences acting upon the actual administration of government" (8–9). Dimock argued:

> Public administration is not merely an inanimate machine, unthinkingly performing the work of government. If public administration is concerned with the problems of government, it is also by the same token interested in fulfilling the ends and objectives of the state. (11–12)

Administrative discretion is essential, Dimock (1936c) argued, because of the limits on the time, pace, and aptitude of legislative bodies. He continued:

> The execution of the law is not the only responsibility of the modern-day administration. Therefore, efficiency is not the only desideratum. Those

who view administrative action as simple commands . . . fail to comprehend the extent to which administration is called upon to help formulate policy and to fashion important realms of discretion in our modern democracies. Legislation and administration are not separable into nicely divided compartments. . . . And because they are not separable, the philosophies of public servants and their ideas concerning the ends of the state score heavily in the shaping of public policy. . . . *Administration . . . is an active, originating, inventing, contriving element in the body politic.* (127–28, emphasis added)

The notion of administrative discretion began congealing into doctrine. In their seminal postwar text, Simon, Thompson, and Smithburg ([1950] 1991) assayed the extent of administrative discretion and the value premises governing its exercise. They concluded that discretion is extensive and nearly fully explained by a detailed consideration of the formal and informal controls that establish the framework of accountability within which public administrators function. "Administrators and employees . . . have considerable freedom to decide matters on the basis of their own ethical promptings" (539). The principal contribution of Simon and his colleagues of the Carnegie School was the elaboration of the concept of discretion in terms of official behavior and, in particular, of discretionary acts of decision making and the premises on which decisions are based.

The Ultimate Act of Discretion

Discretion became an article of faith in public administration. Emmette Redford argued that "though administration is permeated and circumscribed by law, discretion is vital to its performance" (1958, 41). Discretion is necessary in administration because "law is rigid, and policy must be made pragmatically" (43). Variability of circumstances, multiple factors, and unanticipated contingencies are characteristic of administration. "The ultimate act of discretion," says Redford, "is often in *the decision whether to follow or not to follow an existing standard*" (1958, 47). Morstein-Marx argued that the core of the executive function is discretion and control, "the former in the sense of providing for the right kind of action, and the latter looking toward the attainment of accountability for the execution of policy" (1959, 185). He advocated "a profitable blend of judgments—political and professional, staff and line, general and special" (186).

Morstein-Marx and Reining carried the argument to the level of middle management:

As the principal support of top-level direction, middle management . . . has to infuse the generality of organization-wide purposes into its individual operations. On this score it can succeed only insofar as it captures in its own thinking the broad-range ends of the organization at large. (1959, 375)

Further,

> Control of operations, even under exceptionally favorable circumstances, is never a purely mechanical process. Human beings do not function like machines. *Attainment of a reasonably standardized group product hence requires considerable leeway in direction.* A great number of factors enter into any kind of organized group action. Only when the middle manager is placed in a position to influence these factors *without undue restraint* can he be expected to live up to his task. (377, emphasis added)

The notion that administration requires the exercise of discretion, the concept of discretion as the exercise of judgment concerning the ends and means of government, and the idea that the exercise of judgment takes place through decision making provided foundations for the idea that decision making should be based on sound analysis that incorporates knowledge derived from scientific research.

Truth for Power

As the concept of administrative discretion became doctrine, planning traditions appropriate to the exercise of that discretion began to take form, laying the intellectual groundwork for revolutionary developments in the role of trained experts in policy-making. Out of war, Depression, and the growing complexity of modern government arose sustained efforts to identify and satisfy the intellectual needs of policymakers—indeed, to establish and publicize that policymakers have intellectual needs associated with their exercising discretion. The policymakers whom social scientists and policy analysts would inform and advise, whether authoritative decision makers at the top or bureaucrats at middle and street levels of administration, were viewed as actors with the power to formulate, evaluate, and choose between or propose actions to be carried out by others.

"Good New Ideas"

The deliberate use of scientists and science-based information to inform public policy-making and implementation is hardly a recent phenomenon (Lynn 1989).[6] Heretofore, however, such uses had been more or less restricted to particular instances or regimes and were not necessarily a normal feature of policy-making. Moreover, a movement to bring "policy sciences" to bear on policy-making had already taken form. Initiated by Lasswell and colleagues and essentially formally initiated in 1951 (Lerner and Lasswell 1951), academic social scientists had begun to address the need of democratic states for systematic information to inform their deliberations, albeit with a far different purpose in mind than facilitating bureaucratic decision making.

The incorporation of policy analysis practice into executive policy-making beginning in the 1960s was nonetheless regarded within the social science community as something new in American politics. This new movement brought together knowledge derived from recent developments in systems, management, design, and economic sciences, improving competence in administrative leadership and efficiency in resource allocation: tools for managing complexity, identifying and solving problems, and allocating resources for maximum effect. Such tools were thought likely to be most effectively wielded by administrators with discretion to propose, decide on, and implement actions to be taken by others in pursuit of the goals of public policy. What was in fact new, at that time, was the deliberate incorporation of policy analysis and policy analysts into the central direction of large, complex government organizations. A new group of staff officers—policy analysts, answerable only to the organization's senior executives—were given privileged access to the executive and were empowered to speak for that executive in a variety of forums. The visibility of these officers attracted new attention to the processes by which the substance of public policies is determined.

Among the early demonstrations of the potential value of systematic analysis was the RAND corporation study of how to reduce the vulnerability of U.S. strategic nuclear forces. A number of the analysts' recommendations were immediately adopted by the U.S. Air Force. Quade (1964) drew a lesson from these RAND analyses that became a theme of the emerging policy analysis movement: "In an analysis aimed at policy-making, the relevance of the many factors and contingencies affecting the problem is more important than sophisticated analysis techniques. *A good new idea—technical, operational, or what have you—is worth a thousand elaborate evaluations*" (63, emphasis added).

In one of the first policy analysis texts, worth quoting at length in view of the subsequent criticisms of policy analysis discussed below, Quade (1964) identified pitfalls of analysis in the seemingly tractable domain of military planning. Analysts must recognize, he argued, that problems "frequently belong to that class in which *the difficulty lies more in deciding what ought to be done than in deciding how to do it*" (301, emphasis added). The most serious error of practice would be to look at an unduly restricted range of alternatives, to apply "some mechanistic test to alternatives suggested by others" (302), and to uncritically accept "official" figures. Nor is it the case that if enough factual research is carried out, a valid generalization will somehow automatically emerge. "It is a pitfall," says Quade, "to become more interested in the model than in the real world. . . . A model is but a representation. . . . More must be left out than can be included" (309). Analysts should not overvalue methods that facilitate computation, nor should they use techniques that are more complicated than necessary. "It is a serious pitfall for the analyst to concentrate so completely on the purely objective and scientific aspects of his analysis that he neglects the subjective elements or fails to handle them with understanding" (314). Finally, "an analyst is in a position to bias the conclusions of a study. . . . Doing this deliberately to impose his personal preferences is unethical" (316).

A New Administrative Technology

An expanding literature offered additional definitions of policy analysis:

In a contemporaneous formulation that captured its evolving essence, Lane (1972) defined policy analysis as "the answers to the question: What happens when we intervene in the social system this way rather than that and why?" (71). He saw the movement as having several themes: a concern for government's purpose, mission, and objectives; the illumination of the wider social costs and the latent or unintended consequences of government interventions; consideration of alternatives, especially those of interest to groups "unable to present their own case effectively"; consideration of competing values; the normative basis of political advocacy, or "de-mystification of government and politics"; exposure of the consequences of assumptions and conventions; a consumer rather than producer orientation; and an orientation toward intervention, in other words, toward control and action (79–83).

Wildavsky described "the art of policy analysis" as follows.

> Policy analysis must create problems that decision-makers are able to handle with the variables under their control and in the time available . . . by specifying a desired relationship between manipulable means and obtainable objectives. . . . Unlike social science, policy analysis must be prescriptive; arguments about correct policy, which deal with the future, cannot help but be willful and therefore political. (1979, 16)

Lynn (1987) saw the proper role of social science–based policy analysis as improving the basis on which policy decisions are made by employing theory, empirical knowledge, and analytic craftsmanship to clarify issues, alternatives, and consequences in a precise and dispassionate way. If policy analysts do not perform this type of work, which is essential to the clarity and effectiveness of public policy, no one else in politics will do it.

A theme that proved especially inspirational to policy-oriented social scientists of that era was Aaron Wildavsky's characterization of policy analysis as "speaking truth to power." Given access to policy-making by enlightened officials in all agencies and branches of government, many policy-oriented social scientists came to view policymakers ("power") as members of a social engineering firm, whose business it is to correctly apply scientifically grounded "truth" to solving social problems. When policymakers needed help with this important work, they would be able to turn to the growing ranks of professionally trained policy analysts, who, being bilingual in the languages of science and policy, would "speak" to them in terms they could understand. The products of this communication would comprise new forms of "knowledge for action": policy analysis, program evaluation, and policy-relevant research. Serious consideration was given to the possibility that policy analysis might integrate the disparate social science disciplines, thereby reaping the benefits of interdisciplinary inquiry.

The popularity of policy analysis and policy-relevant scientific research strongly reinforced a positive view of social science, viz., the world of human, social, and political interaction can be known through rigorous, transparent protocols that guide policy researchers in their search for general principles and robust propositions that inform action by empowered policymakers. Associated with this view of knowledge was a compatible view of action: action is enabled by power, and power is executive power.

Policy and program analysis, development, planning, and evaluation began to be incorporated into the administrative routines and functional structures of public bureaucracies, thereby ensuring that policy analysts would have a place at a great many tables. The number of policy analysts in government grew rapidly, inspired by President Johnson's apparent intention to institute scientifically grounded policy analysis, planning, and program evaluation as regular functions of the public executive and as instruments of political leadership. Sundquist (1978) coined the term *research broker* to describe the role of packaging and retailing the intellectual products of the research community to policymakers. In his view, knowledge potentially useful to policymakers, while often available in the research community, is inaccessible to or unrecognizable by policymakers. Hence policy-making is often less thoughtful and well-informed than it might be. By identifying, assembling, and translating potentially relevant bodies of knowledge into intelligence relevant to the immediate needs of policymakers, research brokers perform an essential role in the policy-making process.

Policy analysis practice became the subject of a growing literature. Heclo (1977) labeled the new breed of policy analysts as "reformers." "Such analysts," he observed, "are often the agency head's only institutional resource for thinking about substantive policy without commitments to the constituents, jurisdictions, and self-interests of existing programs" (151). "Their most enduring problem," he added, "is one of attracting political customers to use their analysis while maintaining constructive relations and access to the program offices being analyzed." Meltsner (1976) studied the activities of policy analysts at work, emphasizing the social role of the analysts in the bureaucracy. Based on observing policy analysis in the Department of Energy, Feldman (1989) argued that the role of policy analysts in a bureaucracy is not to inform decision making—even the analysts themselves do not see this as their function—but, rather, through negotiating and crossing institutional boundaries, to contribute to the definition of organizational interests and to the interpretation of events and actions. While their technical, problem-solving skills are important, so, too, is their skill in performing their social/institutional role.

The literature on policy analysis practice suggests that its emerging ethos was progressive, critical, pragmatic, optimistic, and reformist. Never monolithic in its methods, policy analysis practice has evolved in response to the political and social realities that shape public policy agendas. Policy analysis in practice has been fueled by intuition, argument, and ethical promptings, clearly associated with the world of political action, both normative and prescriptive, often identified with interests otherwise unrepresented at the table. Says practitioner Robert Nelson (1989), "In many cases, policy analysts make their greatest contribution, not with highly sophisticated economic analyses, but with *simple arguments that challenge practices and ideas that have simply become part of agency tradition, culture, and ideology—even in the face of common sense*" (408, emphasis added).

The Diffusion of Practice

As a result of high-level recognition, a market for policy-relevant research and analysis rather quickly emerged. Apparently, the appearance, at least, of reliance on research-based analysis was good politics. "At all levels of government and at every stage of the policy process, analytical studies of problems and evaluations of programs have become commonplace" (Heineman et al. 1997, 1). Policy analysis organizations inside and outside of government have proliferated; advocacy-oriented policy research has grown in popularity; and nonprofit and proprietary policy research firms have grown in numbers and influence. More recently, the emergence of sophisticated new means of communication has facilitated instantaneous dissemination of policy-relevant research and political mobilization based on policy research findings.

Whereas the earliest generation of policy analysts took advantage of executive agency monopolies on data and program information, data sets now are accessible for public use, and techniques for analyzing data, once restricted to technocratic elites, also are widely available. Small, community-based non-profit organizations are frequently as eager to conduct poverty research and service evaluations as large public agencies. Community groups demand facts, information, and access to expertise. Information-based planning and collaboration are sponsored by philanthropic foundations, and both governments and foundations require needs assessments, feasibility analyses, impact assessments, and forecasts as conditions of grant awards. Courts look to the adequacy of planning and analysis as grounds for adjudicating a growing array of class-action lawsuits.

Policy analysis is now taken for granted in political discourse procedure, causing far-reaching implications that unfortunately are often missed by those most closely involved in policy analysis training and practice. Though teaching cases record the rich contextual details of policy deliberation and administration, methods training and doctrines continue to be based on the traditional trilogy of economics, political science, and statistics (and very occasionally sociology and organization theory). The contextualization of abstract concepts is often left to elective courses, workshops, field placements, and internships. However, the societal implications of this narrow curriculum have not been overlooked by the critics of the policy analysis movement, the stridency of whose commentaries has increased over time.

Consequences and Controversies

In assuming a featured role in American politics, policy-making itself and the new, influential policy analysis methods became the objects of scholarly attention. Two questions in particular came to the fore: (1) In view of the growing political interest in their contributions, what should social scientists study? (2) What is the authority of social science knowledge as a basis for public policy-making? Fueled by public and private grant support for both academic and think tank scholarship and research, as well as by the continually evolving agendas of academic disciplines and subfields, policy-relevant scholarship has prospered, yielding influential new concepts, models, and methods for research and analysis. The employment of this scholarship and the mediating role of policy analysts in its applications have, however, provided abundant grist for the mills of academic controversy.

New Issues for Social Science

From its inception, policy analysis as an administrative technology attracted attention from across the social science community (see, e.g., Charlesworth

1972; Nagel 1975). Emerging from its behavioral phase, for example, political science begin to discover an interest in the content of public policies. A renewed, rigorous concern for institutions emerged in sociology, political science, and economics. New subfields and research agendas took form: policy-making as decision science and as bureaucratic politics, policy formation as political process, legislative behavior as institutionalization of public choice and democratic control, and public deliberation as social learning and mobilization. As a result of this policy-oriented scholarship, understanding of the institutional context for the creation and dissemination of policy advice has changed dramatically and helpfully in recent decades. Here I offer examples of this new understanding.

Discretion and performance.   The issue of administrative discretion is now a good deal more complex than it was in Dimock's day. Is there too much administrative discretion (yielding unaccountable bureaucracy) or not enough (resulting in micromanaged bureaucracy)? Is structure-induced equilibrium a problem (causing gridlock) or a benefit (producing stability and reliability)? Are public executives requisite (as entrepreneurs and innovators), or are their contributions epiphenomenal (mechanistic and inconsequential)? If bureaucracies are suffused with unaccountable authority, is this situation an inevitable concomitant of our system of governance (Brodkin 1987) or inadvertent, inappropriate, and remediable (Gruber 1987)? To the extent that bureaucratic discretion appears to be choked by constraints and unduly restrained by custom, is this as it should be, representing effective social control through collective choice processes (Noll and Weingast 1987), or is it inimical to effective (i.e., visionary, creative, innovative, ethical) governmental performance and, therefore, in need of reform (Goodsell 1995)?

Theoretically, scholars of governance may now begin with a relatively parsimonious view of the public sector, as reflecting a logic of collective choice and a process of institutionalization, and systematically introduce elements of conceptual complexity, including those suggested by bureaucratic theory and by sociological and social-psychological perspectives on organizational and interorganizational behavior. Generic management problems such as overcoming resistance to change, motivating cooperative behavior, or coordinating and integrating distinct horizontal activities can be addressed with due regard for the details of their context. As Weiss (1996) has shown, a process as seemingly straightforward as instilling a sense of mission in an agency can now be understood at a much deeper level as involving complex processes of socialization.

Based on recent empirical research, a formidable array of variables potentially associated with governmental performance has been identified: resource levels and structures of financial administration; judicial institutions and practices; organizational structures; policy designs; intergovernmental relations;

the composition of policy networks; and the discretionary choices of managers. There is respectable evidence to support an argument that the qualifications of managers and the nature of managerial behavior are endogenous to the general system of policy-making and public administration and that the particular qualities of individual managers and of individual acts of management are, as some sociologists have long insisted, epiphenomenal. That specific executives appear to exert an independent influence on what government does may be a self-indulgent and illusory view. Perhaps administrative discretion is not the essence of the modern state after all.

Policy and behavior.   A new, critical perspective on the nature of questions that ought to engage social scientists has been penetrating deeply into policy studies at the vital center of public policy schools but especially into studies conducted outside of public policy schools. Judgment, perception, interpretation, reflection, and framing are, it is argued, the forms of cognition that dominate policy formation and implementation. Cognition, moreover, is less important to effectiveness in policy-making than the ability to exercise leadership without authority and without the dubious support of an intrinsically limited social science.

Welfare studies provide an example of this new type of policy-relevant inquiry. How do we redirect public assistance administration toward the promotion of work, healthy living, and self-reliance? How do we promote collaboration among autonomous actors involved in the lives of the poor in order to reap the benefits of cooperation? New approaches to policy scholarship seem especially promising in policy domains where human behavior is not ordered primarily, or at all times, by material incentives or by enforceable rules.

Empirical research based on structuration theory, for example, has attempted to establish that local social structures, not formal governance, determine how policies are implemented. "The structures of front-line social systems act as filters, neutralizing elements of new initiatives that do not make sense from a front-line perspective" (Sandfort 1997). Left unclear are whether and how these structures adapt to exogenous changes in organizational contexts and what kinds of mechanisms induce change in local structures. In general, the research problem is to identify those collective dispositions that are reflective of local, socially constructed realities, assess their malleability to internal and external changes (such as reallocations of resources), and identify their consequences for organizational performance.

Public policies and programs, including many of our most important social programs, are now recognized as frequently implemented not by bureaus and public employees but by networks of local offices, public schools, neighborhood collaborations, service delivery areas, regions, special districts, and other organizations in the public, nonprofit, and proprietary sectors. Policymakers often acquire voluminous data on the performance of local organization networks. It is almost always true that some offices have a higher level of performance than others. Why? The answer hinges on the number and characteristics of people served, the skill or motivation of workers, the effectiveness of local site management, the clarity of higher level policy direction, the effectiveness of systemwide coordination and control, and the use of private and nonprofit sectors. Some of these factors may weigh more than others in the overall scheme of things. Policymakers and managers need to know which factors are most influential in order to obtain better overall performance. Their ability to decentralize operations and to bring services closer to the people who are served depends on knowing how to ensure accountability and good practice across often far-flung, diverse locations.

Knowledge of which factors are most influential in the performance of local organizations is not obvious and cannot be obtained by simply conversing with people in the field or by studying raw administrative data. Obtaining useful answers requires not only good data but the use of appropriate statistical models and methods to identify causal factors and significant relationships linking governance and performance while controlling for contextual details. A deeper understanding of public policies requires, therefore, sophisticated social science that is both rigorous in conceptualization and respectful of evidence from qualitative and quantitative methods. Policy analysis must be clever in integrating knowledge and insights from diverse sources.

If such conclusions seem straightforward to proponents of policy-oriented research and its application to policy-making and analysis, they are far from clear to their critics.

New Issues for Statecraft

An apparent shift of power over the direction of the state toward executive actors with a superior command of information and analysis could be expected to inspire reactions ranging from imitation to competition to opposition and critical scrutiny by partisans and scholars (who are often the same people). Thus from the onset, those who believe that policy analysis is essential to statecraft have contended with criticism.

The initial spread of analytic practice into military force structure and national security planning aroused relatively little controversy in the social science community. Any kind of enlightenment of defense decision making, especially if it was on behalf of efficiency, seemed benign if not heroic. Controversies over policy analysis methods and practices became intense when policy analysis appeared to be a foundation for American intervention and strategy in the Vietnam Conflict,[7] and even more so when policy analysis began to be incorporated into domestic agency planning in federal agencies such as the

Department of Health, Education, and Welfare; the Department of Labor; and the Department of Housing and Urban Development.

It is worth remembering that the original case for social science–based policy advice seemed straightforward to its proponents. A former (and future) public official, Charles Schultze (1968), in explicit rebuttal of Lindblom's popular and imprecise conception of politics and policy-making as inevitably and appropriately a process of "muddling through," observed:

> The most frustrating aspect of public life is . . . the endless hours spent on policy discussions in which the irrelevant issues have not been separated from the relevant, in which ascertainable facts and relationships have not been investigated but are the subject of heated debate, in which consideration of alternatives is impossible because only one proposal has been developed, and, above all, discussions in which nobility of aim is presumed to determine effectiveness of program. (75)

Schultze saw "analytic efforts" as "instruments for shaping decisions by merging analysis, planning, and budgetary allocation" (77). Systematic analysis is outside of but complements "the advocacy process" by articulating the relationship between values and program characteristics. However, systematic analysis is in tension with political dialogue because "it emphasizes resource efficiency and stresses economic opportunity costs" (92). Following this argument, policy analysts should recognize, but not slavishly follow, political constraints. Policy analysis ought to modify the political process by, in effect, introducing a new set of participants, policy analysts, into the decision-making process and by empowering executive decision makers against self-interested subordinates and their constituencies who comprised, in the term popular at the time, iron triangles of concentrated, unreviewed political influence.

The apparent reasonableness of this perspective notwithstanding, critical reaction to institutionalized policy analysis was virtually instantaneous. The initial controversies had an intramural feel to them: mainstream scholars criticizing their overzealous colleagues.

"Metaphysical madness." The first generation of critics seemed positively angry that academically qualified policy analysts such as Schultze, Rivlin, Schlesinger, and Kissinger should be influential in policy-making.

Lawrence Tribe (1972) criticized policy analysis for its overemphasis on economic assumptions and instrumental rationality and for neglecting "distributive ends, procedural and historical principles, and the values . . . associated with personal rights, public goods, and communitarian and ecological goals" (105).

In a 1972 symposium, "Integration of the Social Sciences through Policy Analysis," a roster of concerns was cited. For example, Kariel (1972) saw the possibility that policy analysts might lose their integrity; rather than representing sound epistemology, they might instead come to represent "accredited interests. . . . They may . . . be led to conclude that research consists of language acts which test and disrupt given states" (106–7). McCord (1972) called attention to the historical misuse of social science: "at times, social science has acted as the handmaiden of policies aimed at the suppression of revolution, the degradation of an ethnic group, or the conversion of ethically torn men into killers" (120).

Richard Nelson (1977) criticized "traditional" policy analysis for being "relatively blind to exactly the kind of disagreements, and conflicting interests, which need to be perceived in order to guide the search for solutions that, over the long run, do not harm significant values or groups" (75–76). He advocated de-emphasizing "choice and decision" in favor of

> the saliency of organizational structure . . . and . . . the open-ended evolutionary way in which policies and programs do and should unfold. . . . Central high-level decision making [is] immune to . . . social sciences' standard research methods. . . . There is little hope to comprehend basic patterns of governance and policymaking within the thin slices of time typically considered by contemporary social and policy sciences. (79)

Rein (1976) insisted that the most demanding task facing policy analysts is "identification of their own values, along with an understanding of how these values blatantly and subtly bias analysis . . . The concealment of values, by tactical ambiguity or denial—which takes the form of a retreat into an impartial, dispassionate, value-free scientific stand—threatens moral integrity" (169).

Observing with cold contempt the "metaphysical madness" of policy scientists aiming to supplant politicians and statesmen (and inadvertently conceding the premise of the policy analysis movement that analysts are indeed influential), Banfield (1980) argued that the popularity of social science–based policy analysis in both the executive and legislative branches could not be justified by "the existence of a body of knowledge about how to solve social problems" (6). He observed:

> Professionals, because of their commitment to the ideal of rationality, are chronically given to finding fault with institutions . . . and, by virtue of their mastery of techniques of analysis, to discovering the almost infinite complexity and ambiguity of any problem [until problems are viewed as] too complicated for ordinary people to deal with. (18)

Based on a clever study by David Cohen and Janet Weiss (1977), Banfield worried that "an analytical society may increase its problems while decreasing its ability to cope with them" (14). Mesmerized by policy science, statesmen might be tempted to devalue wisdom, prudence, and good judgment in their exercise of executive discretion.

His thinking significantly altered by a lengthy period in government, Yehezkel Dror (1983) came to the conviction that "policymaking should be viewed as an existential phenomenon, or phenomena cluster, much too complex and dynamic to be fully caught in concepts, models, and theories" (x).

This general line of criticism has not abated. Recently, Lindblom (1990) and Schön and Rein (1994) have recommended radical revision in policy analysis practice and in the training of policy analysts. Lindblom criticizes policy analysts who see their task as "solving the decision maker's problem for him" (271). He recommends, instead, cooperative inquiry or "probing" by scholars and policymakers and forms of assistance to policymakers tailored to their needs and competencies: a missing body of facts, a synthesis of the issues, probing critiques of the policymaker's own analyses. Say Schön and Rein in a similar spirit:

> We believe that policy researchers should seek first to understand policy practice—not to draw from it rules of effective policymaking, but to describe and explain the kinds of inquiry in which policymakers engage. Policy researchers should focus on the substantive issues with which policymakers deal, the situations within which controversies about such issues arise, the kinds of inquiry carried out by those practitioners who participate in controversy or try to help resolve it, and the evolution of the policy dialectic within which practitioners play their roles as policy inquirers. (193)

"Tools of tyranny." In recent years, scholars who identify themselves as postpositivists have emerged as the most strident critics of mainstream policy analysis. Their critique has its foundations in critical theory, postmodernism, and various non- and postpositive epistemologies. DeLeon's critique is representative:

> The quotidian policy sciences have become an elite, sequestered activity, one whose services to democracy seemingly come as an afterthought to their primary fealty to their governmental agencies. . . . Their traditional positivist methodologies as well as their putative removal from politics have increasingly distanced the policy analyst from the policy recipient

. . . as they self-consciously recluse themselves from the hurly-burly but imperative normative aspects of politics. (1997, 65)

Policy analysis, says Torgerson in a similar vein (1986), is "haunted" by its original "dream," which bears "the unmistakable imprint of the positivist heritage," viz., "the abolition of politics" (34). "Professional policy analysis," he says, "is not really of this world—this all-too-human world of conflict, confusion, and doubt. . . . [T]he analyst . . . becomes one who performs remote operations on an essentially alien object" (35).

The postpositivist animus toward unreconstructed policy analysis has two primary objects (Lynn 1999). The first is a doctrinaire allegiance to positivist dogma and its consequence: the existential removal of policy analysis from the contaminating influence of social and political reality. The goals of public policy are matters of value, postpositivists argue, not facts and logic. Thus, given their dependence on positivist science, which insists that facts and values be kept separate, the goals of public policy cannot be included within the scope of what the policy analyst is concerned about.[8] As a result, conventional policy analysis is "blinded to political reality" (Torgerson 1986, 37). Policy analysts, according to Danziger, cling to the hope that "policy debate can be confined to technical questions on which experts can agree" and believe that certain objective rules of behavior will automatically lead to optimal results (1995, 440). Forrester (1993) indicts the staples of conventional policy-planning practice—means-ends models of instrumental rationality; problem solving; rationalistic, "scientific" models; cybernetic, information-processing models; and "satisficing" models of "bounded rationality" (19)—for failing to address in a systematic manner the ethical and normative issues associated with policy-making.

With respect to epistemology, the postpositivists argue, first, that facts and values cannot and should not be separated in democratic deliberation. Thus policy analysts must take a "value critical approach" in which, as deLeon puts it, "ideology, values, and belief become part and parcel of the formal analysis" (1997, 79). Second, facts to postpositivists are social constructions, not objective features of the material world awaiting discovery and manipulation. Assertions of fact must be recognized as essentially arbitrary pseudodiscoveries that disguise a social and political agenda. Social facts do not exist independent of investigators as sociopolitical beings. Science is not "passive reception and organization of sense data" but rather itself a product of the social world, "grounded in and shaped by normative suppositions and social meanings" (Fischer 1993, 167).

The second object of postpositive animus is the tendency toward clientelism of mainstream policy analysis. Postpositivists view the partnership between policy analysis and the hierarchical state and its executive agencies as devastating to democracy and to policies that would otherwise emerge from unimpeded discussion among informed, autonomous citizens. Unconcerned with social values, policy analysts are said to serve the state willy-nilly, heedless of the normative needs of citizens and unprincipled in their policy advice.

Postpositivists believe the hierarchical structures of a top-down, mass society corrupt democracy by enacting elitist policies favoring the few (Fischer 1993, 166). The touchstone of postpositivist practice is the involvement and empowerment of citizens, especially of those citizens most directly affected by public policies, in the processes of policy-making. They would substitute for bureaucracy what they variously term authentic democracy, unimpeded inquiry, and ethically illuminating, communicative practice. The public policy professional would no longer pose as expert, no longer define practice as serving a bureaucratic client. Instead, policy analysts would facilitate and help inform civic discourse leading toward democratic choice.

Tilling the Epistemological Garden

Because policy analysis is an administrative technology with uniquely significant consequences for the direction of the state, controversies over its means and ends are inevitable. Moreover, they are bound to be intense. Policy analysis exists in a multidimensional Euclidian political space such that its deviation from any axis of normative idealization can be argued to constitute evidence of impermissible, even corrupt, "bias." Indeed, to make their point, critics attempt to maximize the perceived distance of practical policy analysis from critical idealization. Thus it is often difficult to believe that the supporters and critics of practical policy analysis inhabit the same reality, much less understand the basis of the argument.

Now arrayed against policy analysis and positive science as the basis for "knowledge and action" is a flowering of epistemologies based on hermeneutic, phenomenological, symbolic interactionist, and, in general, postmodern philosophies that would redirect attention toward the social construction of reality and its implications for knowing and acting. The language of neutral, unbiased observation and inference has been supplemented by a language emphasizing frames, lenses, interpretive templates, and schemas. Knowledge is generally accepted to be context- and "knower"-influenced, and investigation can be conceptualized quite reasonably as interpretation of sensory experience, which might benefit from the insights of critical theory.

A clash of ideologies. Almost certainly, the critics' political ideologies influence their criticism. This is particularly true of the postpositivist critique of policy analysis. Its literature often has a cloistered quality, its authors largely ignoring the wider policy analysis literature and the realities of practice. Their critique, therefore, tends to be based on a decontextualized caricature, virtually a parody, of actual policy analysis training and practice, from which observations and examples are often wholly lacking. That caricature is chilling but false, so strained, so far removed from the ethos of policy analysis as generally taught and practiced, so inconsistent with the history and literature of policy analysis, and so subservient to its own political agenda, that postpositive charges of bias on the part of traditional policy analysts seem either naive or disingenuous (Lynn 1999).

The words *needs, politics,* and *elites* are, for example, staples of postpositivist discourse. The fact that such terms are usually undefined suggests that postpositivists view *politics* and *citizens' needs* as unambiguous, the definition of their meanings self-evident. That the reification of such terms is no different epistemologically from the positivists' use of terms such as *utility* or *significance* or *cause* is never acknowledged. Moreover, in the name of politics, the postpositive critique of policy analysis puts forth a vision of collective deliberation that leaves out legislatures, elected executives, organized interests, policy networks, the plethora of elites that claim privileged roles, and other political institutions, not to mention money, media, opinion polling, and citizen apathy. By substituting one set of taken-for-granted terms for another, the postpositivists reveal their own inescapably political stance.

The controversy dividing positivists from postpositivists is predominantly ideological. The politics of mainstream policy analysis unapologetically strengthens the liberal democratic state through bringing knowledge to bear on important policy questions. The politics of the postpositivists apparently is replacing the liberal democratic state with an imagined show-of-hands democracy in which no actor has power over others and in which expertise has no privileged role.

Blind spots. Traditional policy analysis is hardly invulnerable to criticism, however. The primary conceit or blind spot of the policy analysts of the first generation was to see themselves as an extension of executive power, necessarily opposing the centrifugal, self-serving forces of legislative politics. The U.S. Department of Defense under strong leadership standing against the military-industrial complex was paradigmatic, and it could easily be imagined that every agency head at every level of government stood in a similar relationship to interest-oriented legislatures and iron triangles of stakeholder influence. Policy analysts were needed to define and analyze the "public interest" and to evaluate alternative ways of achieving it, identifying those ways that were likely to be the most cost-effective.

Contributing to the intensity of the controversies over policy analysis have been some defining features of the policy analysis methods and practice. The lightning rod has been the seemingly privileged role of economists and economic reasoning. With confidence in the prescriptive power of their paradigm, economists have asserted hegemony over an ever-wider range of intellectual precincts, from choices of tactical aircraft to choices among air quality improvement strategies, to selections among day-care, health care, and education investments. Their often patronizing attitude toward "good intentions," their arrogance toward traditional professional and bureaucratic elites, and their tendency to ignore or dismiss "traditional" public administration, the policy sciences movement, and nonprescriptive social science in general account for much of the hostility the policy analysis movement has received.

The early policy analysts, moreover, did tend to place undue faith in the appearance of scientific rationality. As Heineman et al. (1990) note:

> Social scientists and, more recently, policy analysts have often assumed that the objective scientific quality of their analyses would carry weight in the policy process and protect them from the effects of political partisanship. Because it rests on a superficial view of the scientific enterprise and a faulty conception of the policy process, such a posture can lead to considerable frustration for the practitioner of policy analysis. (22–23)

In their own defense, policy analysts would argue that if policy-making is based to a greater extent on "what's right" rather than "who's right" (an early aphorism popular in the McNamara Department of Defense), then the appeal to transparent methods of analysis makes perfect sense despite the limitations of those methods. Contrary to postpositivist claims, policy analysis can be argued to have an antielite bias. But misinterpretations of their apparent "scientism" are understandable.

Shortcomings in policy analysis practice can easily be magnified out of proportion to their importance and must not lead to the outright abandonment of policy analysis as an administrative technology.

Policy Analysis as Contextualized Craft

With administrative discretion a necessary element of political administration, credible bases for its exercise are essential. Thus the modern American state has come to exhibit a dependence on expertise and a bias for apparent rationality. The legitimacy conferred by rational analysis and by expert endorsement of political action ensures that policy analysis in various forms will remain deeply woven into the fabric of civic discourse, policy-making, and public administration. Because a bias for rationality on the part of untrained decision makers renders them vulnerable to specious, statistics-laden arguments they do not understand, the professional role of the policy analyst is to advocate for and practice careful, transparent, nonparochial analysis of the means and ends of public policy. Policy analysts provide an indispensable antidote for official vulnerability due to the lay official's ignorance of science's own biases and for the unscrupulous, self-serving use of political information by political actors.

But the professional practice of policy analysis can never be divorced from its political context. As a professional practice, policy analysis is inevitably and necessarily endogenous to liberal political economy. That is, policy analysis is associated with power and requires the sponsorship and endorsement of liberal political economy. Any presupposition that policy analysts as professionals should act in deliberate defiance of the state or in ways that would undermine it is unsustainable. Advocating replacement of the liberal state should be left to policy intellectuals who can sustain themselves through academic affiliation alone.

If training and practice are to adapt to changes in the context of policy discourse and choice, however, teachers and practitioners must employ three seemingly antithetical tactics: (1) adopt a more scientific approach, (2) demonstrate the political relevance of their work, and (3) identify more clearly as a unique "contextualized craft" that is neither wholly scientific nor wholly political. Past resilience of policy analysts to criticism provides grounds for optimism in regard to their future adaptability.

Policy analysis as science. Among the most thoughtful conceptions of the role of science in policy analysis is that of Robert A. Heineman and his colleagues (1990). "As long as human dignity and meaning exist as important values," they argue, "social science cannot achieve the rigor of the physical sciences because it is impossible to separate human beliefs from the context and process of analysis." They continue: "Essentially, when science is applied as a label to the pursuit of policy analysis, what is being described is *the careful accumulation of data, rigorous study of possible interpretations and alternatives, and the articulation of reasons for the recommended course of action*" (37, emphasis added). The challenge is to be "rigorous" and "reasonable" in performing policy analysis.

A possibly underappreciated dilemma facing a problem-oriented, interdisciplinary professional practice such as policy analysis is the need to avoid the kinds of conceptual and procedural errors that nonspecialists are prone to commit. Avoidance of these fallacies requires that policy analysts demonstrate mastery and realism with respect to both the advantages and limitations of the tools at their disposal. Thus, policy analysts should aspire to a correct understanding of the social scientific concepts they employ, such as goal displacement, cognitive dissonance, opportunity cost, the collective action problem, selection bias, statistical independence, social network, social role, information asymmetry, and incentive compatibility. Policy analysts should incorporate such concepts into their analyses for the generality and power they contribute to policy arguments.

A second dilemma facing policy analysts is sustenance of policy analysis legitimacy as an academic enterprise, exercising the intellectual obligation to be critical, perhaps deeply so, of politics as a social process while maintaining access to and credibility within that flawed system. Many policy intellectuals are prone to pessimism concerning American politics, with its seemingly inherent irrationality, its dominance by partisan interests, the unseemly roles played by money and media, the apparent impossibility of translating the public's desires into public policy in any straightforward or timely way. Policy analysts are easily tempted into the embrace of such critical perspectives and into roles as missionaries for the reform of the political process. While I do not want to deny the validity of personal motivations for practicing policy analysis as a profession, I believe that to adopt reflexively critical perspectives would be self-defeating. This is to say that policy analysis as a profession succeeds by being intellectually and dependably pragmatic and realistic in its aspirations more than by being revolutionary. Its most passionately held convictions must not been seen to require the transformation of liberal democratic politics.

Policy analysis as politics.   A related but subtly different dilemma is encountered when policy analysts become engaged with the political world: maintenance of intellectual integrity in the politically partisan, interest-driven world whose sponsorship and regard are essential to policy analysts' opportunity to contribute. Critics have long pointed out that policy analysts are vulnerable to transformation into instruments of political manipulation, becoming the co-opted authors of rationalizations and pseudoscientific quantitative symbols for use in partisan debate, committed to the appearance but not to the substance of sound argument. Of course, auditors, lawyers, physical scientists, and other publicly engaged professionals are no less vulnerable to political manipulation. The inherent strength of any profession include its ethical foundations and its perceived value to the public interest; these are the ultimate protections for professionals in a political world.

In their efforts to avoid the undertow of political manipulation, policy analysts resort to various forms of protective cover. One of the most effective is to appeal to the putative objectivity of the scientific methods that are at the heart of their craft. They may point also to their lack of direct material interest in the policies they aspire to inform. They may appeal to their commitment to "the public interest" or to normative goals such as a better-informed or more democratic politics. None of these arguments is beyond criticism. Social science is far from "objective"; notions such as "public interest," "information," and "democracy" are social constructions; and the well-being of the agency that employs them *is* a direct material interest.

The general point is that policy analysts must have a sufficiently strong professional identity to sustain their argument that they bring into the political world valuable skills that are needed for effective governance and for which there are no good substitutes. Specifically, policy analysts represent the view that rigor and rationality are valuable contributions to political discourse and should be valued in the same ways that fiduciary accountability, the absence of conflicts of interest, legal sufficiency, and honest numbers are valued. Policy analysts must make their own work seem politically relevant.

Policy analysis as "contextualized craft." The most appealing alternative to more scientistic forms of policy analysis has come to be known as the "craft perspective." Observes Kathleen A. Archibald:

> Rigor and technical virtuosity are admired and often even set up as the sole ideal, but when it comes to examining pitfalls [of analysis], we find that the most serious pitfalls will not be circumvented by greater rigor or improved technical skills. Competencies usually considered "softer"— imagination, judgment, interpretive skills—are just as important. (Quoted in Majone and Quade 1980, 193–94)

Policy analysis, she says, is "an interpretive discipline" (190). Giandomenico Majone (1980, 1989) sees policy analysis as essentially "craft work" involving evidence, argument, and persuasion. "Policy analysis is more art than science," says Eugene Bardach in his recent compact textbook. "It draws on intuition as much as on method" (1996, 1).

The craft perspective is not in opposition to the notion that policy analysis has scientific foundations. Heineman et al. insist that "the very concept of analysis . . . presupposes the importance of rational argument and rigorous methodology" (1997, 5). Argues Majone:

> To attempt to reconstruct policy analysis on the basis of rhetorical categories—to view the analyst as a producer of arguments, capable of distinguishing between good and bad rhetoric, rather than as a "number cruncher"—is not to deny the usefulness of . . . [m]odeling, mathematical programming, simulation, cost-benefit analysis, and decision analysis. . . . However, . . . the traditional skills are not sufficient. (1989, xii)

In other words, rigor, rationality, and transparency of methods remain foundation values of policy analysis. The craft perspective adds the important emphasis that policy analysis is sustained by the particulars of contexts in and for which it is carried out. Herein lies perhaps the most complex challenge to maintaining an adaptable, constructive professional practice.

Perhaps the most perceptive way to view this challenge is to be found in the work of John Friedmann (1988). To Friedmann, the metaproblem of social planning is how to make technical knowledge relevant to social policy-making. He arrays various traditions for solving this metaproblem along two dimensions: whether the emphasis is on providing guidance to social institutions or on transforming those institutions, and whether the political premises are conservative or radical. Because its emphasis is guidance—assisting powerful actors to produce better policies—and its politics are pragmatic and incrementalist rather than revolutionary, traditional policy analysis, Friedmann argues, stands in sharp contrast to policy planning traditions that actively seek either the transformation or the restructuring of society.

Friedmann's conception of social learning provides a constructive and appropriate alternative to the traditional advisory and conservative approach of the early policy analysis movement.

> Social learning . . . is a complex, time-dependent process that involves, in addition to the *action* itself (which breaks into the stream of ongoing events to change reality), *political strategy and tactics* (which tell us how to overcome resistance), *theories of reality* (which tell us what the world is like), and the *values* that inspire and direct the action. Taken together, these four elements constitute a form of *social practice.* It is the essential wisdom of the social learning tradition that practice and learning are construed as correlative processes, so that one process necessarily implies the other. In this scheme, decisions appear as a fleeting moment in the course of an ongoing practice. (181–83)

The social learning tradition focuses on task-oriented action groups, such as legislative subcommittees, agency leadership teams, and task forces or executive committees, that is, substructures of larger social entities. In the course of deliberating on and carrying out actions, the members of these action groups engage in tacit and largely informal learning. But their learning cannot be divorced from their actions and their practice. "The social learning approach works with a process concept of knowledge," says Friedmann. "Its central assumption is that all effective learning comes from the experience of changing reality" (216).

The social learning paradigm requires a de-emphasis on both the instrumentation of knowledge and the quest for efficient knowledge markets. It favors instead disinterested and powerful research communities who are closely tied not with select policy elites but with society itself and who are dedicated to the continuing process of societal transformation. In a social learning paradigm, the concept of research broker yields to the concept of change agent. The premium is to be placed on preparing individuals so inclined to play roles as change agents operating throughout policy networks rather than as research brokers seeking proximity to executive actors. The policy analyst, following this logic, would seek to encourage, guide, and assist social actors in the process of changing reality. They would see themselves as "professionals or paraprofessionals . . . who bring certain kinds of formal knowledge to the ongoing social practice of their 'client group.' To be effective, change agents must develop a *transactive* relationship with their client conducive to *mutual learning*" (185).

The social learning paradigm has quite radical implications for those who would clear pathways for knowledge into policy. Its premise is that policy formation is not intentional; it is not formally goal-oriented. The properties of policies are a resultant of collective action, by-products of the practice of governance by collective entities for which individual influence is epiphenomenal. An understanding of group dynamics, rather than of individual cognition and problem solving, is of paramount importance.

Policy analysis is and will remain pragmatic and crafty. The exigencies of the political world will continue to ensure a reality check on practice, and practice will evolve accordingly. For this reason, policy analysis practice will continue to be driven by problems as they arise in context and by its distinguishing values of rigor, rationality, and transparency. The contexts for practice are often hierarchical, polarized, and interest-driven rather than being the kind of idealized contexts envisioned by postpositivists and social learning theorists. Thus there will continue to be an important role for executive- and decision-oriented policy analysis and for policy-relevant positive research directed at the thinking and choosing of policymakers.

But public policy-making is far less "federal" and hierarchical than it used to be, and our knowledge about the complexity of our political institutions is deepening. Moreover, decades of right-of-center politics have shifted civic discourse decisively from public programs to communities, neighborhoods, and social groups as well as to decentralized incentives, choice, and quasi markets as means for accomplishing public purposes. Research, training, and practice should more incisively reflect those shifts. One of the original ideas associated with the policy analysis movement, "backward mapping" (Elmore 1979), may turn out to be one of the most useful for its future: a vision of social outcomes as foundations for identifying the social practices, resource allocations, institutions, and policies that might appear to be appropriate to achievement, and engagement in the kinds of political communication that might increase the chances of their adoption.

NOTES

1. The term *administrative technology* refers to such replicable methods as merit-based personnel selection, executive budgeting, the administrative department or bureau, regulation and rule making, the executive order, the categorical program, formula grants and block grants, the administrative procedures act, performance audits, and policy analysis.

2. Scholars of policy analysis have been too little inclined to develop in any depth the ideas underlying policy analysis methods and practice. In developing the arguments in this essay, I shall pay special attention to several seminal contributors, and in particular to the work of Marshall Dimock, Edwin S. Quade, John Friedmann, Giandomenico Majone, and Robert A. Heineman and his colleagues.

3. Observed Roscoe Pound in 1919, "As the eighteenth century and the forepart of the nineteenth century relied upon the legislature and the last half of the nineteenth century relied upon the courts, the twentieth century is no less clearly relying on administration" (Pound 1919). A fuller discussion of this issue is in Skowronek 1982.

4. The Decision of 1789 was an act of Congress to give President Washington broad discretion with respect to national defense.

5. I am indebted to Anthony Bertelli for his insights on these issues.

6. For example, the Lewis and Clark Expedition, which "replaced a mass of confusing rumors and conjectures with a body of compact, reliable, and believable information on the western half of the continent," established an elegant precedent for using science to alter the terms of public discourse (Dupree 1957, 27). Shils (1949, 222) observed that "it was the First World War which showed, particularly in the United States, that academic social scientists could be used by Government and by all organizations interested in controlling and modifying human behavior." President Herbert Hoover's seminal project *Recent Social Trends in the United States* and the extensive activities of the New Deal–era National Resources Planning Board brought social scientists into the service of the state. The use of operations research techniques provided the good and well-known means to evaluate military operations during World War II, and economists were employed by the Office of Price Administration.

7. This is a misperception. The policy analysts in war-related agencies were typically the most sophisticated and, because of their analyses, ardent critics of U.S. military strategies in Vietnam, a historical reality that is inconvenient for postpositivists and, therefore, suppressed by them.

8. Little noted by current critics of policy analysis is that one of the most important contributions of early "systems analysis" in military force planning was the rigorous examination of the purposes for maintaining forces in the first place.

REFERENCES

Banfield, E. 1980. Policy science as metaphysical madness. In *Bureaucrats, policy analysts, statesmen: Who leads?* ed. R. Goldwin. Washington, D.C.: American Enterprise Institute for Public Policy Research.

Bardach, E. 1996. *The eight-step path of policy analysis (A handbook for practice)*. Berkeley: Berkeley Academic Press.

Brodkin, E. 1987. Policy politics: If we can't govern, can we manage? *Political Science Quarterly* 102 (4): 571–87.

Charlesworth, J. 1972. *Integration of the social sciences through policy analysis*. Philadelphia: American Academy of Political and Social Science.

Cohen, D., and J. Weiss. 1977. Social science and social policy. *Educational Forum* 41.

Danziger, M. 1995. Policy analysis postmodernized: Some political and pedagogical ramifications. *Policy Studies Journal* 23:435–50.

DeLeon, P. 1997. *Democracy and the policy sciences*. Albany: State University of New York Press.

Dimock, M. 1936a. The meaning and scope of public administration. In *The frontiers of public administration*, ed. J. Gaus, L. White, and M. Dimock, 1–12. Chicago: University of Chicago Press.

———. 1936b. The role of discretion in modern administration. In *The frontiers of public administration*, ed. J. Gaus, L. White, and M. Dimock, 45–65. Chicago: University of Chicago Press.

———. 1936c. The criteria and objectives of public administration. In *The frontiers of public administration*, ed. J. Gaus, L. White, and M. Dimock, 116–33. Chicago: University of Chicago Press.

Dror, Y. 1983. *Public policymaking reexamined*. New Brunswick, N.J.: Transaction Books.

Dupree, A. 1957. *Science in the federal government: A history of policies and activities to 1940*. Cambridge: Harvard-Belknap Press.

Elmore, R. F. 1979–80. Backward mapping: Implementation research and policy decisions. *Political Science Quarterly* 94 (4): 69–83.

Feldman, M. 1989. *Order without design: Information production and policymaking*. Stanford, Calif.: Stanford University Press.

Fischer, F. 1993. Citizen participation and the democratization of policy expertise: From a theoretical inquiry to practical cases. *Policy Sciences* 26:165–87.

Forrester, J. 1993. *Critical theory, public policy, and planning practice: Toward a critical pragmatism*. Albany: State University of New York Press.

Friedmann, J. 1988. *Planning in the public domain: From knowledge to action*. Princeton: Princeton University Press.

Gaus, J., L. White, and M. Dimock. 1936. *The frontiers of public administration*. Chicago: University of Chicago Press.

Goodsell, C. 1995. *The case for bureaucracy: A public administration polemic*. 4th ed. Chatham, N.J.: Chatham House.

Gruber, J. 1987. *Controlling bureaucracies: Dilemmas in democratic governance*. Berkeley: University of California Press.

Heclo, H. 1977. *A government of strangers: Executive politics in Washington*. Washington, D.C.: Brookings Institution.

Heineman, R. A., W. T. Bluhm, S. A. Peterson, and E. N. Kearny. 1990. *The world of the policy analyst: Rationality, values, and politics*. Chatham, N.J.: Chatham House.

———. 1997. *The world of the policy analyst*. 2d ed. Chatham, N.J.: Chatham House.

Kariel, H. 1972. Commentary. In *Integration of the social sciences through policy analysis*, ed. J. Charlesworth. Philadelphia: American Academy of Political and Social Science.

Lane, R. 1972. Integration of political science and the other social sciences through policy analysis. In *Integration of the social sciences through policy analysis,* ed. J. Charlesworth, 71–87. Philadelphia: American Academy of Political and Social Science.

Laski, H. 1923. The growth of administrative discretion. *Public Administration I,* 92–100. Quoted in Dimock 1936b.

Lerner, D., and H. Lasswell, eds. 1951. *The policy sciences.* Palo Alto, Calif.: Stanford University Press.

Lindblom, C. E. 1990. *Inquiry and change: The troubled attempt to understand and shape society.* New Haven: Yale University Press.

Lynn, L. 1987. *Managing public policy.* Boston: Little, Brown.

———. 1989. Policy analysis in the bureaucracy: How new? How effective? *Journal of Policy Analysis and Management* 8:373–77.

———. 1999. A place at the table: Policy analysis, its postpositive critics, and the future of practice. *Journal of Policy Analysis and Management* 18:411–25.

Majone, G. 1989. *Evidence, argument, and persuasion in the policy process.* New Haven: Yale University Press.

Majone, G., and E. Quade, eds. 1980. *Pitfalls of analysis.* New York: John Wiley and Sons.

McCord, W. 1972. Commentary. In *Integration of the social sciences through policy analysis,* ed. J. Charlesworth. Philadelphia: American Academy of Political and Social Science.

Meltsner, A. 1976. *Policy analysts in the bureaucracy.* Berkeley: University of California Press.

Morstein-Marx, F., ed. 1959. *Elements of public administration.* 2d ed. Englewood Cliffs, N.J.: Prentice-Hall.

Morstein-Marx, F., and H. Reining Jr. 1959. The tasks of middle management. In *Elements of public administration,* ed. F. Morstein-Marx. 2d ed. Englewood Cliffs, N.J.: Prentice-Hall.

Nagel, S. 1975. *Policy studies and the social sciences.* Lexington, Mass.: Lexington Books.

Nelson, R. R. 1977. *The moon and the ghetto: An essay on public policy analysis.* New York: W. W. Norton.

———. 1989. The office of policy analysis in the Department of the Interior. *Journal of Policy Analysis and Management* 8:395–410.

Noll, R., and B. Weingast. 1987. Rational actor theory, social norms, and policy implementation: Applications to administrative processes and bureaucratic culture. In *The economic approach to politics: A critical reassessment of the theory of rational action,* ed. K. Monroe. New York: Harper Collins.

Pound, R. 1919. The administrative application of legal standards. *Reports of the American Bar Association* 44:445–65. Quoted in Dimock 1936b.

Quade, E. 1964. *Analysis for military decisions.* Santa Monica, Calif.: RAND Corporation.

Rainey, H. 1991. *Understanding and managing public organizations.* San Francisco, Calif.: Jossey-Bass.

Redford, E. 1958. *Ideal and practice in public administration.* University: University of Alabama Press.

Rein, M. 1976. *Social science and social policy.* New York: Penguin.

Sandfort, J. 1997. *The structuring of front-line work: Conditions within local welfare and welfare-to-work organizations in Michigan.* Manuscript.

Schön, D., and M. Rein 1994. *Frame reflection: Toward the resolution of intractable policy controversies.* New York: Basic Books.

Schultze, C. 1968. *The politics and economics of public spending.* Washington, D.C.: Brookings Institution.

Shils, E. 1949. Social science and social policy. *Philosophy of Science* 16.

Simon, H., V. A. Thompson, and D. W. Smithburg. [1950] 1991. *Public administration.* New York: Alfred A. Knopf; New Brunswick, N.J.: Transaction Publishers.

Skowronek, S. 1982. *Building a new American state: The expansion of national administrative capacities, 1877–1920.* New York: Cambridge University Press.

Sundquist, J. 1978. Research brokerage: The weak link. In *Knowledge and policy: The uncertain connection,* ed. L. Lynn Jr. Washington, D.C.: National Academy of Sciences.

Taylor, F. 1911. *The principles of scientific management.* New York: Harper.

Torgerson, D. 1986. Between knowledge and politics: Three faces of policy analysis. *Policy Sciences* 19:33–59.

Tribe, L. 1972. Policy science: Analysis or ideology? *Philosophy and Public Affairs* 2:66–110.

Wildavsky, A. 1979. *Speaking truth to power: The art and craft of policy analysis.* Boston: Little, Brown.

Contributors

W. Andrew Achenbaum is Dean of the College of Humanities, Fine Arts, and Communication and Professor of History at the University of Houston. Achenbaum is one of the better known scholars on the history of aging and old-age policy. Representative works include *Crossing Frontiers: Gerontology Emerges as a Science* (1995) and *Old Age in the New Land: The American Experience since 1790*, which was chosen as an Outstanding Academic Book by *Choice* in 1979.

achenbaum@uh.edu

Martin Bulmer, a leading British sociologist, is Foundation Fund Professor of Sociology at the University of Surrey. Bulmer is also Academic Director of the Question Bank at ESRC Centre for Applied Social Surveys (CASS), National Centre for Social Research in London. His books include *The Uses of Social Research* and *The Chicago School of Sociology*. Bulmer is a member of the editorial boards of the *British Journal of Sociology* and the *American Behavioral Scientist*, and editor of *Ethnic and Racial Studies*.

m.bulmer@soc.surrey.ac.uk

Sheldon Danziger is Henry J. Meyer Collegiate Professor of Social Work and Public Policy and Director of the Center on Poverty, Risk and Mental Health at the University of Michigan. From 1983 to 1988, he served as Director of the Institute for Research on Poverty, University of Wisconsin. Danziger is coeditor of several volumes and coauthor of *America Unequal* (1995) and *Detroit Divided* (2000).

sheldond@umich.edu

David L. Featherman was appointed Institute Director and Senior Research Scientist at the Institute for Social Research (ISR) at the University of Michigan in June 1994. He is also Professor of Sociology and Psychology in the College of Literature, Arts, and Sciences. Prior to 1994, he served as President of the Social Science Research Council (SSRC) in New York City. Featherman's publications include books and articles about social mobility in America and seven volumes of a coedited series, *Life-Span Development and Behavior*.

feathrmn@isr.umich.edu

Judith M. Gueron is President of the Manpower Demonstration Research Corporation (MDRC), which she joined as its first research director in 1974. MDRC is a nonprofit, nonpartisan organization that designs and evaluates education and employment-focused programs aimed at improving the self-sufficiency and life prospects of low-income Americans. A widely published, nationally recognized expert on poverty, welfare reform, and job training, Gueron is the senior author of *From Welfare to Work* (1991).

16 East 34th Street
New York, NY 10016

Laurence E. Lynn Jr. is Sydney Stein, Jr., Professor of Public Management at the Irving B. Harris Graduate School of Public Policy Studies and School of Social Service Administration, University of Chicago. Lynn has served on the faculty of various schools, including Harvard University's John F. Kennedy School of Government, and has held senior positions with the federal government. Lynn's most recent book is *Teaching and Learning with Cases: A Guidebook* (1999).

llynn@midway.uchicago.edu

Deborah A. Phillips is Associate Professor and Chair of the Department of Psychology at Georgetown University. Previously she was Senior Study Director, Board on Children, Youth, and Families, of the National Research Council's Commission on Social and Behavioral Sciences and the Institute of Medicine. Phillips is on numerous task forces and advisory groups that address child and family policy issues, and she acts as Co-Principal Investigator of the Virginia site of the National Institute of Child Health and Human Development's Study of Early Child Care.

dap4@georgetown.edu

Maris A. Vinovskis is the A. M. and H. P. Bentley Professor of History, Professor of Public Policy, and Senior Research Scientist at the Center for Political Studies in the Institute for Social Research, University of Michigan. Vinovskis has authored or coauthored eight books, edited or coedited another seven volumes, and written approximately ninety scholarly articles and essays. His most recent book is *History and Educational Policymaking*.

vinovski@umich.edu

Sheldon H. White is John Lindsley Professor of Psychology in Memory of William James at Harvard University. A developmental psychologist, he has done research on children's learning, attention, and memory. White has chaired a series of committees concerned with the development of a research program for Head Start, and he has been chair of the Board on Children and Families of the National Research Council.

shw@wjh.harvard.edu

Index

administrative discretion
  development of, 187
  historical use of social sciences in, 13
  necessity of, 189–90, 207
  in Nixon White House, 6
  potential misuse of, 204
  roles of policy analysts and researchers in, 13
  use of, as definition of policy-making, 13
  use of, today, 198–200
Administrative Procedures Act, 189, 214
administrative state, modern, 4, 5–6, 8, 10, 13
  emergence of, 1
  expansion of, 8–9
  reduction of, 6
  and sociology, 3, 5, 7
administrative technology, 187, 188, 195, 198–99, 206
Aid to Families with Dependent Children Program (AFDC), 140, 168
Air Force (U.S.), 44, 194
American Enterprise Institute for Public Policy Research, 66
American Social Science Association (ASSA), 29, 31, 38
Atomic Energy Commission (AEC), 44

Behavioral and Social Science Survey Committee, 51
Bloom, Benjamin, 91, 96–97, 113
Bronfenbrenner, Urie, 11, 85, 90, 110, 113
Brookings, Robert S., 33, 36
Brookings Institution, 2, 66

challenged, by conservative think tanks, 66
  and President Johnson, praise of, 51
  as private foundation, 36, 41, 69
Bureau of the Budget (BOB), 48, 55
Bureau of the Census, 41
Bush, President George H. W., 104, 105

Carnegie Corporation, 32–33, 41, 126, 127
Carter, President Jimmy, 12, 55, 61, 68, 125, 138, 141, 143, 149
Cato Institute, 66
Center for National Policy, 66
Center on Budget and Policy Priorities, 66
Central Intelligence Agency (CIA), 47–48, 68
Chicago Commission on Race Relations, 23
child care, 105, 132, 153
  state expenditures for, required, 147
  subsidized, in welfare-to-work programs, 144–46, 148, 149, 159, 160, 175, 177
  and working poor, 173
Child Development movement, 94
Clinton, President Bill
  and Head Start, 105–6, 111, 112
  and health care and social services, 128
  presidency of, 7, 12
  and welfare reform, 12, 137–38, 139, 146, 148, 150, 152, 159, 171
Committee on Economic Security, 120
Committee on Education and Labor, 97, 112, 113

Community Action Program, 49, 50, 86, 90, 108, 113
Community Work Experience Programs (CWEP), 145, 160, 168, 171, 176–77
Comprehensive Employment and Training Act of 1973 (CETA), 141
Congressional Budget Office (CBO), 5–6, 56, 68, 142, 179
Congressional Research Service (CRS), 56, 68
Cooke, Robert, 86, 88, 89, 98, 111, 113
Council of Economic Advisors (CEA), 47, 48, 53, 68

Department of Agriculture, 41, 43, 52, 68
Department of Defense (DOD), 44, 52, 53, 55, 207
Department of Education, 6, 81
Department of Energy, 7, 197
Department of Health and Human Services (HHS), 89, 104, 169
Department of Health, Education, and Welfare, 52, 112, 202
Department of Housing and Urban Development, 202
Department of Labor, 202
developmental psychologists, and Head Start
    roles of, 11, 83–84, 87–88, 107–10
    demonstration, 93–95
    evaluation, 99–105
    idealization, 95–99
    representation, 90–92
Dewey, John, 20, 93, 99, 191
Dickens, Charles, 91
Du Bois, W. E. B., 18, 22–23, 25, 31, 34

Earned Income Tax Credit (EITC), 144, 154, 160, 161
Economic Policy Institute, 66
Eisenhower, President Dwight D., 47, 48
Elementary and Secondary Education Act of 1965, 49, 50, 59
elites
    academic, 108
    and conservative policy, 66
    and economists, 207–8
    and leadership, pre–World War II, 9
    local civic, 27–28
    and policy, 204
    and policy analysis, 208
    as postpositivist term, 207
    as presidents of foundations, 8
    as scientists, 42–43
    and social learning, 212–13
    and social science, 16, 31–32, 37
Ellwood, David, 148–50, 159, 161, 169
employer demand, 137–38, 142, 147, 152–55, 156, 159
employment
    age-based, 130
    Carnegie Corporation publications on, 126
    counseling during, 160
    and Head Start, 90
    and less-educated workers, 152, 154–55
    and poor, raising of, 141
    and professional civil service, 190
    professionals from field of, 121
    public, viewed as unnecessary, 143
    reform of, 126
    report on (1934), 121
    study of, 151
    surveys, 30
    teaching skills for, 140
    unemployment, 120–22, 132, 140, 141, 142, 153, 154, 181
    of welfare recipients, 138, 144–47, 150, 153–58, 167–68, 172–77, 182–83
epistemology
    genetic, Piaget's, 94
    ignoring of, by policy analysts, 203
    from perspective of policy-making, 187
    and policy analysis, 206–8
    and postpositivism, 204–5
experts
    claims of, 5
    and community groups, 198

dependence on, 208
faith in, as social analysts, 16, 28–30, 34
and federal policy-makers, 40–72, 179, 187–88, 193, 205
and Head Start, 86–87, 89–90, 107–8
postpositivist view of, 205, 207
and Social Security, 125
and societal aging, 126–27, 130
surveys of, 24
and unemployment, 121–22, 166, 167

Family Assistance Plan (FAP), 11, 138, 140–41, 149
Family Support Act of 1988 (FSA), 12, 138, 139, 144–47, 160, 171, 182
    bipartisan consensus on, 144
    and Manpower Demonstration Research Corporation, 145, 160, 178, 180
    and responsibility, increased expectation for, 139
    social science research influence on, 151–52
    time limits, excluded from, 146–47
Food Stamp program, 140–41, 143
Ford Foundation
    and Behavioral Science Program, 46–47
    creation and development of, 71
    and Manpower Demonstration Research Corporation, 12, 165, 168, 169
    role of, 8–9, 46–47
Ford, President Gerald, 58–59, 61, 68

General Accounting Office (GAO), 179
    and Congress, 48
    growth and decrease of, 56
    and Reagan administration, 6, 55
    restructure of, 68
Gerontological Society of America, 126, 129
gerontology, 11, 123–25

GI Bill, 46, 71
"graying of society," 11, 119–20, 122, 123, 130
Great Depression
    and policy-making, 1, 17
    and Social Security, 120–21
    societal aging theories since, 130
    views of, 131
Great Society era, 3, 83
Great Society legislation, 3, 49, 50
Great Society programs, 49, 51, 54, 71
    disillusionment with, 59, 67
    and federal government, expansion of, 68
    impact of, 4
    intellectual challenges to, 58–59
    and social sciences, impact on, 50, 91
Greenberg, Polly
    and criticism of developmentalists, 107–8
    and Head Start, 86–87, 94–97, 110–11

Hall, G. Stanley, 93, 99, 109
Harrison, Shelby M., 19, 25, 30
Havighurst, Robert, 125
Head Start, 83–118
    Blueprint Committee, 102, 104–5, 110
    and President Clinton, 105–6, 111, 112
    and cultural diversity, 84–85
    and developmental psychologists, 11, 49, 83–84, 87–88, 90–105, 107–10
    Early Head Start, 85, 106
    establishment of, 85–90
    evaluation of, 99–105
    goals of, 88–89
    as Great Society program, 4, 49
    purpose of, 84–85
    and social experimentation, 4
    stereotypical clientele of, 84
    and Westinghouse Learning Corporation, 11, 58, 72, 81, 100–102, 107, 113
Heritage Foundation, 2, 66, 69
Holmes, Justice Oliver Wendell, 190

Hoover, President Herbert
   and Commission on Recent Social
      Trends, 3, 14, 19, 30–31, 41–42,
      119, 120, 214
   policy implementation of, 47
Hoover Institution on War, Revolution,
   and Peace, 66, 69
Hudson Institute, 66
Hull House (Chicago), 2, 18, 20, 24, 91
Hunt, J. McV., 96, 97

Illinois Crime Survey, 28, 30, 38
immigration, 17, 22, 31
income tax, 4, 144, 150, 151, 154. See also
   Earned Income Tax Credit; negative
   income tax
Institute for Contemporary Studies, 66
Institute for Government Research, 41.
   See also Brookings Institution
Institute for Social Research (ISR), ix, 36
   anniversary of, vii
   and David Featherman, 219
   founding of, vii
   Health and Retirement Study, 129
   Panel Study of Income Dynamics, 129,
      148
   and Survey Research Center, vii, 70–71
   and Maris Vinovskis, 220
Institute of Medicine, 105
interest groups, 4, 13, 131
   and aging society, 128, 131
   Australian, 127
   and program founders, 180
IQ tests
   and disadvantaged families, 92
   legitimization of, 29
   limitations of, 98
   modification of, 96–99, 100, 102, 104,
      107, 112

Job Corps, 49, 86
Job Opportunities and Basic Skills Training Program (JOBS), 145, 146–47,
   160, 171
Johnson, President Lyndon B., 52

and academics, 49–53, 69
and interest group politics, 4
and juvenile delinquency, 20–22
and social science, 3, 5, 40, 49–53, 54,
   196
staff of, 55, 57
and War on Poverty, 54, 139
and welfare state, 1

Kennedy, President John F., 52
   and academics, 10, 49–53, 69
   and social science, 3, 40, 49
Kissinger, Henry, 57, 58, 202
Korean War, 45, 71

Laura Spelman Foundation, 2, 8, 14, 19,
   32
Legislative Reference Service (LRS), 48
Legislative Reorganization Act of 1946,
   48

Manhattan Institute for Policy Research,
   66
Manpower Demonstration Research
   Corporation (MDRC), 12, 165–86
   and community work experience pro-
      grams, 176–77
   establishment of, 165–67
   and Ford Foundation, 12, 165, 168,
      169
   and Judith Gueron, 12, 220
   and National Work Supported
      Demonstration, 167, 169, 181
   and private sector subsidies, 176
   time limits of, 177–78
   and welfare-to-work programs, 145,
      172–74
Mayhew, Henry, 91
McMillan, Margaret, 99, 112
Medicaid, 49, 144, 146
Medicare, 49, 129, 131
Merriam, Charles E., 33
   as "father of American quantitative
      political science," 25
   and political science, 25–26, 35

and Recent Social Trends, 19, 30
and Social Science Research Council,
    26
and social science, 26, 35, 37
and University of Chicago, 19

National Academy of Sciences, 52, 115
National Academy on an Aging Society,
    129
National Bureau of Economic Research
    (NBER), 2, 19, 36, 41
National Defense Education Act
    (NDEA), 46
National Impact study, 100
National Institute of Education (NIE),
    57, 60, 62, 80
National Institute of Mental Health, 52
National Institute on Aging, 127, 128,
    129
National Institutes of Health (NIH), 9,
    43, 44, 45, 52
National Research Council, 105, 116
National Resources Planning Board
    (NRPB), 42, 78, 214
National Science Foundation (NSF), 43
    and age, 125
    goal of, 5, 9
    and grants, 44
    and social science
        curriculum, 59
    funding of, 9–10, 44, 52, 57
National Security Council (NSC), 48, 68
National Urban League, 97, 113
negative income tax (NIT), 12, 140
    and President Carter, 141
    critics of, 143
    debates over, 4, 57
    definition of, 160
    and experiments, 138, 143, 181
    and funding, 181
    and New Jersey NIT Experiment, 4
    and Program for Better Jobs and
        Income, 141
    and research techniques, 138–39
    and social scientists, 143

and Supplemental Security Income
    Program (SSI), 149–50
New Deal, 189
    and academic advisors, 70
    and Brain Trust, 42
    and economists, 70
    elimination of, 7
    and federal government, growth of, 68
    opponents of, 42
    and public action, 111
    and resources, 122
    Social Security, 11
    and social welfare, 123
New York Bureau of Municipal Research,
    41
Nixon, President Richard
    academic advisors to, 49, 57, 61
    and Family Assistance Plan, 11, 138,
        140, 142, 147, 149
    and federal government, growth of, 68
    and Head Start, 89
    and Office of Management and the
        Budget, 6, 48, 55
    and social science, 5–6, 57, 58, 59
    and welfare state, 1

objectivity, scientific
    in twenty-first century, 1
    disillusionment regarding, 62, 70
    and policy, 2, 3, 4, 210
    and Recent Social Trends, 30
Office of Adolescent Pregnancy Programs
    (OAPP), 62
Office of Child Development, 86, 90, 101
Office of Economic Opportunity (OEO)
    and Head Start, 86, 89, 90, 96, 112
    and social sciences, funding for, 52
Office of Education, 46, 52, 81
Office of Management and the Budget
    (OMB), 6, 48, 55
Office of Naval Research, 71, 74
Office of Policy Development (OPD), 55
Office of Price Administration, 43, 214
Office of Scientific Research and Devel-
    opment (OSRD), 42, 45

Office of Strategic Services, 43
Office of Technology Assessment (OTA), 56, 72
Ogburn, William F., 3, 4, 11, 19, 30, 35
Omnibus Budget Reconciliation Act of 1981 (OBRA), 12, 138, 143

Perry Preschool Project, 93, 95, 103
Personal Responsibility and Work Opportunity Reconciliation Act of 1996 (PRWORA), 12, 137, 172
philanthropy
    and delinquency, 21
    East Coast, 2, 8
    and intellectual elite, 8, 31
    and social science, 16, 32, 34, 36–37, 198
    and Social Science Research Council, 26
Piaget, Jean, 94, 97, 99, 101
Pittsburgh Survey, 19, 24–25, 29, 30, 34
policy-relevant research, 188, 196, 197
positivism, 2, 187, 196, 204–7, 213
postpositivism, 204–8, 213, 214
poverty
    and elderly, 120
    and Head Start, 84, 86, 91, 92, 93, 106, 108, 110–11
    and policy-making, 50, 58
    and social science, 83
    studies on, 17, 20, 21, 22, 198
    and welfare reform, 137–61, 170–78, 182–83
    See also War on Poverty
Program for Better Jobs and Income (PBJI), 12, 138, 141–43
Progressive movement, 17, 24
Progressive Policy Institute, 2, 66
public service employment (PSE), 141

race, 123, 126
    African American/black, 18, 22–23, 25, 84, 132, 153, 156
    and age, 123
    Asian American, 84

and Carnegie Corporation, 126
    Caucasian/white, 23, 84, 132, 153
    Hispanic, 84, 127
    Native American, 84
    research on, 22–23, 33, 157
    and riots, 4, 23
    and RAND Corporation, 44, 66, 69, 194
Reagan, President Ronald
    and academics, 61, 63
    and agency staff, decline of, 55, 61–62
    domestic policies of, 55, 68
    and social science, 5, 6, 55, 61–62
    and societal aging, 125
    and welfare, 143–44, 151, 167, 177
Recent Social Trends, 16, 19, 214
    and aging, 11, 119, 120, 122
    and positivist social science, 3, 4, 30
reformers, middle-class, 27
research and development (R&D)
    civilian, 8, 9
    funding of, 6, 42, 44, 46, 68
    and National Science Foundation, 5, 44, 46
    university-based, 9
Research Applied to National Needs (RANN), 57
research broker, 4, 6, 8, 13, 14, 196, 213
Richmond, Julius B., 85, 86, 89, 93, 112
Rivlin, Alice, 58, 202
Rockefeller, Nelson, 57, 58
Rockefeller Foundation, 2, 32–33, 41
Roosevelt, President Franklin D., 42, 111, 120–22
Roosevelt, President Theodore, 111
Ruml, Beardsley, 19, 32–33, 36, 37
Russell Sage Foundation, 33, 66, 69
    and intellectual elite, 8
    and Social Survey Movement, 2, 19, 24

Schlesinger, James, 58, 111, 202
Settlement House movement, 17, 20, 24, 27, 34, 35, 91

Shriver, Sargent
  as Office of Economic Opportunity
    director, 85–86, 91, 111, 112
  testimony before Congress, 97, 112
Skinner, B. F., 91
Social and Rehabilitation Service, 52
social engineering, 21, 24, 196
social learning, 199, 212–13
Social Science Research Council (SSRC),
    2, 8, 19, 26, 41, 52
Social Security, 122–23, 129–30
  and Europe, 125, 132
  and Generation X, 131
  and health care, 129
  and social sciences, 11
  Social Security Act, 119, 121, 170
  Social Security Administration, 6
  Social Security Board, 122, 123
  and societal aging, 11, 125, 126
  studies of, 129
  and welfare expenditures, 71
Social Survey movement, 16, 19, 29, 34,
    35
  foundation support of, 24
  Pittsburgh Survey, 24
  and policy-making, 2, 24
  Recent Social Trends, 30
  Russell Sage Foundation, 19, 33
societal aging, 11, 119–36
Society for Research in Child Develop-
    ment (SRCD), 110
Sugarman, Jule, 85, 89, 90, 94, 112
Supplemental Security Income Program
    (SSI), 149–50
surveys
  and analysts, 4, 7
  black, 22
  development, 16, 18–19, 23, 43
  Health and Retirement Study, 129
  of household incomes, 133
  local, 30
  National Adult Literacy Survey, 157
  National Household Survey of Drug
    Abuse, 157
  public opinion polls, 24

  and race relations, 23
  Russell Sage, 25
  university, 35
  and urban social conditions, 17, 30
  view of, 53
  and welfare, 156
  See also Illinois Crime Survey; Social
    Survey movement

taxpayers, 31, 159, 171, 172, 173, 174
Temporary Assistance for Needy Families
    (TANF), 147, 172
Thorndike, Edward, 99
Truman, President Harry, 44, 47, 48, 123

universities, and social science research,
    2, 16, 20, 34–36, 40, 41, 63
  abstract nature of, 7
  associations, 51
  and government, 4, 43, 46, 50, 67,
    68–69
  as decentralized, 9
  federal support of, 8, 9, 44, 62, 68, 70
  growth of, 10, 29, 31, 34–36, 37, 68
  and Head Start, 103, 108, 110
  interdisciplinary programs of, 130
  and objectivity, 62, 66
  and philanthropic foundations, 8,
    32–33
  and professionalization of social sci-
    ences, 29
  and Social Science Research Council, 26
  survival of, 5
  and World War II, 43, 46
University of Chicago, 2
  and John Dewey, 93
  and empirical sociology, 19
  graduate school of, 35
  and Robert Havighurst, 125
  and Hull House, 91
  and Lawrence E. Lynn Jr, 220
  and Charles E. Merriam, 19, 25
  and William Ogburn, 3
  and philanthropy, 8
  and Beardsley Ruml, 33

University of Chicago (*continued*)
  and social scientists, 36
  and W. I. Thomas, 19
  and L. L. Thurstone, 19
Urban Institute, 2, 66, 69
urbanization, 17, 31, 124

Vietnam Conflict
  and government, trust in, 7, 62
  and policy analysis, 201, 214
  and political leaders, 50, 59
  and social scientists, 65, 69

War on Poverty, 4, 11, 137, 138, 139–40,
    142
  and community action, 108
  and developmental psychology, 96
  and economists, 54
  and federal management of social pro-
    grams, 99
  Head Start, 83, 86, 93, 96, 99, 112, 113
  and welfare, expansion of, 143, 151,
    152
  and Westinghouse Learning Corpora-
    tion, 100
Washington, President George, 214
Weikart, David, 93, 99, 103
welfare, 11–12, 137–64, 165–86
  and age, 130
  "end welfare as we know it," 137, 139,
    149, 150, 152
  and expenditures, 49, 54, 71
  "make work pay," 142, 144, 149, 150
  and population, 12
  and research, 11–12, 13
  reform of, 6, 11–12, 144, 137–64,
    165–86
    and Clinton administration, 12, 137
    Head Start, 105, 106
    and Nixon administration, 57
    Russell Sage Foundation, 33
    and work, 144
  and Social Security, 123

studies on, 200
welfare state, 1, 7, 12, 127, 189
welfare-to-work programs
  child care, 144
  and Clinton administration, 137–38
  evaluation of, 151–52, 170–78,
    182–83
  goals of, 145
  and health problems, 157
  and Medicaid, 144
  and research, 138–39, 179
  state requirement for, 145, 168
  and transitional jobs, 155
workfare, 12, 138, 171
  evaluations of, 145, 168, 176–77
  mandatory, 176
  optional, 167–68
Westinghouse Learning Corporation, 11,
    58, 72, 81, 100–102, 107, 113
Wilson, President Woodrow, 41, 70
Work Incentive Program (WIN), 168
World War I
  and economics, 41
  and Great Migration, 23
  psychology of, 19, 29
  and social science research, 17, 27, 30,
    41, 50, 70, 214
  and surveys, 16
World War II
  and economics, 139, 152, 153, 214
  and federal funding, changes in, 43–
    47
  and federal government
    changes in, 47–48
    growth of, 68
  and policy-making, encouraged, 1
  and social insurance, 123
  and social science, 2, 6, 8, 9, 10, 34, 36,
    40–43, 50, 67–70, 71, 214

Zigler, Edward, 110
  and Head Start, 11, 85–86, 87, 90,
    91–92, 95, 96, 98